D0345358

THINK GLOBAL, FEAR LOCAL

THINK GLOBAL, FEAR LOCAL

SEX, VIOLENCE, AND ANXIETY IN CONTEMPORARY JAPAN

DAVID LEHENY

CORNELL UNIVERSITY PRESS

ITHACA AND LONDON

Copyright © 2006 by Cornell University

All rights reserved. Except for brief quotations in a review, this book, or parts thereof, must not be reproduced in any form without permission in writing from the publisher. For information, address Cornell University Press, Sage House, 512 East State Street, Ithaca, New York 14850.

First published 2006 by Cornell University Press

Printed in the United States of America

Design by Scott Levine

Library of Congress Cataloging-in-Publication Data

Leheny, David Richard, 1967–
    Think global, fear local : sex, violence, and anxiety in
contemporary Japan / David Leheny.
        p. cm.
    Includes bibliographical references and index.
    ISBN-13: 978-0-8014-4418-0 (cloth : alk. paper)
    ISBN-10: 0-8014-4418-7 (cloth : alk. paper)
    1. Fear—Social aspects—Japan. 2. Violence—Social
aspects—Japan. 3. Sex—Social aspects—Japan.
    4. Japan—Social conditions—1945– I. Title.
HN723.5.L45 2006
306.0952′090511—dc22

                                        2005028794

Cornell University Press strives to use environmentally responsible suppliers and materials to the fullest extent possible in the publishing of its books. Such materials include vegetable-based, low-VOC inks and acid-free papers that are recycled, totally chlorine-free, or partly composed of nonwood fibers. For further information, visit our website at www.cornellpress.cornell.edu.

Cloth printing   10 9 8 7 6 5 4 3 2 1

FOR MY PARENTS, JOSEPH AND SANDRA LEHENY

CONTENTS

ACKNOWLEDGMENTS

This book would not have been possible without the tolerance, encouragement, and support of a great number of friends and colleagues. First among these are those in Japan who gave generously of their time and wisdom. Itabashi Isao and Kawamoto Shiro of the Council for Public Policy have been friends and advisers since I began to work on terrorism, and although our views on counterterrorism often diverge, I hope they know how grateful I am for their unfailingly shrewd advice. I also greatly appreciate the help of Gotō Hiroko of Chiba University, who saved me from countless errors in my research on juvenile crime and also introduced me to other experts working on the problem. Ishida Hiroshi and Satō Kaoru have been most generous hosts at the University of Tokyo's Institute of Social Science, and the late Satō Seizaburō of the National Graduate Institute for Policy Studies kindly helped me on this project during my affiliation there in 1999. This book would not have been possible without their help.

Each of the cases reported in the book was a struggle for me, and the reader has been spared at least some of my errors due to the sharp eyes of several colleagues who kindly took the time to provide their reactions. Leonard Schoppa, Peter Katzenstein, Derek Hall, and an anonymous referee for Cornell read the entire manuscript and gave crucial comments on the book's structure and logic. Thomas Berger, Andrew DeWit, Sharon Kinsella, Jonathan Lewis, Manuel Metzler, Laura Miller, Howard Schweber, Ethan Scheiner, Joe Soss, Kay Warren, and Julia Yonetani (who even fixed one of my faulty translations) read drafts of specific chapters and gave essential and badly needed advice.

The initial idea for the terrorism component of this book arose specifically because of an International Affairs Fellowship from the Council on Foreign Relations and an International Affairs Fellowship–Japan from the Council on Foreign Relations and Hitachi, Inc. I also received generous institutional support from the U.S.-Japan Program at Harvard University, from the Abe Program at the Social Science Research Council and the Japan Foundation's Council for Global Partnership, and from the Graduate School at the University of Wisconsin–Madison. At Hitachi, I thank especially Carl Green, Akimoto Yushi, and Kojima Toshirō. Frank Baldwin, Tak Toda, and Carlton Vann of the Abe Program have been wonderfully supportive throughout this project.

Conversations with friends and colleagues were extremely helpful in shaping my ideas and pointing me in new directions. I thank especially Allison Alexy, Michael Barnett, Verena Blechinger, Kathy Bukolt, Tom Carter, Martha Crenshaw, Don Downs, Scot Folensbee, Ed Friedman, Sabine Frühstück, Tom Hayden, Rob Hellyer, Paul Hutchcroft, Izutsu Shunji, Juliette Kayyem, Kitano Ryūichi, Ellis Krauss, Chika Kubota, Kate Marquis, Alex Moon, Morimoto Yoshiyuki, Nakamura Mayumi, Emiko Ohnuki-Tierney, Leigh Payne, T. J. Pempel, Susan Pharr, Lisa Sansoucy, Gina Sapiro, Michael Schatzberg, Deborah Shamoon, Jessica Stern, Jelena Subotic, Paul Talcott, Katherine Tegtmeyer-Pak, Julia Thomas, Mark Thompson, June Toda, Tsuji Yoshiyuki, Mirelle Warouw, Mark Wong, and Louise Young. Among them, I must single out Martha Crenshaw, who helped me better conceptualize how political negotiations are treated outside of counterterrorism agreements. Crawford Young deserves special thanks for having nominated me for the Council on Foreign Relations fellowship. I also thank audiences at Harvard University, the University of Michigan, the University of Wisconsin, Hitotsubashi University, New College of the University of South Florida, the University of Tokyo, Allegheny College, the German Institute for Japanese Studies, the University of Virginia, Stanford University, and the annual meetings of the Association of Asian Studies and the American Political Science Association. My brilliant research assistant in Tokyo, Ide Hiroko, was an invaluable source of information and an active sounding board.

At Cornell University Press, I thank especially the incomparable Roger Haydon. He has been a superb taskmaster: stern but good-humored, and always aware of how the arguments might be sharpened and clarified. Karen Hwa and John Raymond did a wonderful job in cleaning up the manuscript, and Kay Banning deserves a shout of thanks for the index.

I wrote a great deal of this book at coffeehouses, and I feel I owe some thanks to the staff at the Starbucks on Waseda-Dōri and the one formerly on Rikkyo-Dōri for being so hospitable. The gang at Mosquito in Takadanobaba, especially Masako and Michio, did me the great honor of making me feel at home in 2003–2004.

My older sister, Vivienne, read every word of the manuscript and provided some of the best editorial guidance I could ever hope for, and my younger sister, Cara, provided invaluable comments on the comparative legal issues raised in the book. They deserve far more gratitude than my birthday gifts to them will likely indicate.

But this book is for my mother and father. More through example than through words, they taught me the importance of both tenacity and curiosity. Although this book is poor compensation for their years of parenting, especially because they would probably prefer a book that wasn't obsessed with sex and violence, I hope they know that I dedicate it with love and respect.

The blame for remaining errors, of course, is mine alone.

JAPANESE TERMS AND CONVENTIONS

Japanese names are given in Japanese order (family-given) except in those cases, such as for Japanese authors of English-language books, in which individuals have identified themselves in given-family order. I have also omitted macrons in words commonly used in English (e.g., Tokyo rather than Tōkyō).

The following Japanese terms appear with some frequency in the book.

Enjo kōsai:	"Compensated dating," sometimes understood as prostitution
Fushinsen:	Unknown or suspicious boat
Fūzoku:	Entertainment industries, but frequently used for the sex industry
Hodō; hodōin:	Police guidance (to juveniles); guidance officer
Jiko sekinin:	Self-responsibility
Jūsen:	Housing loan corporation
Kenzen ikusei:	Healthy or wholesome upbringing
Kogal (from *kogyaru*):	Stylishly attired high school girls and young women, often with dyed hair, elaborate makeup, and provocative clothing.
Kōban:	Police box
Kōsakusen:	Operations boat
Yakuza:	Japanese organized crime groups

ABBREVIATIONS

ATA   Antiterrorism Assistance Program

CPP   Council for Public Policy

DPJ   Democratic Party of Japan

ECPAT   End Child Prostitution in Asian Tourism

JDA   Japan Defense Agency

JRA   Japanese Red Army

JSP   Japan Socialist Party

LDP   Liberal Democratic Party

MOFA   Ministry of Foreign Affairs

NGO   nongovernmental organization

NPO   nonprofit organization

NPA   National Police Agency

PSIA   Public Security Investigation Agency

SCAP   Supreme Commander for the Allied Powers

THINK GLOBAL, FEAR LOCAL

Cat and crow deterrents doubling as tire guards in Tokyo, June 2004.

CHAPTER ONE

FEAR, NORMS, AND POLITICS IN CONTEMPORARY JAPAN

Posters in Tokyo's subways extol the merits of off-peak commuting; even those responsible for Japan's superbly reliable mass-transit system seem to want no part of it at rush hour. Particularly around 8 a.m., but also in the early evening, cars fill to nearly double their apparent capacity, and even one unsteady rider can cause a miniature avalanche as the train reaches a station, with people stumbling into one another like densely packed dominoes. I have always envied those who can somehow sleep, even while standing up, during a commute, and I also envy those who get rich by dreaming up the "virtual pet" games or text messaging on cell phones, both of which serve to make the crowded commutes more bearable, at least for those passengers who can keep one thumb free. Some passengers find the commute nearly crippling in the discomfort it produces, whether from the claustrophobic environment or, especially for women and girls, the possibility of physical violation by another passenger. My problem is germs. I have spent most of my rush-hour commutes in Tokyo gripping a bar or handle to keep myself upright, always fearing the inevitable wet, hacking cough from a two-pack-a-day smoker immediately next to me. I find myself preparing for rush hour by purchasing germicidal wipes to clean off the effluvia that I imagine will coat me by the time I finish the ride.

Fortunately, my work schedule at the University of Tokyo in 1996 was sufficiently flexible for me to take a 6 a.m. train to the office and then return home at 3 p.m., thereby avoiding the seething throng. The train from my office in Hongo terminated at Ikebukuro Station, one of Tokyo's major transportation hubs. With a lively if somewhat grimy nightlife, Ikebukuro is also a popular after-school gathering spot for the city's teenagers. One autumn day, my subway car was unusually empty. I was sitting alone at one end of the car while three or four other adults sat at the far end. At the second stop after I boarded the train, two attractive schoolgirls, perhaps sixteen or seventeen years old, sat down in the seats across from me. After the doors closed, they stood up and one silently took off her school uniform's jacket and held it around her friend, who then began to strip. This routine is not unusual in coed junior high school classrooms, where students often change before physical education classes, taking turns holding jackets around one another to protect classmates' privacy. And the girls were practiced enough at the maneuver that all of this was handled remarkably smoothly; I can barely unzip my hooded sweatshirt on a moving subway without falling over.

While I watched—they were about four feet directly in front of me, so it was difficult not to watch—the first girl stripped out of her school uniform down to her underwear, pulled some clothes out of her bag, and changed into them: a different school uniform. She then took her jacket and held it around her classmate, who went through the same routine. I kept looking over to my left, to see if the other people on the train were watching (they were), and whether they seemed alarmed (they did). Within three minutes—the time to the next station—the two girls had completed their little exercise and had sat back down. Passengers arriving on the train in the subsequent stops would have had little idea that anything odd had happened.

I wish I could report that I was scandalized by the girls' behavior, but my intense anxiety reflected more my guilt and revulsion over the voyeuristic pleasure I took in the moment than any real outrage that teenagers might act like that. My astonishment also left me feeling almost vertiginously confused: How could I understand Japan so little, even after living there for several years, that I was unable even to frame a guess as to what these girls were doing? The quick and possibly correct consensus among the Japanese friends I later told was that the girls were traveling to Ikebukuro to engage in *enjo kōsai*, or "compensated dating," a heavily publicized practice in which schoolgirls would reportedly date and possibly sleep with adult men in exchange for cash or presents. According to these friends, by changing their uniforms, the girls were simultaneously disguising their identities so that their teachers would not recognize them at a distance, and using sexier uniforms, or those from higher-class schools, so that they could command higher prices.

Like me, the Japanese press found the girls fascinating, and for reasons I will detail later the outcry surrounding compensated dating vastly exceeded the actual scope of the phenomenon. The scandalous behavior of schoolgirls emerged during an anxiety-drenched decade for Japan, in which visible social transformations reinforced concerns over the country's economy and failures of political leadership. Although I was troubled by the brief encounter on the train, it was not out of any concern for the girls. Rather, my reaction seemed to confirm that something was wrong with me, perhaps that I had the predilection for young Asian women that is often assumed to be the carnal root of a white male researcher's interest in Japan. The local debates surrounding "compensated dating" in 1990s' Japan suggest that something vaguely similar was happening to local audiences as well. For many Japanese observers and writers, the emergence of a generation of self-sexualized schoolgirls confirmed that something was wrong with Japan, something that would make these girls behave so extraordinarily. The specter of licentious schoolgirls, engaged in varying levels of criminal mischief, began to merge with larger fears about wayward youth and what their recklessness meant for Japan's future.

In 1996, of course, Japanese might have been forgiven for feeling distinctly uneasy about their country's future. The shallow but frustratingly durable recession that punctured the myth of the nation's economic invincibility was well into its fifth or sixth year; a cult of apocalyptic lunatics had released a weapon of mass destruction on Tokyo's subway system; a major earthquake had claimed the lives of over six thousand people; and North Korea's saber rattling had grown more intense, later culminating in a test-fired missile that passed through Japanese airspace. Anyone wishing to make a case that the country was on a downward spiral could find ready emblems for disaster, whether in the firms that were ominously discussing "restructuring," the swirling and incoherent party politics that had seemingly replaced postwar electoral stability, or the two schoolgirls undressing on the subway.

In this book, I explore how political actors used the fears bubbling up during Japan's nervous 1990s to justify enhanced powers for the state. Japan's newly demonstrative schoolgirls and murkily defined foreign threats (in particular, presumptive Chinese criminals and North Korean spies) became crucial symbols of a nation under attack. Both seemed to threaten the nation's security, the former by destroying Japan's social fabric from within, the latter by invading it. But such views were contested by civil libertarians, leftists, and others eager to remind the public of the costs of an overly heavy-handed state. Although officials had long wanted the power to police Japanese youth more strictly and to undo the legal and constitutional limits on security forces, they had confronted predictable obstacles from those political forces that feared the state more than they did other potential menaces.

In both cases, however, officials received help from a powerful deus ex machina: international efforts to combat transnational crime. By using the legitimacy of these initiatives—to protect children from commercial sexual exploitation, to constrain transnational terrorist networks—Japanese officials found ways to attach local scapegoats to global solutions. There is nothing revolutionary in observing a relationship between fear and politics, one often revolving around the extension of state power, but I implicate global initiatives to improve the world in the strategies that local actors employ to define and to use fear. In these international efforts, local fears found political cover; by cracking down on schoolgirls and unleashing the military, Japan was simply observing its international responsibilities.

Transnational Crime, Global Solutions

Japan is, of course, far from alone in confronting an array of transnational crime and security problems. Demonstrating impressive resolve in the wake of the September 11 attacks, Prime Minister Koizumi Jun'ichiro promised President George W. Bush extensive support for U.S.-led counterterrorism activities, primarily at the military level but also in law enforcement. Within a few months of the attacks, Japan's Ministry of Foreign Affairs (MOFA) trumpeted a wide array of steps taken against international terrorism, including unprecedented military support for the U.S. attack against the Taliban in Afghanistan and accession to the International Convention for the Suppression of the Financing of Terrorism. Japan had been seen in some circles to have an overly "soft" approach to terrorism, and new government initiatives were clearly aimed at proving otherwise.

Another arena of transnational crime—child prostitution and pornography, especially that involving children in developing nations—had also witnessed significant Japanese countermeasures. Just two years before the September 11 attacks, the National Diet of Japan had passed a law to ban child prostitution and child pornography, largely in response to broad criticism that the government was soft on pedophiles and sex tourists. The new law promised a crackdown on those involved in the sexual exploitation of children, and was followed by widely publicized arrests of Internet website operators and others deemed culpable in these crimes. Although not a topic with the same Wagnerian overtones as the U.S.-led "war on terror," the sexual exploitation of children, especially the hundreds of thousands in sex markets in Southeast Asia, has been an explosively and justifiably emotional issue for global human rights movements. Japan's ratification of international agreements was taken as evidence that the government was moving in the right direction.

Indeed, it was; and I do not mean to argue that these policies were simply crass and cynical efforts to quiet international condemnation. But a closer look suggests that these steps against international crime are both politically and morally more qualified than they might appear at first blush. Subsequent developments in both cases indicate that the government's decisions were premised on implicit social and political bargains that would likely meet with less international acclaim. In the case of terrorism, for example, the government's efforts have been deliberately aligned with the achievement of long-desired changes in the country's overall military security policy. Similarly, although the child prostitution and pornography law ostensibly aimed at cracking down on adult predators of children, the larger social debate in Japan—and subsequent police efforts—suggest that the primary goal was to clamp down on the increasingly ostentatious sexuality of Japanese teenagers.

This is not, I believe, because there is something wrong with Japan but rather because agreements on crime lend themselves exceptionally well to deployment against people or problems already judged to be threats; they provide opportunities to interested officials. When international organizations, states, or transnational social movements ask that other governments engage in tighter policing, they almost certainly have in mind the solution to a commonly recognized problem. The idea that such enhanced authority comes with the legitimacy of international agreement and sanction may be important, particularly if movement activists can inject into national political debate a real sense that the transnational problem is one worth solving. But when states enhance law enforcement authority, they arrogate to themselves increased legal authority to investigate, prosecute, and punish people for a growing list of offenses.

Particularly in democratic nations, there is the risk that people will resent increased state capacity to arrest and imprison them because of a transnational problem that may or may not have much to do with them.

It would be easier to gain popular acceptance if the enhanced state authority were to respond in some way to a widely recognized problem. Instead of focusing on an amorphous transnational problem, such as terrorists and drug or sex traffickers, leaders may find it effective to rely on more familiar bogeymen. The trick—and it is an important one—is to ensure that adherence to the international norm can be tailored to handle the country's specific fears. Particularly since 1990, with the economy in a long recession and with widespread insecurity about social change and declining national prestige, there has been no shortage of such concerns for the Japanese government to employ.

Threats and Politics

Fear may be a powerful motivator, but more often than not its use is relatively banal. Without goals any more sinister than keeping their gardens clean, for example, my neighbors in Tokyo had decided to try to scare away the various pests that were despoiling them. By the time I arrived in Bunkyo Ward in fall 2003, virtually all of the neighboring residents had grown weary of the stray cats and spaniel-sized ravens that used their gardens as public toilets. Having heard that the crows and cats were frightened of dancing lights, they filled large plastic bottles with water and placed them around their yards. The hope was that the bottles would catch rays of sunlight, sparkling in ways that would spook the animals and keep them at bay. The practice was widely debated on Japanese websites, with one showing a photo of a cat sitting calmly next to such a bottle. The raging issue was not whether people should scare the cats and crows, or even whether fear was the key to prevention, it was whether the bottles did the trick.

Like most people, I routinely work on both ends of the fear spectrum. On the one hand, this book is evidence of my position as receiver; my colleagues went out of their way to express, usually in regretful tones, the likelihood that they would deny me tenure if I did not write it in a four-month spurt in 2004. Lurking in the back of my mind (and occasionally leaping to the forefront) while I wrote was the academic purgatory that would be the logical if exaggerated extension of a "no" vote: successive short-term appointments, no job security, and professional bitterness that might extend to nearly biblical proportions. Of course, I do something similar to my students, explaining to them that if they do not do all the required course reading, they will likely fail my class. I then hint darkly that an F in my class will likely doom them to a lifetime without gainful employment, health insurance, or the means to raise a family. It is a cheap gimmick, one that many of my students have unfortunately figured out, but it works often enough to make it my best technique, certainly more effective than suggesting that they might actually learn something. I do it largely because I can; power corrupts, and frustratingly narrow power corrupts in frustratingly narrow ways. But at a certain level, I believe what I am saying to the students just enough to feel relatively comfortable that it is not a lie. Instead, I am giving a truthful but only partial and vaguely probabilistic account of risk and worst-case scenarios, strongly implying to the students that the best way to avoid future problems is to do what I want them to do.

Obviously, officials, pundits, and political critics do this all the time. For many, this is not about creating fear but rather about encouraging citizens to recognize threats and to adopt the speaker's views about the proper solutions. We need people to fear global warming now so that they will make the sacrifices necessary to preserve our fragile environment. Or we need people to understand that foreign students might really be terrorists in training or lying in wait, so that we will be willing to take the necessary steps to monitor them. Threats are crucial underpinnings to politics, but they are neither natural nor self-explanatory. Even if the public agrees, for example, that rates of teen pregnancy represent a serious threat to the American social fabric, competing interest groups and political figures frame the issue alternately as evidence of insufficient sex education or as symptomatic of the country's moral decline. Anyone who has witnessed a U.S. presidential inauguration, or "question time" in the British Parliament, or a Japanese candidate holding forth from the top of a campaign bus in downtown Tokyo understands that politics is largely about performance. A crucial element in that performance is reassurance, or suggesting to the public that one's political agenda carries within it the solutions to social problems.[1]

Good theater needs its villains. In his classic study of drunk-driving legislation, Joseph Gusfield argued that proponents of tighter rules tended to use increasingly "scientific" evidence of the dangers of drunk driving to convince voters that only stiffer penalties and bans would save lives. In doing so, however, they also dramatically created a picture of "the drunk driver"—probably an incurable alcoholic who has no real control over his or her actions and is therefore a killing machine until society steps in to say no. The dramatic process of banning an action also involved the construction of a villain, an ideal type of person to be targeted by the laws. Gusfield's own fieldwork on drunk driving patrol with the police, however, revealed a far messier reality: a wide variety of violators, as well as greatly divergent tactics and methods employed by the police officers. The government's proposed drunk-driving law, however, rested on assumptions and constructions of a specific kind of person who "would" be a drunk driver and therefore of proper approaches to handling this kind of person.[2]

Particularly when leaders wish to increase the power of the state to investigate, prosecute, and punish people, they must be able to point to the types of threat that proposed new laws will counter. And this is easier if the ideal threat is one that citizens already fear; for this reason, we may need to consider scapegoats as the predictable if unintended outcomes of international norms on crime and justice. Although this term is widely used in the social psychology literature, referring to those individuals pushed out of groups in order to maintain cohesiveness,[3] I am interested in a more general social usage. The literary theorist René Girard has argued that the designation of a scapegoat allows large-scale action against a specific figure, not simply because it permits people to displace their own sins onto the scapegoat but also because a thorough investigation of a society's sins would lead to endless rounds of recriminations, conflicts, and revenge.[4] When government leaders argue for new rules against a specific activity, they are talking about more than the criminalization of money laundering or the viewing of sexually explicit images of children. They are also making implicit and sometimes explicit claims about what kind of person—a terrorist, a pedophile, a hacker—would actually do this and, as a result, should come under greater scrutiny by the state.

Many fears are universal: of physical assault, of losing our children, of violent death. But the bogeymen that embody them (gun-toting teens, Muslim terrorists, U.S. soldiers) reflect both their cultural context and the active efforts to shape them. In the case studies in this volume, I look closely at how political and intellectual figures define the problems for Japanese society and the threats that certain groups pose. Though controversial, government approaches to child prostitution and to post-9/11 security have involved the establishment of ideal types of villains for which there are obvious and clear solutions. We have, for example, the licentious schoolgirls who are not bound by traditional mores and whose entry into sex markets can be halted only with their punishment. We have North Korean sailors who operate as professional spies and saboteurs, as soldiers really, and whose actions can only be understood as terrorism. And in both cases, we have a clear solution: for the former, rules enabling the penalization of the juvenile offenders, and for the latter, looser constraints on the use of deadly force by police and military forces. In both cases, failure to act now will likely lead to worse consequences in the future: either Japan's internal social decay or a devastating attack from an enemy.

This is not an unfamiliar phenomenon in the United States. Even before the September 11 attacks, cultural critics suggested that media-driven panics—including those surrounding pedophilia, plane crashes, and young black men—have been crucial tools for political and economic actors eager to market certain commodities or policies as solutions.[5] Since al Qaeda's strikes on New York and Washington, a growing number of scholars have expressed concern over the constitutional and diplomatic consequences of the Bush administration's use of fear.[6] The American experience, however, suggests that opportunities to employ fear are not limitless. In the aftermath of the attacks, lawmakers, security officials, and law enforcement officials had a remarkable chance to remake their environment, and the USA Patriot Act (actual name: Uniting and Strengthening America by Providing Appropriate Tools Required to Intercept and Obstruct Terrorism, 2001) that ensued was controversial enough that even the President's Republican allies in Congress attached a sunset provision, requiring an affirmative legislative vote for the law's powers to be extended. Even when people are afraid, they probably will still differ on what ought to be done and how much leeway should be afforded to governments that can use security powers to menace responsible citizens as well as their enemies. Particularly in democratic societies, where voters have at least some authority to reward and punish their leaders in regular and predictable ways, those who would use fear to expand their powers need to consider their prospects for doing so. Scholars, critics, and analysts need to consider how those opportunities are produced. If international efforts to combat transnational criminal problems can provide these opportunities, it suggests both that the world is less perfectly "globalized" than is often supposed and that international action may be less praiseworthy than most of us would like to believe.

Norms and Choices

Scholarship on transnational problems formerly fell into a familiar international relations debate regarding patterns of conflict and cooperation. Realists (or, more precisely, neorealists) envisioned a conflictual world, with cooperation likely to obtain only when states might collectively balance against a threat.[7] Liberals and neoliberals, in contrast, viewed interests as arising from motives other than interstate competition, so that different states might achieve "absolute" gains instead of the "relative" gains in which one state's success is, by necessity, other states' failure.[8] Especially since the end of the cold war, however, other theorists have asked how state action might be driven more by unexamined norms, or standards of behavior that simply are taken to be "normal" for states. Why, for example, do all states have flags and national anthems? Why do all states—including those tiny states that have no real use for the expensive hardware—have fighter aircraft?[9] Why have transnational social movements managed to get states to cooperate (if imperfectly and incompletely) on environmental issues, human rights, and weapons proliferation? These researchers have argued that interests come not from self-evident structures like the international state system or the international marketplace but rather from ideas and institutions created and continually remade by human behavior.

In this view, state interests are "socially constructed." Had the rules for states been written and institutionalized differently, international behavior would be dramatically altered.[10] For example, states now formally agree that racism is bad, and many governments even practice what they preach. This is a relatively recent development that cannot be easily ascribed to the independent enlightenment of different nations. Instead, social movements have used the authority of international organizations and agreements to make it illegitimate for states to tolerate formally encoded racism, so a state—such as South Africa under apartheid rule— that engages in this practice is abnormal and subject to penalties.[11]

For something to be normal or abnormal, however, there has to be a category to which these terms are related. There are normal styles of dress for lawyers at work, and others for NASCAR spectators. A normal ending for a Hollywood action movie, not a German art-house film, involves the hero's killing the villain, often after casually tossing in a tagline like "I told you, don't screw with my weekends." The same person might be willing to attend a meeting and say either "Hi, my name is Dave, and I'm an alcoholic" or "My paper builds upon but challenges some conventions in the constructivist tradition." It matters a great deal, however, which is said at an Alcoholics Anonymous gathering and which comes out at the annual meeting of the American Political Science Association. Different norms apply.

Different norms apply because they depend on institutional contexts that produce identities. Ronald Jepperson defines institutions as "socially constructed, routine-reproduced (*ceteris paribus*), program or rule systems.

They operate as relative fixtures of constraining environments and are accompanied by taken-for-granted accounts."[12] By creating actors with different identities, institutions establish and reward different types of appropriate behavior. The same person might be a husband, son, AA member, political scientist, and church deacon: his behavior will differ according to context because different things are expected of him. Similarly, a singular institution, such as a university, produces different identities, such as administrators, professors, deans, and students. I know, as a professor, what is proper and improper, permitted and prohibited, and yet I cannot recall anyone telling me what it is I am supposed to do. I have simply been in university settings for so long that I take it all for granted. Sometimes— such as when I am asked by undergraduates I do not know well to write letters of recommendation—I do something professorial even though it is time-consuming and not self-evidently in my personal or professional interest. I do it, however, because I know that this is the sort of thing that professors do. I feel bound to do it, and if the student's request seems both annoying and troubling, it also seems legitimate. If we conceive of states too as institutions, we realize that there are implicit rules regarding their organization, leaders' proper behavior, and the types of programs and policies they are expected to follow, simply because they are states.

"Constructivists" or "norms scholars" seek to explain these phenomena and have become especially influential in international relations theory since the end of the cold war. Some have focused on the role of international law in shaping states' behavior and even their notions of sovereignty,[13] while others have been especially interested in the coordinating effects on policy of international institutions,[14] transnational movements,[15] or international scholarly communities.[16] The critical response has been tough but instructive. Realists and liberals have critiqued norms theorists for intellectual sloppiness, focusing especially on their inability or unwillingness to make specific predictions. They have also suggested that constructivists have failed to make clear the mechanisms by which institutions create or states adopt norms.[17] Indeed, scholars within the constructivist tradition have noted that there will need to be greater attention at the domestic level to the ways in which different governments approach international norms and respond to them.[18] Recent advances in international norms theory have aimed at specifying the discursive and communicative strategies through which actors convey and internalize global standards.[19]

My sense, however, is that at least part of the critique against constructivists has grown out of their subject matter, seen as somehow utopian and as simply not belonging in the rough-and-tumble world of global politics.[20] For realists, the world is a dark, scary, law-of-the-jungle place; even the cooperation-minded liberals have often prided themselves on their ability to trace how global trade deals, for example, reflect the cruel and Machiavellian considerations of self-interested economic actors across nations. Constructivists, on the other hand, have tended to explain why states band together to stop apartheid, or nuclear weapons, or environmental degradation. Their case selection, unfortunately, has lent itself to caricature by tough-minded scholars who view norms analysts as idealists obsessed with the world's becoming a better and better place. A stereotyped norms analysis goes something like this: a hardy band of left-wingers, typically northern Europeans dedicated to social welfare and peace, joins together with a few especially enlightened Americans and some well-educated representatives of the developing world. Working with grassroots nongovernmental organizations (NGOs) that are nearly ubiquitous in these studies, they manage to bring some issue to the agenda of regional intergovernmental organizations, then to the United Nations, and then force through some kind of convention or treaty that ostensibly binds governments to put an end to the scourge.

In reality, of course, processes like this actually occur, and constructivists should hardly be ridiculed for trying to explain important political and social phenomena that have shamefully been neglected by the more prevalent schools of thought in international relations theory. But if norms matter, they also have less predictable and laudable effects. Newer research on norms has examined their unintended consequences, such as the gendered norms that, in the Balkan war, led international organizations to evacuate women and children but to leave young adult men behind, often to be slaughtered.[21] Moreover, people contest even those norms that they mostly accept; by interpreting them in a manner consistent with their overall political views, they recast them as components in local debates over justice, rights, and morality. In Guatemala, for example, the intellectual worlds of leftists and indigenous rights activists collided over the meaning of democratic and nationalist norms in the 1980s and 1990s.[22] Even International Monetary Fund anticorruption efforts worked in South Korea largely because the government sold them as a break from the legacy of Japanese colonialism, building from nationalistic claims about honesty rather than an idealized view of fair business practices.[23] By looking only at formal agreements or legal changes consistent with certain international norms, we miss other potential consequences, some with life-or-death implications.

The meaning of norms can in this sense be "de-linked" or "decoupled" from their original purposes; even as they maintain legitimacy through the connection to an internationally accepted institution, people's interpretations will vary depending on political, social, and cultural context.[24] Without attention to the act of decoupling, constructivists risk further caricature, and this is particularly true in cases of security and crime. After all, few things seem more distinctive to specific states and societies than collectively enforced rules on crime, security, and morality. Unless they examine in some detail the local definitions of sin, crime, and punishment, constructivist accounts of the myriad international agreements dealing with these problems have to rest on the shaky idea that leaders and citizens across the world understand deviance, threat, and disorder in the same ways. Even a quick glance suggests otherwise. Criminalization and punishment are standard and even necessary functions of the state,[25] but states differ in their proscriptions. A government's designation of criminal acts and the appropriate punishment is ideally supposed to reflect "national values," though these are more properly understood as the constantly evolving outcomes of debates and power struggles in each nation.

In Saudi Arabia, for example, where women have made important social and economic gains, the government faces pressure over women's role both from modernizers and from Wahhabi clerics who provide much of the regime's legitimacy. As a result, women might work as journalists but still have to veil themselves in public because of the potential they pose for "evil and catastrophe."[26] And the mythical construction of Brazil as a multiethnic democracy has pushed lawmakers to criminalize racism, including racial insults, in spite of clear and durable evidence of other structural barriers to full integration.[27] U.S. controversies over the criminalization of abortion would be considered absurd in Japan, just as strict Japanese prohibitions on firearms would be considered extreme in the United States. In each case, we are often tempted to quickly sum up these crucial and very different debates over a central state function by saying, for example, that Saudis are strict Muslims, or that Japanese are pacifists. These institutionalized outcomes, however, reflect compromises and negotiations between competing factions in each country and ought to direct us to pay careful attention to the debates that shape the laws. International norms may affect the national debates, but they almost certainly will not replace them.

By examining how it is that more morally troubling norms become relevant, or, as in this book, how "good norms go bad," we can undermine the simplistic critiques that unite norms literature with idealism. Other scholars have examined how self-interest helps to drive the creation of norms and identity,[28] though I aim at something slightly different. Japanese policymakers working on international terrorism or international sex markets may be confronted with complex interests and incentives, as members of an international community of police and also as Japanese with responsibility for protecting Japanese notions of justice and crime. As this book makes clear, they handle this tension by reinterpreting and marketing the norms at home as solutions to problems that Japanese already recognize; doing so reshapes both the legislation and the moral implications of the norm. Instead of trying to explain the genesis of norms and interests, I focus on how policy actors are embedded in dense cultural environments that shape their identities and views of the world, thereby affecting their understanding and use of norms. My concern here is how certain norms become opportunities for officials to exploit domestic fears, not with the creation of an all-encompassing theory of norms and their effects. I thereby leave aside the "big question" of where norms and interests originate, because I feel that we have not yet answered all of the "little" questions of how they actually affect public and political life. I worry that these little questions, particularly with regard to norms about crime and security, may have far more damaging implications than is commonly supposed.

The Cases

Japan's legendary public safety record would seem to make it a poor choice of case for a book about fear and anxiety. The changes Japan has experienced, however, since the death of the Emperor Shōwa in 1989 and the subsequent collapse of the "bubble economy" have generated a remarkable array of accounts of the country's efforts to come to grips both with a mythologized past and an uncertain future.[29] As I argue in chapter 2, the disparate catastrophes Japan faced in the 1990s—financial meltdown, natural disaster, terrorist attack—seemed to feed on one another in the popular imagination, leading Japanese observers to talk about a more general crisis confronting the nation. This set the stage for any number of claims regarding the steps that the government would need to take to rescue Japan from its troubling drift, either tying it to the foundations that had ostensibly supported the nation in its prosperous postwar decades or building new ones to reflect its altered global position.

But the opportunities to do so were affected by global political currents that defined what was possible, or what was normal, for state behavior. Japan has been a common subject for studies of norms in the past,[30] in part because of its vaunted position as the first non-Western nation to join the ranks of the fully advanced industrial powers. The fit is uncomfortable, as has been observed even in recent literary and cinematic efforts to resolve the connection between cacophonous modern Japan and an idealized traditional Japan.[31] A sense of Japan as an outsider suffuses even the academic research on Japan. Occasionally called a "reactive state"[32] because its domestic political changes are sometimes preceded by international pressure, Japan has also been pilloried as a poor global citizen. Critics point to its sometimes abusive environmental policies and unwillingness to protect resources in Southeast Asia,[33] its mendacity as an aid donor,[34] and its tardiness in extending economic and political rights to immigrants.[35] Even in areas, however, where the English-language media have been quick to criticize Japan for its apparent backwardness—such as its handling of sexual harassment and gender discrimination—one can easily point to the use of international norms by domestic activists to achieve important changes.[36]

The cases I examine in this book—child prostitution and child pornography, and international terrorism—leave absolutely no doubt that important Japanese political figures have been strongly affected by ideas of global responsibility and international convergence. But convergence has been both partial and qualified. This is nothing new; transnational flows of ideology, religion, and law have been crucial in Japan's earlier campaigns of "moral suasion," even as political figures and social groups have sought to bend these flows to suit their own views of Japan's proper social behavior.[37] I do not believe this to be any special failure on the part of the Japanese. One need not dig deeper than the past few years to find cases in which the United States, for example, has flaunted international norms (such as those regarding the treatment of suspects in terrorism cases or the environmental measures dictated in the Kyoto Protocol). Even a cursory glance at the northern European nations sometimes described as norms-generating nations reveals the occasional glitch, such as Norwegian whaling.[38]

The search for a nation's susceptibility to international norms is probably quixotic. If we assume that different countries will feature different political institutions and moral and cultural structures and fissures, a government's willingness to adhere to norms will almost certainly vary across issue areas. In the Japanese case, the government—itself motivated by national revulsion toward atomic weapons—seems inclined to adhere to and support transnational agreements against the production and diffusion of weapons of mass destruction (WMD).[39] But its effort to build strong political and cultural ties with its neighbors in Asia has led it to be less willing than, for example, western Europe to link economic aid to demonstrable progress in human rights and democratization.[40] Both tell us something about Japan but not that the country is either a saint or sinner where norms are concerned.

My sense is that contemporary Japan is a particularly appealing location for research on international norms because of the wide acceptance that it is a country going through an era of profound change that challenges existing domestic institutions in a number of ways. As political figures deal with the nation's perceived crises, they clearly see the opportunity to remake the nation more to their liking. Because international law has played a crucial legitimating role in postwar Japan,[41] the connection of local preferences to international standards can serve to justify steps that people might want but are nervous about taking.

Compensated Dating

I would be lying if I were to describe a process of "choosing" compensated dating and counterterrorism as the cases for the book; instead, in a sense, both chose me. My decision to examine compensated dating followed not directly from my having witnessed two teenagers change school uniforms on the train but rather from what happened next. On arriving home, I immediately called a Japanese friend and described the scene to her as completely as I could. Her immediate response was, "Ah, naruhodo," which roughly translates as "Yeah, of course." This, of course, made me feel even more foolish; an event completely incomprehensible to me was, apparently, blindingly obvious to a Japanese. "They were probably doing enjo kōsai," my friend told me.

Enjo kōsai translates roughly as "compensated dating" and has been an important media topic since the mid or late 1990s. Typically, the term refers to liaisons between adult men and high school girls in which girls are paid with money, allowances, or presents, for dating and possibly having sex with the men. By 1996–97, it was an intense media phenomenon, the subject of hundreds of news articles and no small number of statistical surveys, books, opinion articles, and television programs. If my friend was correct, the girls were changing school uniforms on their way to enormous and anonymous Ikebukuro Station (a major enjo kōsai hub, according to the reports), probably putting on sexier ones or using those of upper-class high schools in order to raise their market value and also to disguise their identities. I honestly have no recollection of what their before-and-after uniforms looked like, so I cannot know whether this was correct, though many other Japanese friends have agreed with this possibility.

For reasons that I explain in chapters 3 and 4, the number of girls actually engaged in enjo kōsai was almost certainly exaggerated by the media, and I remember a Japanese friend's telling me at the time that the problem was probably overstated. With that in mind, I walked around Ikebukuro Station a few days later and noticed two things. First, virtually all of the high school girls I saw looked like the ones on the train: dyed hair, school skirts hiked up to the point of being micro-miniskirts, "loose socks," and varying degrees of suntans. Second, simply going by the numbers, I knew that most of these girls were not engaged in enjo kōsai. But I could not tell who was and who was not, or, to put it more bluntly, I could not tell who were the good girls and who were the bad girls. My guess was that if I could not tell, neither could their parents or anyone else, which probably would have been disconcerting.

As I began to read more about the phenomenon, I was struck by how the discussions of enjo kōsai focused primarily, and sometimes exclusively, on the schoolgirls. To be sure, there were occasional English-language reports that trotted out stereotypes of the pedophiliac tendencies of Japanese "salarymen" (white-collar businessman), but in the Japanese coverage, the spotlight aimed squarely at the girls—why they would behave like this and what kind of society had produced them. Moral responsibility appeared to lie with these "little sluts" (as one Japanese friend half-jokingly described them to me) rather than with their adult boyfriends or customers. This posed a variety of interesting conceptual issues, especially when the government passed a law two years later to crack down on child prostitution and child pornography. At first glance, and because of some of the public proclamations of lawmakers, the new bill seemed to be designed primarily to align Japan's behavior with those of other nations that were clamping down on sex tourism involving children. The prevailing debate in Japan, however, had been about enjo kōsai rather than sex tourism, and no one could have mistaken the schoolgirls in Ikebukuro for those children working in the sex districts of Bangkok or Manila. And so I began to examine the relationship between domestic debates over child sexuality and the government's wish to sign on to international agreements to protect children.

Counterterrorism

About three years after the subway incident, I received a fellowship from the Council on Foreign Relations, in a program designed to draw junior faculty members into the U.S. government and to give young bureaucrats a chance to work in a think tank for a year. The program aspires to improve foreign policy through professional development and intellectual exchange. For reasons too complicated to explain, though owing far more to luck than to any special cleverness or foresight on my part, I joined the State Department's Office for the Coordinator for Counterterrorism, where I worked as a regional affairs officer (Central, East, and Southeast Asia) for most of 2000. While waiting for my security clearance to come through, I traveled to Japan with the support of a related fellowship and started researching Japanese counterterrorism policy, because I thought I might do a comparative study of the two countries' approaches to terrorism. This seemed like the professionally responsible thing to do, and I had initially envisioned this as an inquiry into the Japanese government's basic lack of interest in an issue with which I believed the United States government was foolishly obsessed.

This point—one that I would articulate in a number of State Department conversations but fortunately did not publish anywhere—came to haunt me personally, roughly a year after I left the State Department, when al Qaeda hijackers crashed civilian aircraft into the World Trade Center and the Pentagon. I had been my office's token liberal, consistently arguing that terrorism was not a sufficient threat to the United States to justify cracking down on civil liberties at home or aligning ourselves with human rights abusers overseas. And so on September 11, I watched the towers collapse on live television and felt not just horror but also personal responsibility and almost bottomless guilt. Intellectually, I do not believe my views about the importance of civil liberties and human rights to have been mistaken, and I still defend them now, though with far less emotional commitment than previously. The attacks themselves had made me recall the most persistent source of frustration for a counterterrorism official: not having the authority to prevent a catastrophic attack. Had I still been in government after September 11, I too would have lobbied to break down constitutional and legal constraints on my office's powers. Even if politically and morally doubtful about the long-term implications of limiting constitutional freedoms, I would have imagined each legal restriction on my power as the one that might lead to another attack, and I would have believed myself (however unjustifiably) capable of handling increased authority responsibly and ethically. Counterterrorism officials and their political allies in the White House and the Congress quickly moved against the rules and constraints limiting their range of action. For CIA operatives, it was the Church Commission that placed undue restrictions on their use of "human intelligence" from sources engaged in grossly unlawful behavior.[42] For the FBI, targets included rules against racial profiling, Internet searches of suspects, and the firewalls between national security investigations (with lower thresholds for warrants and seizures) and criminal investigations.[43]

These proposals might be effective in individual cases, but I have been fascinated by the way in which their supporters have suggested that they are definitive parts of a proper counterterrorism strategy. Everything I witnessed in Washington, like all of my research on terrorism since then, has convinced me that it is simply far too varied a phenomenon for there to be a "solution." Indeed, lumping groups like the Shining Path, Aum Shinrikyo, and Hamas together into one conceptual category and then trying to figure out the best way to solve it strikes me as being about as plausible as a single cure for cancer, halitosis, and obsessive-compulsive disorder. And yet proponents of specific types of counterterrorism tools—which, as international norms, had until recently centered almost entirely on law enforcement and intelligence—usually claim and almost certainly believe that these are the ones that will work in general. "Homeland security" rules are among the most obvious recent examples. When apparent al Qaeda militants killed nearly two hundred people by bombing a train station in Madrid in March 2004, European counterterrorism professionals increased their somewhat frantic efforts to cooperate on the basis of something akin to the developing American conception of homeland security. Clearly exasperated at the belated interest of Europeans in the phenomenon, Jack Clark, a U.S. professor at the Marshall Center for Security Studies (a graduate training program run by the U.S. Army for Europeans), told National Public Radio:

> They don't understand the concept. They don't understand what it encompasses. They don't understand, for example, the private-public . . . partnership that is necessary to secure critical infrastructure. They—my point is that they are just coming to realize how dangerous the situation and how vulnerable Europe is, and it's scary to them. They really don't know how to deal with it.[44]

Even though the U.S. Department of Homeland Security was, in early 2004, less than two years old and still not able to point directly to any clear successes against terrorism, Clark assumed that the U.S. approach was actually the right one to take, and that other countries would do well to emulate it. I have no wish to fault Clark for this; after all, my colleagues and I tended to talk like this all the time. Even with no clear evidence of the "correct" way to respond to a problem, policymakers can quickly rationalize their preferred approaches as the best answers and the legal constraints or challenges they face as the most obvious problems to tackle. They may indeed be speaking strategically, consciously playing up the risk in order to justify their goals; at the same time, I think they really believe what they say. In the same way, I am not really lying when I tell my students that they cannot succeed in my classes without working hard; although I am making the comment strategically, I believe at a certain level that I am correct.

Since September 11, I have been struck by the certainty with which Japanese policymakers have adopted certain aspects of a more muscular U.S. approach to counterterrorism, even as they redefine more conventional and better-known threats to justify remarkable and widespread changes in their government's approach to security. Within weeks of the September 11 attacks, the administration of Prime Minister Koizumi had proposed new "counterterrorism" laws that initially focused on direct support for the United States but that ultimately included wider latitude for law enforcement authorities. They also aimed specifically at adhering to developing international institutions and conventions on the handling of terrorism. The Japanese media had portrayed the September 11 attacks primarily as strikes on the United States, not on the civilized world; despite the deaths of twenty-four Japanese citizens, few saw this as a "Japanese" problem. Supporters of these laws emphasized their utility not only for U.S.-Japan relations but also as crucial for Japan's safety from military or criminal threats. Sometimes implicitly but often explicitly, this has generally meant the mobilization of idealized threats of which Japanese were already aware, especially those of North Korean spies and foreign (particularly Chinese) criminals. For reasons discussed in chapter 6, neither group can easily be defined as terrorists, but both the popular discourse and the specific implementation of these new laws have relied on groups of people that can be meaningfully separated from the majority of Japanese, and who represent threats from which the Japanese state should provide safety.

Methods

If my argument about the strategic employment of these norms and the encouragement of local fears is correct, one needs to examine the larger moral and political debates surrounding domestic adoption of international norms. The apparent acceptance of a norm (through ratification of a treaty or the passage of implementing legislation) is part of a longer process, not the end of it. To engage these issues, we need to take account of the ways in which policy actors interpret the meaning of the norms and apply them to their local or more pressing problems. In my earlier research, which had also examined the meanings that policymakers and audiences ascribe to government initiatives, I relied heavily on interviews. My goal had usually been to get at the interpretive context shaping policy, not at the backroom deals or discussions that often engage other investigators. With uncontroversial topics (my previous book was on Japanese leisure and tourism policy), interviews have been extremely helpful; people expressed surprise at being asked for interviews and have usually gone out of their way to reflect on their efforts.

This time, however, the interview strategy proved largely ineffective because people were understandably reluctant to speak openly with me. Both the sexual exploitation of children and counterterrorism policy are politically sensitive topics in Japan, and a number of people have clearly worried about my revealing secret negotiations or compromises that might be embarrassing, providing ammunition for future public debates or elections.

The most remarkable change occurred after September 11, 2001. In late 1999, I spent three months in Tokyo, researching Japanese counterterrorism policy before joining the State Department's office. At that time, Japanese officials were relatively open with me even though I had no personal connection with them; the topic was unusual enough that they had no particular reason to be nervous about speaking. During my ten months in Tokyo in 2003 and 2004, however, even those with whom I was friendly were usually unwilling to go beyond the "talking points" approved for public discussion of the now emotionally and politically charged topic. Largely for this reason, those people who spoke with me usually did so off the record, and more often than not they relied on relatively safe political rhetoric. My contacts—mostly in the government, NGOs, think tanks, and universities—were for the most part highly educated and well aware of international debates over these key issues. Only rarely did I get the sense that people were dishonest with me; more often, I sensed that they used language they thought would be acceptable to a foreign interlocutor and that they believed sufficiently close to their own positions to be justifiable.

To grasp the assumptions underlying the larger political debates, I therefore relied not only on the transcripts of Diet sessions but on popular Japanese books, especially *shinsho*, and opinion magazines to provide rough heuristic guides. Shinsho are short, inexpensive books (usu-ally around ¥750), often by famous scholars or authors, that deal with specific social, cultural, and political topics. They vary widely in quality but are mostly devoid of academic prose and citations and are written to reach general audiences. Many of the major opinion monthlies are more specifically targeted. *Seiron*, published by the right-wing Sankei newspa-per company, aims directly at a very nationalistic audience; its ideologi-cal opposite, *Sekai*, is primarily written by and for left-leaning academics. Articles that cross the ideological lines of either journal are extremely unusual. *Chūō Kōron*, a favorite among bureaucrats and people in Tokyo's think tanks, has a policy wonkish feel and a fairly but not overwhelmingly conservative bias.[45] Similarly, *Ronza*, published by the liberal Asahi news-paper company, also focuses on pragmatic policy matters, though from a moderately left-leaning position. Towering over all of them is *Bungei Shunju*, with upward of seven hundred thousand readers each month. This magazine includes a wider array of articles, and it comfortably crosses the line between literary magazine and opinion monthly. Al-though it is somewhat conservative in its political orientation, *Bungei Shunju* (like *Chūō Kōron* and *Ronza*) is reasonably eclectic in its willing-ness to publish mildly left-leaning pieces by famous authors or pundits. The articles are longer and more substantive than those in newspapers or weekly magazines but are written specifically to be engaging to read-ers who might peruse them at bookstores.

My interviews and informal conversations in 2003 and 2004 thus served as "reality checks" for me. Rather than relying on them for con-text or to get basic information, I primarily tried to ensure that I was rea-sonably interpreting the claims made in written sources, something I could usually ascertain by the speed with which someone responded to a question. If he or she had a ready response—in either agreement or disagreement with something I had proposed—I assumed that this was something they had already considered, probably because it had entered their private discussions or had been widely acknowledged in the media. On the other hand, when they seemed to be taken by surprise, I guessed either that I had misinterpreted a claim made in the readings, that I was injecting too many of my own (and probably strange and unfamiliar) views into the discussion, or that the argument made by an author had failed to engage popular attention.

Capturing the tone of these debates—for which I also refer to popu-lar films, novels, and other cultural specimens from Japan's 1990s—seems to me essential, because these national conversations shaped the ways in which people understood threats to their security as well as the range of proper solutions. The range of options considered, including the ones that failed to win, will likely tell us as much about the cases as will the direct legislative outcomes.[46] If norms are to matter in politics, they must be interpreted and placed within a framework that political audiences can understand. And so when we note, for example, that the Japanese government passed a law to ban child prostitution and child pornography, that might seem to be prima facie evidence that Japan has "adopted" the norm. But the 1999 law was in fact part of a longer process of Japanese legal and political negotiation over sexuality, innocence, and gender. To grasp how the debate is evolving we need to know which moral bargains and debates informed the 1999 law, not simply that the 1999 law occurred as a result of international pressure. Similarly, Japan's willingness to sign on to new counterterrorism norms makes the government's approach seem like clear capitulation to global standards. But both the contextual debates and subsequent political steps have revealed different motives and political calculations. My goal, therefore, has been to use these popular textual resources to illuminate Japanese debates.

Global Efforts, Local Fears

Before analyzing the two cases, I will begin with a short profile of Japan since the early 1990s. By all accounts, Japan has been in rough shape during this time: a stalled economy, inconclusive efforts at political and economic reform, a massive earthquake that killed over six thousand people, a WMD attack by a cult on the Tokyo subway system, and the rise of Asian rivals such as China and South Korea, not to mention continued scare tactics by the North Korean regime. I am most interested, however, in the public understanding within Japan of its being in "crisis." To be sure, all of the points made above are objective facts, as are continuing demographic trends involving an aging population coupled with a declining birthrate, increasing numbers of foreigners, and more single people. Japanese observers of all political stripes, however, have linked these as components of a basic and usually irreversible trajectory of decline. In depicting Japan since the 1990s, I rely not only on scholarly but also on journalistic and artistic depictions of Japan's putative collapse. Rather than being seen as unrelated problems or freak occurrences, long-term trends and immediate shocks alike have become emblematic of the expected decline of a country for which, until 1990, the future had seemed very bright indeed. And current Japanese anxieties over unwelcome social and political developments cannot be separated from larger fears over the direction in which their country is headed.

For each of the two cases, I first examine the debates before the arrival of a major shift in international norms. Some observers in Japan would likely see the 1990s through the prism of moral decay. This threat—commonly embodied by a dyed-blonde schoolgirl talking loudly into her cell phone while plotting her next tryst—to Japan's social security had provoked a tense debate between Japan's liberals and conservatives over the sources of radical change among Japan's teens. Those on the left explained this largely with reference to Japanese consumerism, while conservatives focused on a putative decline in Japan's traditional values. Similarly, concerns over political violence had generated a stalemate between those arguing in favor of greater leeway for Japan's police forces and military in handling violent showdowns and those searching controversially for political solutions. Japan's "case-by-case" approach to terrorist crises sat uneasily alongside the more active stance of many of its G8 partners, who had pushed a "no-concessions" pledge that effectively criminalized and depoliticized terrorism. In neither case could the debate between domestic forces be considered resolved.

Changes in the international normative environment, however, decisively entered the arguments. A transnational movement against the sexual exploitation of children, primarily addressing sex tourism that victimizes minors, became an opportunity for the Japanese police to crack down on "compensated dating." It did not, however, supplant the conclusion among most conservatives that the schoolgirls, rather than their customers, were to blame; this judgment would dramatically alter the implementation of Japan's relevant laws. The September 11 attacks, though taking place thirteen time zones away from Japan, were heard like a gunshot in the corridors of Japanese officialdom. Responses by the U.S. government mixed with major shifts in Japanese domestic politics, becoming a crucial opportunity to redefine threats to Japanese security. A more assertive military stance was now part of the "war on terror," even if it could be justified only by reframing murky if omnipresent threats from North Korea as "terrorism" similar to the attacks in New York and Washington.

It is, of course, no surprise that leaders have to peddle specific visions of public problems in order to justify solutions consistent with their goals and political interests. Nor should it come as any surprise that these efforts produce scapegoats, on whom the state's coercive gaze may fall most forcefully. But it is less obvious that international efforts to make the world a safer, better, healthier place can provoke these outcomes. In these two case studies, I retrace the ways in which international norms involving crime became local fodder for an extension of the state's role in countering local threats. My point here is neither to undermine the international norms literature nor to say that there should be no norms; instead, I hope to demystify the idea of "unintended consequences," an increasingly common topic in policy research over the past ten years. Even if unintended, some consequences can be anticipated and factored into the analyses of scholars and practitioners.

Before moving into the cases, however, I offer a caveat. By focusing on the public representation of threats, I am not denying their existence. Islamist extremists did attack the United States, the North Korean government has test-fired a missile over Japan, and juvenile delinquency in Japan produces victims ranging from abused schoolgirls to homeless men murdered by rampaging teens. My concern is rather with how these threats are portrayed and how international norms can inspire or empower specific policy constituencies to make use of these symbols. When terrorists are understood to be Arabs and Muslims, the consequences of state action tend to fall disproportionately on them, rather than merely on violent criminals themselves, or on religious or ethnic communities in general. And in state efforts to crack down on sexual interaction between children and adults, the designation of the child as a willing agent of moral violation has consequences for children in general. These are troubling outcomes that I do not wish to lay at the doorstep of unintended consequences. To be sure, the consequences I describe are unintended by international institutions and transnational social movements, but they do result from intentional action. For this reason, I believe that they are predictable if we start to consider how norms relating to crime and security, when applied locally, might be expected to produce scapegoats. Security policies need villains—the people who will justifiably be punished by a state trying to protect its citizens. When these laws become internationalized, we need to consider carefully which villains present themselves to political leaders and citizens alike.

The early morning hours in Takadanobaba, Tokyo, March 2004.

CHAPTER TWO

A "VAGUE ANXIETY" IN 1990S JAPAN

In late 2003, a small number of Japan's artier cinemas began to show Hiroki Ryūichi's superb film *Vibrator*, which is based on a 1999 novel by Akasaka Mari and for which actress Terashima Shinobu won several major prizes, including the Best Actress award from the Japanese Academy. Terashima plays Rei, an unmarried freelance writer whose relentless inner voices chatter away while she makes her midnight trips to her local convenience store to stock up on wine. Only her subsequent bouts of bulimia and the occasional vibration of the cell phone that she keeps on "silent mode" in her shirt pocket temporarily interrupt them. Although the movie becomes an affecting road trip in which she explores her need for companionship with a smoothly (and falsely) self-confident trucker, it never veers far from Rei's intense loneliness, amplified by her rootlessness and alienation from traditional institutions like family, firm, and school.

Rei is too idiosyncratic to be considered typical of women in recession-era Japan, but it is hard to imagine another time or place when she could have been created as a character. Even before 1990, there had been Japanese women like her, working on the fringes of a corporation-based economy, living alone, and separated from "normal" rhythms of labor, marriage, and child rearing. But they were largely invisible: marginalized in wider discussions of what Japan is and ought to be.[1] For this reason, the movie probably could not have been made fifteen years earlier, when Rei would have been largely unrecognizable, except as a cautionary figure, and therefore incomprehensible as a heroine to audiences. She makes sense as a character because she is very much the acknowledged product of a Japan that had experienced the 1990s, with its consequences for lifestyles, social possibilities, and economic fortunes. By 2000, women like Rei were part of a developing narrative about contemporary Japan, in which institutions of social and economic life had broken down, leaving in their wake a new generation untethered by traditional expectations of how their lives are supposed to work.

By the standards of an advanced industrial nation, the 1990s had been a trying decade for Japan, one covered almost entirely by economic recession, punctuated with a cataclysmic natural disaster, a major terrorist attack, and unusual political upheavals. Of course, the era of Japan's "miracle" economic growth from the mid-1950s through the 1980s witnessed myriad national traumas—from the AMPO riots of 1960 over renewal of the security treaty with the United States to the Minamata illness scandals of the early 1970s to the national soul-searching that accompanied the arrest of child murderer Miyazaki Tsutomu in 1989. As they would have anywhere, these crises led to wide debates about what the Japanese government had done wrong, or how corporations had behaved mendaciously, or how society could have produced such a monster. But the 1990s were different, especially to the extent that the disasters seemed not to occur individually but to have cascaded, feeding on one another in the public imagination. For many in Japan, the cumulative effects of the bad news generated a definitive sense of crisis, one that became a unifying theme much wider than independent discussions of what is wrong with Japanese finance, or security, or social relations. By the end of the decade, the question had largely become one of what had gone wrong with Japan.

Indeed, the decade challenged durable notions of what Japan is. As William Kelly and Merry White note, Japanese problems in the 1990s undermined confidence in the "family-nation," an idealized relationship between a benevolent and competent state, enterprising and seemingly infallible Japanese firms, and an ethnically homogenous nation structured around traditional nuclear families. In this view, Japanese technocrats provided optimal guidance to Japanese firms, which were more concerned with maintaining the lifetime employment of their workers (themselves recruited through pure meritocracy) than with the immediate bottom line of profit. Of course, as Kelly and White point out, these ideas were powerful myths connected more to public ideologies than to messier truths.[2] The concept of the "family" used in this conception of the family-nation is a relatively recent and somewhat fragile construction,[3] and Japan has been characterized by far less social mobility than a "meritocracy" thesis might suggest.[4] Japan's employment relations have moreover been the long-term ideal for only a subset of Japan's workers, primarily those in large manufacturing firms rather than those working for the subcontractors on whom those firms rely.[5] And Japan's homogeneity has been a carefully constructed myth[6] that has masked the reality of a country with significant minority and foreign populations.[7]

But the relentlessness of Japan's troubles in the 1990s placed a nearly unbearable strain on these views of Japan as a harmonious and orderly society, and there was certainly no worse year in the decade than 1995. In this chapter, I set the context for the empirical analysis that follows by describing the interrelated discussions that surrounded three crises from that year: bank closures, the Hanshin earthquake, and the Aum Shinrikyo sarin gas attack. Significantly, each of these events was attended by growing evidence of distrust in larger institutions. The 1995 bank closures made it impossible for the government or for firms to deny that Japan faced structural economic problems that were not merely the result of the hangover of bubble-era speculation. The most remarkable aspect of the Hanshin earthquake was the staggering and very public failure of national authorities to act quickly to help victims of the earthquake, making the government appear fundamentally incompetent. And the Aum Shinrikyo incident was followed by extensive efforts by Japanese observers to explain how Japanese society had produced the murderous cult and potentially many others like it. Each of these discussions extended beyond the event itself, briefly touching on the larger themes of economic, political, and social deterioration symbolized by these unfortunate moments. Japan is far more than the sum of these three crises, but the country that emerged from them was a different one than the dynamo that loomed in the world's imagination in the 1980s.

I recognize the risks in writing this kind of chapter. After all, I do not want to badly misrepresent the era as one of unqualified darkness. I am writing this chapter in a coffee shop near Ikebukuro, where people seem reasonably happy and healthy; certainly no one seems terrified about Japan's future. A decade that resulted in record unemployment also produced the intense national mania surrounding the success of pitcher Hideo Nomo in his first year as a Los Angeles Dodger, and firms like SOFTBANK were seen, at least for a time, to be energetic symbols of potential post-bubble economic success. Additionally, I do not intend—as Yumiko Iida has put it[8]—to use eccentric incidents to illustrate larger stereotypes of the country, thereby making Japan exotic, a fundamentally unknowable Other. In fact, I can think of little that is more understandable, even natural, than to allow one's fears to telescope—to look at current crises and imagine an avalanche of disasters. Finally, other books have seemed to suggest that Japan's large-scale crisis was the predictable outcome of fundamentally problematic relationships between society and the individual—in other words, that Japan almost had it coming.[9] This point seems to me to be impressively angry more than intellectually defensible.

In trying to understand how Japanese political actors interpret and employ international norms, it is crucial to show that the country's unexpected and, for many, unnerving turn away from the economic growth culture of the 1960s through the 1980s has provided significant leverage to those promising reform. The rest of this book examines concerns about the government's ability to respond to crises and to rapid social transformation, but these fears are embedded within a larger insecurity about the country's economic footing. All of these issues played a role in the 1995 shocks. My goal here is quite modest; I hope to describe an era in which so many things went wrong that subsequent problems could be magnified as more evidence that Japan had somehow lost its way.

The *Jūsen* and an Economy Gone Awry

When Hyogo Bank became the first of Japan's regional banks to default on its loans in the summer of 1995, its collapse served as a figurative exclamation point. Beginning with the demise of two "credit cooperatives" in late 1994, Japan had started to witness the physical meltdown of a financial infrastructure whose rickety joints had been camouflaged by the bubble economy of the 1980s. Since the end of that bubble in 1990, the idea of the Japanese economy in recession had, for many, been intellectual rather than visceral. To be sure, Japanese banks had been twisting to hide the extent of their bad loans, and major firms scrambled to cut costs without having to take the tell-tale route of laying off workers. But the closings of 1995 effectively recast the economic doldrums as crisis by undermining faith in central political-economic institutions that had, for decades, symbolized the country's economic success.

For each failed credit cooperative or bank there has been a publicly acknowledged villain: a bank administrator who used shady or illegal means to hide the extent of bad debt, a retired bureaucrat who had taken

an *amakudari* (descent from heaven)[10] post in a bank and had failed to
respect the public trust, a behind-the-scenes political fixer who took
bribes and used his influence to keep the institution afloat. But the problems for these institutions have been largely structural: an insufficient
monitoring environment, collusive bargaining between Ministry of Finance (MOF) regulators and the institutions themselves, and systems of
financial connivance that allowed major banks to use smaller firms to
hide the dangerous state of their loans. A key portion of the bad debt
that accumulated in Japan's smaller institutions resulted from "referred
deposits." As Ulrike Schaede has noted, a "large bank would talk its client
into issuing low interest commercial paper (CP) and investing the proceeds in a large-scale high-interest savings deposit" at a credit cooperative or other institution. Doing so would earn, on the books at least, a
quick profit for the client, a hefty fee for the bank, and a substantial
deposit base for the credit cooperative, which could then make high-
interest real estate loans.[11] Because of the seemingly unstoppable ap-
preciation of Japanese and Pacific Rim real estate markets, it seemed
temporarily like a safe strategy.

The collapse of the stock market in 1990 and then of the real estate
market nearly three years later, however, rendered these institutions virtually insolvent, thereby threatening both the major city banks as well as
their clients. And no set of institutions better symbolized this problem
than did the *jūsen* (housing loan corporations). Although these accounted for only a small portion of Japan's bad debt, their ties to Nōkyō
(Japan's major agricultural cooperative association) as well as their rapid
and public collapse made them emblematic of a larger problem facing
Japan. When the National Land Agency tried to clamp down on real estate speculation in 1988, the Ministry of Finance encouraged banks to
stay out of housing loans. To maintain access to this potentially lucrative
market, the banks lent money to the jūsen, which then were able to engage in exactly the activities that the administrative guidance had been
designed to halt. The collapse of real estate values with the end of the
bubble essentially bankrupted the jūsen, which struggled to hide their
red ink, and helped to imperil the financial system as a whole.[12]

The jūsen drama played out under intense public scrutiny. As had earlier scandals, such as the 1975 revelations that Lockheed Corporation
had bribed Tanaka Kakuei during his tenure as prime minister, the dis-
closures provoked overwhelming media attention. And if the scenes of
police investigations, vehement denials, and tearful apologies were familiar sights on Japanese television, the jūsen phenomenon offered

something new. It (and the coinciding financial catastrophes) implicated the "managed market economy" that had been seen for decades as the source of Japan's strength.[13] Indeed, the following year witnessed a major clash between the Liberal Democratic Party (LDP)–led coalition and the Shinshinto (New Frontier Party), which staged a three-week sit-in to block jūsen bailout legislation. Extremely unpopular among citizens, the proposed legislation protected the agricultural cooperatives and put most of the burden for lost loans on the major banks.[14] Many saw the plan as further evidence of the LDP's desire to protect its rural constituency without coming to grips with the economy's structural problems. Indeed, the jūsen problem prompted some critics to suggest the abolition of Japan's Ministry of Finance.[15]

At least by the standards of advanced industrial nations, Japan now faced serious economic problems. I would argue, however, that the events of 1995 reshaped them as a crisis. Major institutions of economic governance were now fair game for criticism. And yet there was great difficulty in generating fundamental reform, which stemmed in part from the earlier success of these previously functional economic institutions. Collusive patterns of bank lending, ministerial cooperation with and guidance of specific enterprises, and major firms' general reluctance to engage in cost cutting through layoffs had for decades been seen in Japan and overseas as keys to the country's economic growth. Perhaps America's most widely noted observer of Japanese politics, Chalmers Johnson described Japan as a "developmental state,"[16] an account that has been labeled revisionist by classical economists skeptical of the state's role in industrialization, though it had become an unusually popular term among political scientists and policymakers.[17] A simplified version would posit the róle of a competent and politically insulated bureaucracy protecting the domestic market from foreign competition and encouraging collusive strategies for local industries to focus on performance in overseas markets.[18] Especially in the 1980s, when a rapidly growing Japan had so threatened the United States that people began to look for signs of the decline of U.S. hegemony,[19] there was little public doubt that Japan's political-economic governance fundamentally called into question key theories of growth and development.

The widespread Japanese challenges to these institutions, particularly after the emblematic meltdown of 1995, do not necessarily mean that Johnson and other theorists of the developmental state were wrong. After all, institutions that had been functional for promoting development might be profoundly dysfunctional for a fully advanced economy, particularly if a bureaucracy noted for picking and supporting industrial winners was having trouble shifting labor and capital from "sunset" industries unable to compete internationally.[20] Increasing tension between the competitive high-tech industries driving the economy and the labor-intensive, low-tech industries benefiting from political protection might even cause a major "regime shift" in the governance of the economy.[21] But even as angry Japanese voters watched with disbelief as their economic system started to crumble, most had good reason to be fearful of prescribed remedies. Most accepted that "reform" would be necessary, but significant numbers had a stake in maintaining certain economic institutions, such as long-term employment in their own firm or continued government protection of their specific sector.[22] Indeed, the term *risutora* (restructuring) has come to symbolize in Japan, as in the United States, wide layoffs—hardly an appealing solution even if no one had a better idea.

But the ripples that began with the collapse of financial subsidiaries such as the jūsen and the credit cooperatives have now permeated Japan's financial infrastructure. To deal with the alarming problem of unreported bad debt, the Japanese government took steps, including the creation of the Financial Supervisory Agency and a series of "big bang" liberalizing measures.[23] But much of the damage has already been done. By 1997 and 1998, the Japanese public had witnessed the previously unthinkable: venerable firms like Yamaichi Securities went bankrupt, letting go their workers. Restructuring deals at other major Japanese firms resulted in wide layoffs as well, with the economy reaching a record unemployment rate of 5.5 percent in 2002.[24]

The pressure to deal with cash-flow troubles and increased competition from imports—especially from the rest of Asia—has taken an exceptionally visible toll on two sets of people: young entrants into the job market and older men.[25] The problems for people in their teens and their twenties is reflected in the new visibility of what are called the *furiitaa*, a word created from the combination of the English "free" and the German "arbeiter" (worker). Although not technically unemployed, the *furiitaa* are mostly young, structurally underemployed people, working a variety of short-term jobs, often living with parents well into their twenties. The growth in their ranks is not necessarily a catastrophe in Japan, but it represents a profound change from earlier ideals of the proper life course, especially for men.[26] Rather than entering a firm that provides at least some employment security in return for long hours and initially low pay, these young people find themselves in an economically precarious position without much promise of a better future or a corporate or union identity to embrace. In comparison to problems facing Japan's growing homeless population, the problems of the *furiitaa* may seem inconsequential. Yet the growth of their numbers and their public visibility pose a profound challenge to the idealized economic institutions of postwar Japan.

For men in those major firms that had kept peace with labor unions by maintaining long-term employment, changes in employment relations have been nearly catastrophic. Although some had their wages or hours cut in the early 1990s, the media focused attention increasingly on those who faced bullying from supervisors who demanded "unpaid overtime" (*sābisu zangyō*) or voluntary termination. Others have been simply laid off, with profound social consequences. By the late 1990s, Japanese suicide rates began to climb at a furious rate, taking an especially heavy toll on middle-aged men, the group most immediately threatened with layoffs. Between 1997 and 1998, the number of men in their forties and fifties killing themselves increased 45 percent, to over ten thousand, just as Japan's overall annual number of suicides climbed past thirty thousand.[27] Particularly for those men who find themselves in debt to loan sharks, suicide can be the appallingly responsible solution, as Japanese life insurance policies generally pay out for suicide unless special waivers are built into the contract.[28]

None of this is a direct or necessary consequence of the failure of the jūsen. But their collapse, as well as their controversial political handling, together made it impossible to deny that Japan was in a genuine tailspin that would not be susceptible to the same kind of hard work (by citizens and the government) that had mythically transformed Japan in the 1960s and 1970s. In public debate, the slowdown of growth, reports of possible bad debt, and deflation had been important topics in the early 1990s, but with the actual failure of financial institutions in 1995 came increasingly public recognition that this was one set of challenges for which there would be no easy solution. And indeed, a mounting sense of futility surrounding the nation's economy would profoundly affect people's judgment regarding Japan's ability to deal effectively with any of its glaring problems in the following years.

The Hanshin Earthquake and Failed Politics

Among these, none was more cataclysmic than the Hanshin earthquake of 1995. Japan is, of course, located on the Ring of Fire and is subject to intense seismic activity. With the obvious exception of World War II, the most traumatic physical event in twentieth-century Japan was the Great Kanto Earthquake of 1923, which killed over 140,000 people. With projections that major earthquakes will rattle Tokyo approximately every seventy years, there has long been a tradition of gallows humor in Japan about when the next one will strike. As I recall, it has been projected that the worst possible time would be a winter evening at rush hour. Fully loaded highway bridges would collapse, sending trucks and cars onto the apartment buildings below them. Subway tunnels would cave in, sentencing passengers to excruciatingly prolonged deaths, especially for those of us, like me, who use Japan's newer lines, built at seemingly impossible depths. Gas mains would burst and burn to death anyone unfortunate enough to be trapped in a building or neighborhood with few escape routes. Darkness and snow would hamper rescue efforts, and the cold would claim the lives of a few people who otherwise might have made it. While traveling on the ultramodern, driverless Yurikamome train to an exhibit of a sunken North Korean spy boat (described in chapter 6) I overheard two middle-aged Japanese men talking about the grim prospects facing Tokyo's reclaimed land areas, such as O-Daiba, on which the train line is constructed. "If there's a quake," one said, gesturing widely at the shopping malls and theme park rides that litter the artificial island, "none of this will survive."

Shortly after 5 a.m. on January 17, 1995, a temblor of about 7.2 on the Richter scale struck Hyogo Prefecture, inflicting especially heavy damage on the city of Kobe. Within moments, television stations across Japan broadcast news of the quake, with increasingly disturbing images of fires, collapsed buildings and bridges, a frenetically shaking office (captured by a security camera at the moment of the shock), and bewildered citizens searching for their loved ones. Casualty reports began to filter in, deaths perhaps in the hundreds, then perhaps over a thousand. Most astoundingly, there was a debate in Tokyo over who had the authority to order in assistance, such as from Japan's Self-Defense Forces (SDF), to help survivors. The Ministry of Foreign Affairs had delayed before accepting international offers of assistance, while waiting for authorization in the multilayered crisis management system. One Japanese student in my office at Tsukuba University, where I was conducting my dissertation research, piled her friends into a car to drive to Kobe to help out, since it appeared that rescue and relief efforts would be up to citizens themselves.

At the center of the political maelstrom was Prime Minister Murayama

Tomiichi, almost certainly the wrong man for the job at that moment. Two years earlier, a massive financial scandal involving LDP kingpin Kanemaru Shin, implicated in taking illegal donations from a trucking company and then hiding roughly $40 million in undeclared assets, had shattered Japan's political landscape. Upset at the sudden downturn of his fortunes within the party, Kanemaru's protégé, Ozawa Ichiro, bolted from the party with a number of other faction members, creating Shinseitō (the New Life Party). Doing so paved the way for the fall of Prime Minister Miyazawa and the convoluted ascendance of Japan's first non-LDP government since 1955, a visibly fragile coalition headed by former Kumamoto governor Hosokawa Morihiro. Although this government was profoundly troubled by internal ideological strife, it achieved some key successes, including a dramatic reform of Japan's electoral system, which Ozawa had hoped would promote a two-party system akin to that of the United States.[29]

The LDP was not the only party threatened by this development. Ozawa, largely seen as the brains behind the coalition, had hoped to demolish the Japan Socialist Party (JSP), and a shift toward single-member districts from proportional representation would likely cost a number of Socialists their seats in the Diet.[30] And so when Hosokawa was himself implicated in a financial scandal, the angry JSP took the opportunity to leave the coalition; now a minority in the Diet, the hodge-podge collection of new parties lasted for only two more months under the leadership of Prime Minister Hata Tsutomu. The JSP and LDP decided to overlook their longstanding differences and formed a new coalition with a new party, New Harbinger Party–Sakigake, in a compromise that resulted in the improbable rise of Murayama Tomiichi as the first Socialist Party prime minister in over four decades. In the process of cementing the alliance, Murayama forced his JSP to drop its longstanding position that the Self-Defense Forces' existence was unconstitutional. For Japanese used to LDP domination, the party's loss of power was strange enough; the rupture of the ideological fault line that had divided Japanese politics for four decades was enough to cause political whiplash. Largely in response to the horror of witnessing this cynical departure from the parties' founding principles, Japanese observers began to agree that Japanese politics had reached a fundamental crisis.[31]

The Hanshin earthquake could therefore hardly have come at a worse political moment. Murayama—more pragmatic than some in the JSP, but still fundamentally uneasy with the existence of the Self-Defense Forces and uncomfortable with executive power—also faced significant political and constitutional constraints on the use of extraordinary prime ministerial authority. And he was simply not the leader who would be willing to shatter taboos against the SDF's rapid deployment, even to save the lives of citizens. Before the government finally sent in national support to beleaguered local authorities, fires burned on, almost certainly killing more victims, as other people presumably died while trapped under debris. In the final tally, the earthquake claimed over six thousand lives, in addition to the tens of thousands injured or left homeless.

Public reaction ranged from anger to disbelief, though it was often marked by the country's deep ideological fissures. Sassa Atsuyuki, a retired National Police Agency (NPA) official, laid the blame directly at the doorstep of Prime Minister Murayama and his inability to manage crises,[32] though Sassa's later discussions of terrorism and other crises, outlined in chapters 5 and 6, described the problem as more structural and less personal. The moderately conservative opinion journal *Chūō Kōron* published several reports on the failure of the Japanese state to deal in any systematic way with emergencies, and pointed to the need for the government to develop institutions allowing, for example, for the more rapid deployment of the Self-Defense Forces to deal with natural disasters.[33] Wary of the sudden boost for enhanced executive authority over the military, left-leaning sources, like the opinion magazine *Sekai*, argued that disaster relief functions for the SDF would fly in the face of public understanding of its role, and that different disaster relief units should be created.[34] Real earthquake preparedness would lie in wiser construction standards and better urban planning to reduce overcrowding.[35]

That committed intellectuals and pundits tend to see events through ideological lenses should come as no surprise. More critical, however, is the way in which the government's inability to cope with the Hanshin earthquake provided a crucial new focus for public dissatisfaction with politics. As in other advanced industrial nations, public trust in government in Japan had been on the decline for decades, with especially dismal views of the corruptibility of politicians.[36] After the earthquake, however, the distrust focused no longer just on greedy politicians but also on a fundamentally dysfunctional, even incompetent, state.

Indeed, the Hanshin earthquake and the subsequent Aum Shinrikyo incident together provoked new legislation for Japanese crisis management, described in chapter 5. But the earthquake also forced the government to respond to public demands for a larger and more autonomous role for Japan's nonprofit organizations (NPOs), whose heroic efforts in

Kobe had enhanced their public stature.[37] Although the decline in public trust in the Japanese government has been a long-term phenomenon, and the weird JSP-LDP combination had already provoked the idea of crisis, the Hanshin earthquake was undoubtedly a watershed event. It had, at least in the eyes of many observers, laid bare fundamental problems of a political system whose stability had commonly been seen as both cause and effect of Japan's long period of postwar economic growth. Even if one withholds judgment regarding the rapid defections and new alliances that typified Japanese politics in the mid-1990s, there is no doubt that the slow response of an economic superpower to a reasonably predictable natural disaster within its own borders was a political failure of the first order. And whatever prescription one had—for a military or nonmilitary capacity to deal with similar events, or for the empowerment of nongovernmental organizations—the earthquake suggested to many of Japan's opinion leaders that their nation was a shadow leviathan, unable to guarantee even their most fundamental safety.

The Aum Shinrikyo Attack and Social Collapse

With Japan still reeling from the Hanshin earthquake, on March 20, 1995, operatives from one of Japan's "new religious movements," Aum Shinrikyo, released bags of sarin gas on four subway cars converging simultaneously on Kasumigaseki Station. Kasumigaseki's symbolic stature in Japan appears even in its name, which translates roughly as the Gates of the Heavens. The home of Japan's major ministries, its vulnerability to such a major attack with a weapon of mass destruction made immediate headlines around the world; even though the attack fortunately killed only twelve people, it injured and could have killed thousands. The failure of Japan's internal security organizations to prevent the attack—in spite of evidence implicating the cult in a similar 1994 attack in Matsumoto City—also became the subject of intense political scrutiny (discussed in chapter 5).

But much of the debate in shock-weary Japan focused on how society could have produced such a group of monsters, a line of questioning that built on time-honored efforts to distinguish between responsible adults and a purportedly unrecognizable generation of youths. In the immediate aftermath of the Aum attack, a wide range of observers asked what had gone wrong in Japan to allow the cult to form, to draw in so many members, to make them so murderously faithful to a guru, Asahara

Shoko, who seemed little more than a short, hirsute, self-evidently nutty charlatan. Particularly notable in these analyses was the alarming spread of Japan's "new religions," or as Japanese religion scholar and historian Helen Hardacre puts it, "new new religions." As opposed to some of the religious movements in Japan after World War II, most of them espousing New Age–type dogma, the "new new religions" have often posited apocalyptic forces and seem to draw in part on entertainment-produced images of the end of the world.[38]

Some Japanese writers have taken the rise of Aum as evidence of a rootless society that provides opportunities for the manipulation of citizens. Religion scholar Nakamura Yūjirō, for example, suggests that Asahara was able to encourage young people to kill for him in part because of the spiritual "vacuum" in modern Japan.[39] Among a wide variety of voices, though primarily from the left end of the political spectrum, education scholar Kariya Takehiko has argued that the Aum attack is a consequence of the Japanese educational system. In this view, schools that that do not teach children to think critically or to question have left them helpless against a guru like Asahara.[40] One of Japan's foremost commentators on the relationship between politics and the media, Yoshimi Shun'ya, suggested that there was something in the structure of Japan's everyday consciousness that had created Aum. Referring to Max Picard's *Hitler in Ourselves*, Yoshimi pointed to common media-inspired images of power, technological triumph, and spiritual emptiness that fueled Aum's rise. Without placing the blame on any specific institution or group, he argued that a modern fascination with the occult, science fiction, and apocalyptic violence are themselves emblematic of deep uncertainty in the Japanese consciousness.[41] Novelist Haruki Murakami interviewed several members of Aum, though not any directly related to the attack, and he found that references to science fiction and the occult appeared regularly. As one former member, who had joined Aum after reading some of its gloomy promotional literature, put it, "What I liked most about the Aum books was that they clearly stated that the world was evil. I was happy when I read that."[42]

None of Murakami's respondents contrasted Japan with the rest of the world, or suggested that their unhappiness was a specifically Japanese phenomenon. And yet foreign and Japanese observers alike imposed this conception of a damaged modern Japan on them. Some of the soul-searching likely follows from unifying theories of Japanese uniqueness that have occasionally been expressed in biological terms, though more normally in social ones.[43] Although widely critiqued,[44] these theories of national distinctiveness ("Japanese are group-oriented," "Japanese society is structured around the family and village") have been important themes in political discourse.[45] Sometimes used with pride to explain particular Japanese successes, such as the country's relatively low crime rate or its economic miracle, these theories have also been useful when something goes wrong. The Japanese are x, so y happened: cause and effect.

Wider questions about cults in other nations rarely entered the debate. For example, the spooky similarities between the police raid on Asahara's Aum compound and the apprehension of Charles Manson and the Manson Family in the United States in 1969 could have become a device for cross-national comparison of murderous cults.[46] Aum had many followers in Russia, a connection noted in Japan mostly because of growing evidence that this was where Asahara's minions had gained access to weapons and matériel.[47] Yet the focus was almost invariably on something about modern Japan that had created Aum—a focus that allowed observers to channel their various frustrations with the country onto a small group of young fanatics.

This depiction of the Aum generation as a distinctively Japanese set of wayward youth involved longer-term debates about social change. In the 1980s, the rise of a "new species" (*shinjinrui*) of materialistic yuppies generated a critical panic among pundits who found their work and leisure ethics badly out of place with the austere practices of their parents, who had ostensibly built the Japanese miracle. Some of the concern, as Sharon Kinsella notes, was certainly related to increased concern about women's professional and personal behavior.[48] By the late 1980s, it was already clear that Japanese women were marrying and becoming pregnant later than before.[49] Within ten years, partly because of public concerns about Japan's declining birth rate, this phenomenon had gone from demographic curiosity to evidence of national decline. Some Japanese commentators began to label such young people as "parasite singles" who prefer to mooch off their parents than to grow up and marry.[50] The public debates have usually focused on the women involved, making them gendered symbols of a selfish generation that refuses even its most basic responsibility of reproducing the nation.[51]

These demographic trends had started before 1990, as had the rise, for example, in pregnancies before marriage. But by the 1990s, they were becoming central features in Japanese political and public discourse: unnerving aspects of modern Japan like increases in juvenile crime and divorce. As had the jūsen failures and the Hanshin earthquake, the Aum attack provoked wildly different judgments of the proper solutions, in this case meaning better policing of religious movements or more liberal, individualistic education. Underlying these arguments, however, was an increasingly widespread sense that the attack represented a genuine crisis in Japanese society. Even if people were not, as Yoshimi prescribed, interested in finding the "Aum inside ourselves," there clearly were searches for the features inside of Japan that had produced Aum. Increasingly, this meant attention to a generation that threatened Japan not only through selfishness and irresponsibility but also through their alienation from traditional values and the willingness of some to use brutal violence in acting out their frustrations.

The fear appears, and is critiqued, in the last film completed by one of Japan's most famous directors, Fukasaku Kinji, before his death. Based on the 1999 novel by Takami Kōshun, *Battle Royale* depicts Japan in the near future, when juvenile delinquency has become so severe a problem that the government has passed a law to annually send one junior high school homeroom to a deserted island, where they must slaughter one another within three days. Fukasaku uses flashbacks to summarize Takami's interior monologues, which had explained the character relationships of the children in the novel, but he focuses more on the alliances and deception occurring on the island. Even weirder are the flashbacks that depict the life of their pitiless teacher (director and comic Kitano Takeshi) as a sad, lonely mess. His own family is in shambles, shaping his vindictive and murderous behavior toward his students. Some of the kids are a bit rough around the edges, but there are only one or two genuinely bad eggs in the class. Released by the deeply conservative studio Tōei—whose last controversial film had been *Puraido: Unmei no toki* (Pride: The Moment of Fate), a biography lionizing Japan's wartime prime minister, Tōjō Hideki—*Battle Royale* is an unexpectedly and weirdly antiauthoritarian action film. In the near future, Japan is so deeply dysfunctional as a society that it scapegoats and kills its own children.[52]

Aum Shinrikyo's attack neither created nor concluded long-standing debates over Japan's wayward youth. It did, however, serve as something of a turning point in these discussions as well as larger ones about Japan's direction. Coming so soon after the first major financial failures in decades and the Hanshin earthquake, the sarin gas attack helped to redefine debates about Japan's specific problems, turning them into larger themes about Japan's future. These events did not change core ideologies, which is to be expected. The September 11 attacks in the United States convinced U.S. conservatives that the country needed to take a stronger stand against its enemies, a belief most of them already had. U.S. liberals, on the other hand, pointed to flaws in foreign policy and prescribed more attention to economic and social justice, which already typified their views of the world. Confronted with the events of 1995, conservatives in Japan pushed for greater coercive authority and more fidelity to traditional values, whereas progressives argued that Japan's coercive systems had already produced a generation capable of carrying out the attack. The idea of crisis, however, had become ubiquitous.

Saving Japan from Itself

By mid-1995, the ground had been laid for a wide-ranging pessimism about the country's future. Rather than focusing on specific financial challenges, curricular problems in education, or individual political scandals, Japanese writers and pundits began to discuss the problems as part of a larger social malaise. In some cases, the authors used these concerns to argue for specific political agendas, while in others they served largely to underscore amorphous critiques of postwar Japan. But the idea of overarching crisis had become part of a broad national consensus, albeit one with differing opinions about what the crisis meant and how Japan should best deal with it.

Shortly after the gas attack, well-known anthropologist Aoki Tamotsu argued in *Chūō Kōron* that the Aum attack was symptomatic of a shift in Japanese society from a broad-based ideology of development to a fear of general decline. The Hanshin earthquake had only exacerbated an amorphous fear of collapse, punctuated by hollow claims of reform that would ostensibly deliver Japan from its troubles.[53] In a published conversation[54] with famous anatomist and pundit Yōrō Takeshi, Aoki went further and argued that the outcomes of the sarin incident reflected a larger Japanese fear of disorder:

> Japanese think that problems are going to be solved, and so when something remains unresolved, we are really unsettled. Because we have an almost religious faith in order [*chitsujō shinkō*], any disturbance in that order really shakes us psychologically.

Yōrō responds, "I have felt the same way about Japan for a long time."[55]

Some pundits were eager to point fingers, to explain what had produced disorder—and to offer solutions for bringing Japan back. The most important of these, Ishihara Shintarō, is famous in the United States for his anti-American comments in his book *The Japan That Can Say No*, and reviled in much of Asia for his frequently xenophobic rants.[56] But his recent success as a politician—after resigning from the Diet in 1995, he became the governor of Tokyo in 1999 and was reelected in 2003—owes more to his populist rhetoric and his reputation as a refreshingly and politically incorrect straight talker.[57] In summer 1995, he argued that the crises should force a fundamental rethinking of Japan's relationship to the world. Japan had for too long debased itself by obeying a constitution forced on it as punishment for the war, even to the point that the government had dawdled in response to the Hanshin earthquake. Unlike Sassa, however, Ishihara does not limit his critique to the Murayama cabinet. He writes that "what is really wrong, I think, is more than just the politicians. It's also the citizens who do not even try to show or express the frustration and anxiety that they know in their hearts to be true." Ishihara argues that it will be critical for people to rethink who makes their decisions for them, and whether their political needs should really be determined by an international system set up for the benefit of others.[58]

In a subsequent piece, Ishihara pressed the antiregime message that later made him so popular with Tokyo voters. The problem was with an ossified bureaucracy and a political elite too ensconced in their tired ways to really fix Japan's problems.[59] Neither of these sentiments was particularly new to Ishihara, who had long critiqued the pacifist constitution and any politicians or bureaucrats with the temerity to disagree with him. The government's inability to cope with mounting political and economic crises, however, had given his arguments new traction.

Japan has, of course, long had a strain of nationalistic thought, and its upsurge in the 1990s might reflect the breakdown of traditional cold war rivalries[60] more than it does tension and conflict within Japan.[61] But the idea of a general crisis for Japan—economic, political, even spiritual (all three figure in different ways in Ishihara's articles, for example)—became generally accepted fodder for conservative politicians. Indeed, Koizumi Jun'ichirō's remarkable popularity, at least for part of his tenure, reflected his reputation as a straight shooter who worshipped no sacred cows, whether bureaucrats or elites in his own Liberal Democratic Party, in his efforts to fundamentally reform Japan. His visits to the controversial Yasukuni Shrine—which houses the souls of Japan's war dead, including a number of war criminals—surely displayed political calculations involving the interests of Japan's Far Right. But to his supporters, they also showed him to be a maverick, one who is prepared to take bold steps even when they are diplomatically risky.[62]

Notably, conversations among the Left accepted the basic premise that conservatives like Ishihara emphasized: that Japan was mired in a crisis of national decline that went beyond any specific event. In May 1995, *Sekai* published an instructive chat between commentator Kawamoto Sanjurō and author Yamada Taiichi, entitled "Aimai na fūan no jidai" (The Age of Vague Anxiety). Like Aoki, who argued that Japan's faith in order had been ruptured, Yamada and Kawamoto point to a crisis, typified by lack of faith in long-standing institutions. In their view, however, an ideology of development had consumed Japan in much of the postwar era, and Japanese were starting to see the costs. They would for this reason reach a new conclusion, one that would typify a number of the Left's claims in the following years: decline might be a good thing for Japan. Yamada says:

> The highest value in Japan is for calm [*heion*]. So if we don't experience a real decline [that can shake things up], our sense of values will become completely ambiguous. It's gotten so that we're not really working for ourselves or for our own standards, but rather, since the end of the war, for this unchanging goal [of economic development]. And now the downside of this approach is continuing to become more apparent. But we don't have any ability on our own to change this paradigm. I think most Japanese are subconsciously hoping for foreign pressure or for national decline [*shūmatsu*], something from outside that will force us to change.[63]

This became a frequent refrain of progressives, that the breakdown of Japan's faith in certain institutions had opened space for real social change, the kind that would make Japan a better, healthier, kinder place. In 1998, Kina Shōkichi, a top Okinawan music star, sat down for a chat with third-generation Korean-Japanese, left-learning commentator Shin Sugok. Although *Sekai* had asked them to speak primarily about the meaning and nature of Japanese culture, Kina and Shin went much further, tracing the breakdown of traditional structures in Japan and arguing that the society was experiencing a new vitality, introduced by previously marginalized groups. Japan's old system had ostensibly treated rebels especially badly, but the crisis that shattered faith in these institutions had created a new and better Japan, one that might genuinely respect diversity and the rights of all—ethnic outsiders, foreigners, women, and gays and lesbians.[64] This type of argument became a common one for foreign commentators eager to see a fresh, "cool" Japan birthed by the acknowledged crises of the 1990s.[65]

The Speed of Calamity

Any brief description of a full decade in a country is bound to be misleading. Japan entered and left the 1990s with the world's second largest economy, extraordinary health care, nearly perfect adult literacy, and admirably low crime rates. Its problems would be the envy of most nations. I could have organized the chapter around other developments that might be equally representative of other broad themes. The country's reading habits changed dramatically, with fiction sales plummeting and self-help books (often by U.S. personal development gurus) picking up some of the slack. The imperial family's stature grew, in contrast to that of royals elsewhere. An aging population has made new demands on a social welfare system that has traditionally depended on family support for the elderly. Unlike 1990, there are now so many foreigners—both visible and "stealth *gaijin*" (as one Korean-American friend described himself)—that I now feel blissfully unnoticed in Tokyo.

I have concentrated on the traumas of 1995, because I believe that it is worth considering how Japan's "crisis" became a pervasive, all-encompassing phenomenon. Each of the incidents challenged fundamental institutions that had always been partially fictive—the benevolent corporation-employee relationship, the competent if sometimes dishonest state, the meticulously effective school—and left far more questions than answers. The Hanshin earthquake and the Aum attack figure into virtually any Japanese conversation about the most critical events of the 1990s, producing myriad and often conflicting lessons about what Japan should have done differently. Additionally, virtually nothing about Japan since the 1990s can be seen as completely independent of its long recession, with profound consequences for employment relations, housing, and the causes of death. The timing of these 1995 problems could scarcely have been crueler, leaving many in Japan wondering just how bad it could get. And indeed, without the prospect of fundamental reform—painful, uncertain reform—there was little reason to believe that things would not get worse. In this context, it has become easier for officials to argue that the state needs to take firmer steps to stop growing disorder (two examples of which provide the core of this book) in order to bring back some semblance of normality to a country seen as sliding into entropy.

Of course, one's perspective on either a reenergized, nationalistic Japan or a Japan whose institutional failures had shown the way to a more progressive future depends on one's preexisting views of what was right and wrong with Japan. But after 1995, virtually everyone in Japan agreed that there was *something* that had changed, and that this something went far beyond a simple business downturn, or a small group of mass murderers, or a bumbling response to a natural disaster that would likely have killed thousands in even the best of circumstances. People can be wrong of course. They almost certainly were in 1990s Japan, at least insofar as some sought to find the magic explanation that could account for so much going so wrong so quickly. But people create their own reality; whether there were real witches in Salem was less important, at least in terms of consequences for the town, than people's belief that there were. A pervasive sense of crisis can have profound consequences, particularly for those (politicians, bureaucrats, young people, women, foreigners) ultimately believed to be part of the problem. Shopping for wine and waiting for the solitary comfort afforded by the vibration of a cell phone could now be political symbols—of women rejecting a coercive society or of a selfish generation concerned more with leeching off the nation than with reproducing it.

Although I have no desire to understate the challenges faced by Japan—after all, I do not envy an employment environment in which killing oneself might well be a financially responsible decision—I hope to qualify the meaning of crisis for the nation. I would agree with those analysts who argue that the financial, political, and social crises shattered some of the myths about Japan's family-nation. But I think that they have been replaced not by more "realistic" understandings of what the country is but rather by newly idealized conceptions that have been filtered through long-standing debates and political positions over what kind of country Japan is supposed to be. This is, unfortunately, no less challenging for foreign observers like myself than for the Japanese writers and commentators who are themselves embedded in and implicated by the national structures and institutions they critique.

The speed of calamity in 1990s Japan throws the clash of Japan's views into sharp relief, but it is far from a uniquely Japanese phenomenon. For example, Philip Roth's later novels, such as *The Human Stain* and *American Pastoral*, are unintelligible without consideration of how social and political upheavals in the 1960s undermined one set of myths about America, only to replace them with others. Japan's changes, however, altered the environment in which the country's policymakers, writers, and audiences came to view demands from overseas. In the next four chapters, we turn to cases in which Japan faced pressure to adhere to developing international standards of law enforcement, specifically with reference to the sexual exploitation of children and to terrorism. In both cases, officials found it easier to tackle current issues when they could align international pressure with prevailing fears about the direction in which the country was moving. International norms could justify steps that might have been otherwise constitutionally difficult, while their deployment against popularly accepted fears made them politically acceptable.

The prototypical *kogal* look, Ikebukuro, May 2004.

CHAPTER THREE

"WHATEVER IT IS, IT'S BAD, SO STOP IT"

Among the many unsettling changes facing 1990s Japan—the recession, late-marrying women, the striking growth in the number of foreign residents—the reported rise in juvenile delinquency was a particularly popular topic of conversation. There had, of course, been earlier crime waves by Japanese teens, and one might easily date the current problems with teens as having preceded Japan's economic decline. After all, during my first trip to Japan, in 1989 and 1990, a manga with film spin-offs, *Be-Bop High School,* celebrated the rebellious and violent behavior of a pair of uniform-clad high school boys, provoking expressions of concern over how the media were affecting real life. In November 1989, I sat in the teachers' office of a grimy suburban junior high school—where I was temporarily stationed as an assistant English teacher—watching a lanky, spiky-haired teen, brandishing a broom handle, stand behind the gym teacher. My Japanese was execrable, and I was in any case too confused about what I was witnessing to attempt even to use it. Instead, another teacher yelled, "Look out!" The gym teacher sidestepped the blow, which I think the student actually delayed. He had been holding the makeshift weapon for several seconds and only brought it down when the teacher made his move to the left. My guess is that the student made his point just by swinging the broom handle downward like a sledgehammer, crashing it harmlessly into the floor, and forcing the teachers to jump on him to prevent him from taking a second shot.

They handled it calmly, holding the boy and talking him down; things like this had happened before. But one would not necessarily realize that from discussions that were taking place seven years later. As the heady 1980s turned into the shaky 1990s, a possibly short-term rise in juvenile crime, coupled with a small number of particularly gruesome murders by teens, provoked a fundamental national rethinking of the threat that young people posed. In this chapter, I address especially the increasing image of the social threat that teenage girls presented, arguing that newly troubling images of them were inextricably tied both to large-scale anxiety over the juvenile crime wave and the sexual precociousness of girls and young women. My goal is to focus the discussion of anxiety—which in chapter 2 dwelt on larger national concerns—on a specific topic, that of teenage girls and their most famous, if largely alleged, activity, "compensated dating." It was this arena that proved crucial in Japan's adoption of a major international norm of criminal justice, legislation against the sexual exploitation of children. The selection of the issue strikes me as both fair and appropriate, because if the 1990s are acknowledged as a period of remarkable social change in Japan, the decade could hardly find a more apt symbol than that of the *kogal.*

Considering Kogals and the Sex Industry

Generally used to describe teenage girls with dyed hair, an affection for gaudy makeup, and apparent access to high-priced fashion items, the term *kogal* is derived from both English and Japanese. The English word "girl" or "gal" has, in Japanese, longstanding connotations of worldliness and even immorality;[1] the prefix, *ko,* either means "little" or is a shortened version of *kōkō* (high school), therefore referring to high school girls.[2] Either way, the kogal struck the Japanese popular imagination like a thunderbolt, and there is a case to be made that the kogal image epitomized Japan's hazily defined crisis of the 1990s at least as well as did layoffs by top Japanese firms. To some, the kogal represented an element of creativity and originality in a society driven too long by consumerist conformity; for others, she embodied Japan's decisive turn toward the moral precipice. Crucially, as an easily recognized image, the kogal could be exploited—to sell fashion magazines, to market the need for tighter control over juveniles, or to indicate a potential direction for the empowerment of women and girls in a patriarchal society.

Kogals also became central, if sometimes only implied, figures in a debate over Japan's adherence to a developing international norm regarding child prostitution and child pornography. Because of the links drawn between kogals and enjo kōsai ("compensated dating"), in which women and girls are paid for dates and sometimes sex, a number of observers, foreign and Japanese alike, have referred casually to enjo kōsai as prostitution, usually by schoolgirls, though this became a complex definitional issue in Japanese politics. The connection, however, complicated the Japanese application of the international norm against the sexual exploitation of children, which became localized in Japan as a wedge for stopping enjo kōsai. Interestingly, these efforts ultimately came to include potential punishment for the girls, tagging them as perpetrators rather than simply as victims. In chapter 4 I trace the evolution of the international norm itself, as well as Japan's fretful response to it—a response that has been more effectively implemented against local "compensated dating" than against the international sex tourism market that the global movement had aimed to halt. Although the 1999 Law for Punishing Acts Related to Child Prostitution and Child Pornography and for Protecting Children (Jidō Poruno/Jidō Kaishun Kinshi Hō) was a result in part of the efforts of Japanese dedicated to ending the scourge of rich sex tourists' preying on minors in countries like Thailand and the Philippines, its implementation was shaped in large measure by growing fears at home over Japanese girls gone wild.

The kogal was an ambiguous figure for much of the decade, during which popular images of kogals as a menace coexisted uneasily with efforts to explain and to justify their appearance. At a time when Japanese police were laboring to revise laws protecting juveniles from prosecution for most crimes—all the while bumping up against tight constitutional and political constraints—debates over kogals and enjo kōsai provided an extraordinary glimpse at the creation, maintenance, and use of social problems. Were the girls victims or villains? Were they seductresses or merely show-offs? Would they grow up to be terrible wives and mothers, or would they simply be reabsorbed into a putatively conservative national family structure? In this chapter I trace the changes in legal and moral conceptions of children, especially girls, and argue that enjo kōsai as a practice developed in part as the unintended consequence of sex industry regulations designed specifically to protect the innocence of schoolgirls. The kogals—who stand for alternately rebellion against a crushingly patriarchal social order or an amoral slide from traditional values—played a crucial if primarily iconographic role. Although they were largely judged to be a social menace, the debate was far from over, and the legal circumstances were still up for grabs at the time that left-leaning activists pushed their government to protect other Asian children from wealthy sex tourists. The norm itself became a vital element in the argument over this gaudy emblem of a tumultuous era for Japan, particularly as the proscription against child prostitution came to be used as a further critique of girls and young women who entered the sex trade.

The sex industry in Japan is, by almost any measure, enormous. A sprawling literature in English on the subject has developed, ranging from the historically descriptive[3] to the relatively salacious.[4] American journalists seem to be especially interested in the fact that sexual commerce is nearly inescapable; a Japanese news magazine I purchased for an article cited in chapter 6 also included a long photo spread on sex businesses in Nagoya as well as a behind-the-scenes account of one of Japan's most famous male porn stars.[5] One relatively common theme in the popular literature is an overly broad delineation between sexual mores in "the West" and the presumably more free-spirited and tolerant "East."[6] These usually come with some reference to the role of prostitution in Japan's political past or with a generic claim about the difference between Christian and Buddhist judgments about sex. But in Japan, too, there are tough judgments about sex: what is right and wrong, permissible and impermissible, extolled and forbidden. Popular views and public rules about sexuality bear the strong imprint of international—particularly U.S. and European—influences. Sexuality has become another avenue for Japan's modernization, attended by ideas of proper or scientifically defensible sexual behavior.[7] And it has also included fluid but consistently tense notions of innocence, and of the types of women and girls who would sell themselves.

But before the following chapter's investigation of the 1999 introduction of legislation against child prostitution and child pornography, I examine the context then facing Japanese activists, legislators, and policymakers. Concerns over child welfare, new threats posed by juvenile offenders, and judgments about the moral fiber of sex workers all entered the discussion. All of these reflected tensions between conservative efforts to use the state to guarantee protection of the social order and liberal interests in limiting the state's reach into individual lives. Significantly, these tensions bore the heavy imprint of international influences, from Western-derived notions of romance and sexuality to U.S.-written constitutional guarantees of juvenile rights. The international norm met in Japan neither a tabula rasa, an empty nation waiting to be aligned with global standards, nor an untouched land of authentic and essential difference. Instead, it ran into political judgments in a nation already deeply affected by transnational discourses about innocence, sin, sex, and responsibility. And it should tell us something about the limits of norms that Japan in 2004 seemed no more identical, at least in terms of sexual mores, to the United States or France than it did in 1990.

A caveat is in order. The prevalence of uniformed schoolgirls (or adults dressed as such) in Japanese pornography has only compounded the country's reputation overseas as a nation of pedophiles. In this chapter, I do not examine whether Japan displays more or less pedophiliac tendencies than other advanced industrial nations, and I make no effort to explain why people do or do not find teenagers attractive. Others have traced and explained the special role of "cuteness" (*kawaii*) in Japan,[8] which undoubtedly affects the shape and size of sex markets involving schoolgirls or their imitators. With regard to the legal and political issues involved, however, I am loath to draw too clear a distinction between Japan and other countries. Japanese schoolgirl outfits resemble those in the United Kingdom or Catholic schools in the United States, where they have been fetishized for years.[9] Indeed, the late 1990s popularity of the pop singer Britney Spears cannot easily be separated from her appearance in a schoolgirl uniform in one of her early music videos. But the uniform is hardly a prerequisite for the sexualization of children, particularly where marketing is concerned. Brooke Shields initially became a star as an American teen model who appeared partly naked in Calvin Klein ads and in *The Blue Lagoon*. Even judged from a distinctly moralistic perspective, Japan cannot be considered uniquely villainous in its handling of children as sex objects.

Children and their Welfare

Constructing Children in Prewar Japan

Children, as both symbol and social category, played a crucial role in the development of modern Japan's political ideology, starting with the Meiji Restoration (1868). As Kawaji Toshiyoshi, who created the Japanese national police, remarked in 1876, "The nation is a family—the government, the parents; the people, the children; and the police, their nursemaids." Moreover, the Imperial Rescript on Education, which had, on its 1890 promulgation, pushed primarily for public morality, was quickly reinterpreted as a statement for nationalism that held the family as its foundation.[10] Because political documents from this era so clearly rely on children and families as metaphors, one might be forgiven for assuming that they were self-evident categories. Meiji Japan's collision with "modern" mores, however, dramatically altered prevailing conceptions of what children are and what actual and symbolic roles they should play.

Children represent one of the most deeply naturalized classificatory schemes in modern history. When we think about other ways of conceptualizing people, we imply a history. My identity as an American is itself deeply institutionalized, and yet I know that "America" did not always exist, even as linguistic shorthand for the United States; calling oneself an "American" could not have made much sense in the mid-seventeenth century. Similarly, most would likely understand that the idea of a "housewife" has limited relevance in primarily agrarian societies where both men and women work the fields and live near them. But when we think of "the child," we tend to project the concept backward, to take for granted that there is something natural about the term. Children are seen not just as vulnerable—and therefore in need of protection—because of their size and lack of experience, but also as innocent, and therefore less deserving of the world's myriad cruelties than adults.

Partly for this reason, sociologist and former Ministry of Health and Welfare child welfare specialist Kashiwame Reihō has noted that "child" is far more than a clinical, social, or legal category, and is widely used in political rhetoric. Because the child is innocent, incapable of either moral transgression or ethical judgment, advocates of social regulation often invoke the child, who must be protected from "bad areas" where prostitution and vice flourish. This tendency is one of the foundations of contemporary paternalism.[11] Americans like myself can see this at home, of course, where efforts to use the machinery of the state to ban or restrict certain activities or commodities (violent video games, gangsta rap music, guns, tobacco, and the like) focus almost invariably on their putative effects on the young. In promoting widespread testing for drugs at schools, President George W. Bush remarked in his 2004 State of the Union address, "The aim here is not to punish children, but to send them this message: We love you, and we don't want to lose you."[12] Although the state's initiatives are by any measure coercive, they are justified specifically because they protect children from adults and even from their own urges.

According to the late media critic Neil Postman, the concept of the "child" is a recent invention, inextricably tied to notions of shame, morality, and propriety. The idea that children deserve special protection grows from a sense that they are not responsible for their moral actions and need to be shielded from some kinds of influences as well as abuses that they are ill-equipped to confront.[13] Some Japanese scholars, even while citing Postman, have been quick to point out that his understanding of the child comes entirely from a Western European and North American cultural context. In Japan, argues Kashiwame, the concept has a longer pedigree. The written word *jidō* (used as a technical and legal term for "child," and less common conversationally than the more colloquial *kodomo*) is formed out of two Chinese characters, the first referring originally to a soft or unformed cranium, and the second meaning "slave" or "manservant." In combination, the term originally referred to the biological characteristics of children as well as their subservient social position. When encoded in legal texts after the Meiji Restoration, the term referred initially to the age of legal responsibility for crime. But with the drive to classify the new nation with modern specificity, the Meiji oligarchs began to define age groups more precisely. Until the age of three, Japanese were *eiji* (infants); between three and six, they were *gaiji* (toddlers); at seven, they became *jidō*; and they became adults at the ages of thirteen for girls and fifteen for boys.[14]

Another sociologist, Kawahara Kazue, argues that the development of the social concept of the child in Japan is unintelligible without reference to Western influences. In feudal Japan the relevant distinctions had not been between children and adults so much as between castes and genders, so boys from peasant families were conceptualized in roughly the same category as men from the their class, with little connection to girls from upper-class families. There was far less attention to differentiating children from adults in terms of rights and responsibilities than there was between women and men, or between samurai and merchants. The Meiji government's efforts to modernize Japan quickly involved the adoption of foreign categories that destabilized notions of caste and prompted an emphasis on people in generational terms. Subsequent efforts by authors to emulate European children's literature helped to establish clear delineations between children and adults, imputing innocence to the former and probable guilt to the latter. As such, the idea of children increasingly became infused with a romanticism that resembled if not mirrored its European sources.[15]

Throughout this period, oligarchs in the new state pushed through relevant laws. These reflected both the government's push to become a "rich nation with a strong army" (*fukoku kyōhei*) and the government's susceptibility to broad international trends. By 1872, mindful of the need to have healthy children (in part to provide future military forces), the government mandated the provision of a minimal amount of rice for abandoned children until they reached the age of fifteen; two years later, another order provided rice for poor families with more than three children. Laws providing for schools and reformatories (*kankain*) and abolishing labor for very young children followed between 1910 and 1925, particularly after the establishment of the League of Nations, which pushed for more tightly codified protection. Children featured prominently in Japan's first real welfare law, including 1929's Kyūgohō (Relief Law), which focused especially on child protection (*jidō hogo*) for those under thirteen. It included financial relief and basic medical care for impoverished young children and pregnant women and was perhaps the first step toward Japan's modern welfare state. By 1933, the establishment of new laws and ordinances banning specific types of child abuse helped expand the notion of "child protection."[16] These increased protections shadowed the development of sentimentalized notions of children's physical and emotional vulnerability, which had been presented in magazines for Japan's middle class from 1915 onward. Protection was not simply a legal responsibility for a modern state but also the duty of a just and moral society.[17]

Occupation Era and Postwar Reforms

Before World War II Japan had thus witnessed an elaboration of the concept of the child, with political authorities simultaneously extending protection to children while using the child's role as a metaphor for the citizen's in a patrimonial state. U.S. Occupation forces in Japan—who themselves employed paternalistic imagery in their training of a newly democratic Japan—viewed the relationship between the state and children as crucial in Japan's development. As early as September 1945, the Ministry of Education was instructed by the Supreme Commander for the Allied Powers (SCAP) administration that the military youth organizations were to be disbanded, effectively ending one crucial area of national governmental control over children. In complying with the order, the ministry encouraged prefectural governors to establish local children's organizations in order to prevent the children from being "left unorganized in their social life." SCAP also did what it could to decentralize control over social education, leaving it more up to localities and less to the national government.[18]

In compelling the Ministry of Health and Welfare to rewrite Japan's child protection laws, the Occupation authorities appear to have been motivated by a dual concern with standardized protection of children's welfare—imagined in a broader way by these New Deal–educated reformers than by the Japanese bureaucrats who narrowly construed it as support for orphans or the very poor—and a decentralization of authority over their moral behavior. The Child Welfare Law, a civil law promulgated in 1947, thus began primarily as an effort to combine and to expand on Japan's myriad laws and directives on such topics as social payments to poor children, reformatories, juvenile delinquency, child abuse, and the like.[19] In describing the purpose of their initial proposals, a Ministry of Health and Welfare subcommittee explained the shift to a broader vision of child welfare:

> The law's purpose is not limited to children in exceptional or unusual circumstances but rather is focused on comprehensive protection for all children; it is necessary that the law be clear and positive about this. We therefore hope that the phrase "children who need protection" be stricken from the proposal. . . . The law's goal is to advocate the clear and positive improvement of the general welfare of children, so it should be called the Child Welfare Law.[20]

Governments that extol the innocence and vulnerability of all children face a particular problem in policing them. In prewar Japan, the limited child welfare laws had as their mirror the relative ease with which children might be punished. Prosecutors previously had something of a free hand in determining the conditions under which underage offenders could be charged and tried in a regular court and often penalized them in the same ways they would adults.[21] As part of its effort to eradicate Japan's wartime police state, SCAP had abolished the Naimushō (Home Ministry), a multipurpose internal ministry with a strong security bent, and kept a lid on the authority of the National Police Agency that was created from the ministry's ashes. SCAP's social reformers also established the Shōnenhō (Juvenile Law) as an addendum to the criminal code, based in part on existing Japanese legislation but also instituting tighter protection for child defendants. By mandating that all youthful offenders, whether accused of major or minor crimes, be treated in family courts by judges and without prosecutors, the Juvenile Law institutionally made the family court judge a surrogate parent during the hearing. In so doing, it defined the offender not as a criminal suspect but as a child with problems that need to be addressed and solved so that he or she can become a functioning and productive member of society.[22]

Prosecuting Juveniles

Not surprisingly, the Juvenile Law has proved troublesome to authorities because it hampers investigation and prosecution of crimes committed by juveniles, which, according to the NPA's statistics, accounted for half of all reported crimes by 1996. Many of these, however, are nonviolent offenses, such as drug use, and critics argue that the police statistics are purposely misleading in order to justify changing the Juvenile Law to allow the police and prosecutors more leeway.[23] In the early postwar era, juvenile crime was numerically a more significant problem than it was in the late 1990s, and the image of Japanese youth as somehow becoming "worse" by the 1990s is difficult to defend statistically.[24] But the disingenuous use of these statistics indicates something about long-term attempts by the NPA and its political allies to make it easier to punish teens. As early as the 1970s, the Ministry of Justice had sought to revise the Juvenile Law to permit prosecutors to press charges against some juveniles in regular criminal courts. Wary of the loss of control by family courts that this would have produced, the Supreme Court of Japan stepped in to prevent the shifts, swaying the opinions of some of the academics and attorneys on the Justice Ministry's advisory committee. The ministry thus had to be satisfied with the release of a 1977 report that called for a rethinking of the Juvenile Law's status.

In their efforts to reform the Juvenile Law, the Justice Ministry and the NPA had long been stymied by opposition from Japan's civil libertarians and from left-leaning parties in the Diet. These legal experts and lawmakers were, like their counterparts in other advanced industrial democracies, critical of extending the state's coercive power into the lives of citizens. Even those eager for a clampdown on offenders found it difficult to challenge the rhetorical weight of the romanticized child, an innocent likely to be harmed rather than productively deterred by exposure to adult criminal penalties. Indeed, after its initial setback with the Supreme Court in 1977, the Justice Ministry made few overtures to its legislative allies in the Liberal Democratic Party, and the National Police Agency turned its attention to other strategies for countering juvenile crime. Capitalizing on a juvenile crime "peak" in 1983, the NPA took steps to control sex-oriented and entertainment businesses and also established outreach programs at schools and youth centers. This "deterrent" approach was in many ways a remarkable shift for the NPA, which began to develop information networks with teenagers and to lecture them about the possible consequences of their actions.[25]

The late 1990s, however, witnessed a dramatic shift in public percep-
tions about the danger of youth crime. The NPA had been extremely angry about the disposition of a 1993 murder case in Yamagata Prefecture,
in which seven junior high school boys were found innocent (three on
appeal) of murdering a classmate, despite evidence that their alibis were
lies.[26] With the buildup to Japan's May 1995 ratification of the United
Nations International Convention on the Rights of the Child, however,
the Ministry of Justice and the NPA wisely held off on proposing major
changes to the law, settling for administrative reports warning about the
rise of juvenile delinquency and potential risks. As noted in chapter 2,
the 1995 Aum Shinrikyo incident had provoked wide-ranging discussion
of what had gone so profoundly wrong in Japan to have encouraged
bright, educated young people to join a murderous cult. In that context
of heightened alarm about the possible dangers posed by out-of-control
youth, the major impetus for a change in the Juvenile Law came from
1997's infamous "Sakakibara Seitō" case. One of the grisliest of Japan's
postwar crimes, the so-called Sakakibara case revolved primarily around
the murder of an eleven-year-old boy in Kobe. Three days after his reported disappearance, his severed head was found in front of his elementary school's main gate, a cryptic note from the murderer stuffed in
his mouth; the *Kobe Shimbun*, a regional newspaper, received a similar letter a week later.[27]

When the police made the arrest, it was of a fourteen-year-old boy, who
had adopted the weird pen name of Sakakibara Seitō, created from an
especially unusual collection of Chinese characters (Liquor-Devil-Rose
Saint-Fight). He ultimately confessed not only to the murder but also to
four separate attacks on young girls in the same area; he had bludgeoned
one of them to death. The brutality of the murders as well as the suspect's
treatment—his face appeared in the *Shūkan Shinchō*, one of Japan's
weekly newsmagazines, in spite of legal prohibitions against revealing the
identity of a juvenile suspect—prompted a larger debate over the types
of protections afforded to juvenile offenders. According to conservative
critics of the existing Juvenile Law, it had coddled the young for too long,
convincing them that there were no serious repercussions even for murderous behavior.

Seeing the likely risk to the law's child protection provisions, liberals
and civil libertarians immediately tried to shift the debate to education
and family issues, though to little avail. Already armed with carefully selected statistics showing increases in juvenile roles in violent crimes, the
NPA called for an overhaul of the law. The NPA's commissioner general,

Sekiguchi Yūkō, gave a June 1997 speech extolling the virtues of a tougher stance on juvenile crime, provoking public criticism from civil libertarians and legal experts. Concerned about the legal and political ramifications, the LDP's chief cabinet secretary, Kajiyama Seiroku, made a statement on July 1 calling for a calm rethinking of the Juvenile Law.[28]

In that vein, the LDP established a research group in October 1997 to study possible changes to the law.[29] The legislation taking shape allowed for a greater role for prosecutors in the handling of juvenile crime and also shifted the age for the prosecution of crimes in adult courts—to sixteen or older (and fourteen or fifteen in some instances). They would be treated not as children with problems but as guilty individuals meriting punishment. For the next three years, civil libertarians and human rights advocates deployed every argument they could against Juvenile Law revisions. They argued that by placing prosecutors in family law environments that were previously nonadversarial, the proposed changes would violate constitutional due process guarantees.[30] Furthermore, having additional judges in the family court, another provision, would create a more "coercive atmosphere," thereby violating the UN Convention on the Rights of the Child.[31]

At the time, the media were saturated with stories about increased youth crime. In addition to the NPA officials gladly providing facts and figures to show that they needed more coercive power, most people had only to turn on their televisions to find images of the swirling panorama of Shibuya or Shinjuku in Tokyo, where one could see uniformed schoolchildren clearly up to no good. Significantly, the murderer in the Kobe case would not have been among them. Although juveniles like these probably accounted for the alarming rise in the use of drugs (particularly stimulants), the Kobe murderer had been isolated and clearly disturbed. But in the public imagination, they were all symptoms of the same problem: "out-of-control youth."[32]

The prescribed solutions reflected larger political predispositions on the part of analysts. For liberals, it was a reformed educational and family environment that could make children happier, more loved, and self-confident; for conservatives, it was a freer hand for the police to do their part to protect the public. Many were willing to see it both ways, believing that the increase in juvenile delinquency might be symptomatic of problems for which the children should not themselves be blamed, but that they still needed to be taught that their actions have consequences. According to the renowned social psychologist Iwao Sumiko:

To make their daily lives more enjoyable, children need places open to and managed by themselves where they can freely blow off steam. They also need to have their behavior corrected when it is wrong and to be punished when they deserve to be. Juvenile offenders must be made to pay the appropriate penalty. They need to be made to think deeply about the significance of the crimes they have committed and to repent sincerely. These steps are necessary for them to achieve maturity. I do not believe that holding back punishment, or the chance to feel remorse, because the criminal is a youth is truly to that child's benefit.[33]

There is nothing self-evidently unreasonable about this position, and it likely resembled the views of many in the 91 percent of respondents who supported revision of the Shōnenhō.[34] Changes to the Juvenile Law did not turn Japan into a brutal garrison state, one using coercive force indiscriminately against its young; compared to the United States, where some children walk through metal detectors when they enter their schools and where police may search their lockers, Japanese youth live in an almost pre-Hobbesian world. The debates behind the revision, however, reflect sources of tension for a political system premised on guarantees of liberties, a competent police system able to maintain public order, and on the idea of children as innocents who will grow up to be adults and become the nation's future. This was largely a government- and media-driven debate, with the police and Ministry of Justice pushing for tighter surveillance (as they had for decades) and news organizations picking up the most sensational juvenile crimes and embedding them in larger anxieties over Japan's future. Japan had, in its not-too-distant past, already experienced alarming crime waves; this time, however, the ghastliness of the attacks and the pervasiveness of public concern allowed at least one layer of gloves to come off.

Girls, Sex, and the Japanese State

Any gender-neutral discussion of children, however, will paste over the special role that girls often play in popular understandings of vulnerability, purity, and proper behavior. If girls are viewed as being especially innocent, their perceived transgressions suggest something worse than increased criminal activity; they may be breaking down a social order premised on deeply institutionalized patterns of male-female behavior. This too owes a great deal to historical changes in our definitions of girls, proper sexual behavior, innocence, and deviancy. In late- nineteenth-century Japan, the transition from girl to woman was fraught with particular tension,[35] which was reflected in the ideals of family, sex, and marriage. Western-imported notions of "romance" partly recast the structure of ideal man-woman relationships, and the idea of the educated "lady" who would be a life companion had taken up currency among upper-class Japanese men of the era. In her exploration of Meiji and Taishō era romance novels, literary theorist Saeki Junko argues that there was a pronounced shift in the depiction of male-female relationships, away from earlier representations and toward a "modern," almost "platonic," love. In so doing, the literature drops eros out of male-female affairs, turning sex into a filthy commodity for purchase, and converting geisha and yūjo (women in brothels who had, according to Saeki, previously been depicted as equal partners in sexual and emotional relationships) into objects of potential scorn.[36]

Although prostitution was openly legal until the middle of the twentieth century, it was considered a socially legitimate occupation only for girls from poor families. The distinction was crucial; sex work was never for the economically comfortable. In the seventeenth century, the Tokugawa shogunate established the Yoshiwara quarter, an entertainment district in Edo (Tokyo's pre-Meiji name), partly in order to distract would-be opponents within the city limits. From 1899 through the middle of the twentieth century, the Japanese government continued to permit prostitution, providing a system of licensing in order to regulate the size and shape of the industry.[37]

Although some social reformers in the Japanese government were emboldened by anti-prostitution efforts led by the League of Nations after World War I, they made little headway in limiting or criminalizing the sex trade.[38] Indeed, by this time, Japan's licensed sex trade had even spread overseas. As Japanese businesses began to develop new markets in Southeast Asia in the late Meiji and early Taishō eras, small communities of women were among the first to leave Japanese shores, taking up residence overseas and providing sexual services to merchants and laborers working in these trading towns. In a practice not entirely unlike late-twentieth-century sex industry patterns in Thailand, Japanese brothel owners would pay poor families, often from Japan's rural regions, in advance for their daughters' services. The girls and young women would then be taken to Japanese merchant areas around East and Southeast Asia, where they would "work off" their contracts.

These *karayuki-san* (literally, "those who go to China") have been well-known figures in Japanese historical debates, and until around 1970 the dominant image of them was of poor but brave women who were helping their families and, in a way, serving patriotically by offering their bodies for Japan's expansion. The primary challenge to this romanticized view came with the 1972 publication of *Sandakan Hachiban* (generally translated in English as "Sandakan Brothel No. 8") by historian Yamazaki Tomoko. She argued that the terms of employment of the women were extraordinarily coercive and that the judgment of their selflessness and purity diverted attention from the sheer cruelty and shame of these Japanese brothels.[39] In a startling 1996 account designed to revise notions of power in Japanese contract relations, law and economics scholar J. Mark Ramseyer argued that up-front payments in the Japanese sex industry suggest that the women actually had a clear sense of their choices; they and their families were asking for a large initial sum as a "credible commitment" in an otherwise dishonest industry.[40] Whatever the conditions of their entry into sex markets, however, these women's importance in the development of Japanese economic territories around Asia is indisputable.[41]

Morally justified as a choice that poor women might make (ideally, to help their families), prostitution was therefore legal and regulated in prewar Japan. Indeed, the system of licensing laid the foundation for postwar rightists' defense of the *ianfu* ("comfort women") system that has in recent years been decried internationally as sexual slavery.[42]

In the immediate postwar era, in spite of the constitution written by the United States during the Occupation, which guaranteed equal rights to women, there was little pressure for a ban on prostitution, especially since the U.S. forces were the customers of Japanese government–sponsored brothels, through the Recreation and Amusement Association (RAA), in the late 1940s and early 1950s.[43] But this confronted SCAP with a serious problem. At the same time that sex markets were seen as a necessary evil for entertaining thousands of U.S. troops, SCAP also aimed at reducing the Japanese central government's control over moral matters, with reformists strenuously seeking to protect the welfare of children, including of course, prepubescent and adolescent girls.

The solution determined the subsequent shape of Japan's sex markets. Mixed with its general requirements for dealing with children, including fairly elaborate regulations for the administration of child welfare, the Child Welfare Law made muted reference to the protection of children from sexual abuse.[44] Compared with other elements of the law's Article 34 on forbidden actions, the comment on sexual abuse is brief and vague: "activities engaging children in lewd behavior" (*jidō ni inkō o saseru kōi*).[45] This proscription is complemented by Articles 176, 177, 178, and 182 of Japan's criminal code, which forbid sex crimes such as rape, coerced sexual conduct, coerced exposure to obscenity, or encouragement of obscenity, especially in regard to children.[46] Remarkably, the Child Welfare Law is silent on the issue of what constitutes obscenity. Instead, the definition of "lewd behavior" is left to prefectural governments, which are in charge of nuanced regulations on morality.[47]

Significantly, this split—national legislation to protect children comprehensively, including from sexual abuse, matched with local management of what constitutes obscenity—reflects both the Occupation's zeal for social reform and its efforts to decentralize control over moral and ethical behavior. Reacting to the wartime Japanese state's control over citizens, which explicitly used the state-as-family metaphor as a central justification for dominance and authority, SCAP actively sought to replace a Japan based on nearly filial duty to an emperor with one of individual citizens and democratic power. In so doing, SCAP aimed at remaking the Japanese, reconstituting even children as individuals requiring protection but also deserving of rights vis-à-vis the state. Although the Child Welfare Law established special protections for Japan's children, further encoding their place as social and political innocents, it also shaped and limited the subsequent ability of Japanese officials to keep girls away from sex markets.

The Partial Criminalization of Sex Markets

The 1957 Antiprostitution Law marked Japan's shift from regulation to partial criminalization of sex markets, though this in some ways complicated efforts to prevent underage girls from entering the trade. It also served as an emblem of Japan's presumed adherence to international standards of moral regulation. The international movement to ban prostitution led by religious organizations and women's groups was premised on the perceived violation that sex work represented to human rights and was supported by Japanese Christian and women's activists. Pressure from abroad and within Japan pushed the government to pass the law, particularly because of the United Nations stipulation that prostitution ought to be abolished. One sex industry journalist, Itō Hosaku, angrily faults the Japanese government for having bowed too much to international pressure without thinking properly about the place of the sex industry in Japanese tradition:

> The story of "citizen power," particularly of women's groups, in the creation of this law has been handed down to us. But if you look at the weight of historical evidence, it is clear that the winds of "freedom" [*jiyū*] that were blowing violently at this time were being skillfully used by officials for the purposes of national policy.[48]

Even if one sympathizes with Itō's critique of the state's efforts to adhere in some measure to a foreign-born norm, the law's passage was the result of more than just the heavy hand of the state. Prominent Japanese representatives of Christian and women's movements (frequently with international ties) played an indisputable part.[49] Rather than attaching criminal penalties to the act of selling sexual services, the law aimed at establishing "rehabilitation" centers for the women, ostensibly protecting their welfare but also adding a level of social pressure to wean them from the industry. This almost certainly reflected the voices of prominent feminists, such as Ichikawa Fusae, in the debate.[50]

Interestingly, the Anti-Prostitution Law criminalizes nearly every activity involved in the sale of sexual services, *except* for the transaction itself.[51] One can be arrested for providing facilities supporting prostitution, serving as a pimp, soliciting clients, and the like, but the actual sale of sexual services is not specifically labeled as a crime. Prostitution is, however, considered to be bad for "public morality" as well as "sexual morals," and the law aims specifically at "guiding" and "protecting" girls.[52] I have argued elsewhere that this legal framework almost certainly allowed (perhaps deliberately) the concentration of informal authority over the sex industry in the hands of the yakuza, or organized crime groups, since these groups would presumably have the contacts necessary to circumvent tight enforcement of these restrictions on management of prostitution.[53]

The immediate aftermath of the law's promulgation was the camouflaging of prostitution, bringing sex workers into organized businesses that managed to glide through some of the law's many loopholes. Indeed, the police did not crack down on the industry until 1963, when the upcoming Tokyo Olympics made the maintenance of "public morality" something of a political priority; even after this, however, "soaplands" (bathhouses with private rooms) and other sex businesses exploited loopholes and concentrated control over what women in the industry could and could not do.[54] Many observers have noted that the main upshot of the law is that, somewhat predictably, the women selling sexual services have faced severe consequences for their behavior and the men buying the services have not. With the development of soaplands, "pink salons" (erotic massage parlors), and the like, sex industry operators sought to circumvent the restrictions by creating some kind of barrier between themselves and the women sex workers. In other words, they controlled the women and the facilities but had some kind of "plausible deniability" with regard to the actual sexual transactions. In soaplands, for example, women actually rent individual rooms from the establishments and then are able to meet customers through the management. In word if not deed, the management simply provides space for men to have a bath with an attendant; whatever else goes on behind the closed door is between the customer and the room's tenant.

In a study of Japan's legislation on sex, Andrew Morrison argues that the refusal to criminalize prostitution reflects a deep ambivalence within Japan about whether or not prostitution is immoral. Although "ambivalence" is probably an apt characterization, Morrison makes something of a leap in suggesting that this reflects something separate and timeless in Japanese culture, given that the acceptance and regulation of sex work has hardly been a straightforward matter in any nation. Particularly troublesome is his assertion that the laws reflect "traditional unwillingness to view women as anything other than victims in a prostitution arrangement between the men and a *mizu shōbai* [sex-oriented business] enterprise."[55] This is only partly true, in that the "protection" (*hogo*) of women cited for prostitution has a coercive element that resembles arrest; in chapter 4, I examine the process of *hodō* or guidance as it applies to teens. Crucially, the Anti-Prostitution Law, by banning solicitation but not sexual commerce more broadly, has ensured that women are dependent on sex business operators, who are usually male. By doing so, it has likely been a boon to organized crime figures who run many of the firms and who have, by and large, been insulated from direct police interference.

Itō Hosaku, the sex industry journalist who criticized the 1957 law for its capitulation to international pressure, makes a crucial point about its effect on the women involved. By banning streetwalking and solicitation but providing exploitable loopholes for brothel-like establishments, the Anti-Prostitution Law contributed to the growing demonization of women in the sex industry. Previously seen as poor but brave women choosing an undesirable lifestyle to support their families, prostitutes were now being viewed as amoral criminals. Itō remarks that the price of international acceptance was turning prostitutes into "castoffs" (*kimin*).[56] This outcome was not due solely to the law; Japan's steady economic growth in the 1960s and 1970s made it harder to assume that sex workers came from hungry, impoverished families. And so the presumption of virtue and selflessness had to be redefined and reconstrued; there had to be something wrong with these women, something that made them choose to do something so awful.

One of the better-selling nonfiction books of 1996 captures the conflicting impulses and themes surrounding Japan's sex industry. *AV Joyū* (Adult Video Actress) is a collection of interviews with Japanese porn actresses. The author, Nagasawa Mitsuo, clearly sought to make the book more than titillating vignettes. His questions keep returning to the actresses' family lives, and most of them refer either to trauma and dysfunction or to boredom and alienation. Indeed, media coverage focused less on the book's occasionally explicit sexuality and more on the statement it seemed to be making about the collapse of the traditional home. *AV Joyū* depicts the large and available labor force for the sex industry as the direct outcome of the failure of Japanese families.[57]

I cannot say for sure how accurate the book is. Nagasawa pushes the women to talk about their families, and all of the interviewees are aware that their careers are hardly prestigious. For this reason, it is entirely possible that their stories sound alike simply because Nagasawa has tossed them an easy opportunity to justify their decisions. I am quite certain that troubled Japanese families far outnumber Japanese porn actresses, and so I do not believe that this is a sufficient explanation for entry into this career. But for at least a subset of readers and commentators, the book made the women's decisions to enter the sex industry intelligible. Others presumably purchased the book because of its spicy title, fetching cover photo, and the occasionally graphic admissions the women make in their interviews. The Japanese sex market—far from being the ubiquitously accepted phenomenon depicted in some of the more sensationalistic English-language coverage—is a source of debate, not to mention arousal, shame, and rationalization.

The Unintended Consequence of Regulation

In some ways, nothing better represents the extent to which women in the sex industry have become castoffs than the absence of official data about them.[58] Although the Japanese government maintains detailed data on the country's labor force, it has generally avoided any attention to the sex industry. Most of the information available about these women comes from men's magazines like *Spa!* or *Friday*, with a predictable slant on the women's sex lives and their turn-ons and turn-offs. A few journalists, particularly *AV Joyū* author Nagasawa,[59] have made careers out of providing vignettes, sometimes based on interviews, of sex industry workers, and Japanese human rights organizations such as HELP (House in Emergency of Love and Peace) have devoted attention to the specific issues of trafficking and the employment of non-Japanese Asian women in the sex industry. There is, however, little in the way of government research on the industry or the women employed in it. Nevertheless, it is very big business; by the mid-1980s, annual sex industry revenues were estimated to be roughly $40 billion,[60] and the figure is almost certainly much larger today.

The sex industry has become a crucial political topic specifically when the "wrong kinds" of women or girls have been employed. In the early 1980s, a rash of provocative news articles reported incidents of high school girls working in hostess bars and similar establishments. Already alarmed by increases in juvenile delinquency, the National Police Agency pushed for reform of the law governing sex-oriented and other entertainment firms. Because child welfare advocates and civil libertarians had successfully held off the Ministry of Justice's initial attempts to rewrite the Juvenile Law, the NPA moved to take the less controversial step of curtailing the activities of the relevant enterprises. In 1984, it had the LDP introduce into the Diet a revision of the Fūzoku Eigyō Hō (literally, the Enterprises Affecting Public Morals Law, but perhaps more accurately conveyed as Sex-Oriented Business Management Law). This gave the Diet the opportunity to respond publicly to growing reports that schoolgirls were beginning to work in sex businesses by debating the revision of the 1963 law governing licensing of these businesses.[61] The revision ultimately drove the establishment of new technologies—such as the "message dial" systems described below—making it even harder to prevent teens from entering the trade as amateur sex workers.

The law's revision required businesses to shut down operations anywhere near schools or residential zones, and posted heavy fines for allowing in anyone under the age of eighteen.[62] Although *fūzoku* can be defined to mean any "enterprises affecting public morals" (including game centers or pachinko parlors), the toughest stipulations were directed at "bathhouses with individual rooms [soaplands], strip bars and sex show theaters, 'love hotels,' adult toy stores, massage parlors with individual rooms, and the like."[63] Indeed, the NPA made it abundantly clear that this was a revision that—although dramatically expanding its powers against these firms—was meant to be a limited and reasonable response to an increase in juvenile delinquency.[64] By including a grand-father clause, however, the law essentially encouraged new sex-oriented businesses to seek permits between its August 1984 passage and February 1985 implementation.[65]

The revised law also gave an additional boost to a new kind of business, known as the *terekura,* or telephone club. First created in 1983, telephone clubs were originally places where men could call young women—not necessarily the club's formal employees—whom they could watch through a window and arrange to meet with outside of the club. Because of the ban on sex-oriented businesses in residential areas or near schools, the telephone clubs were able to take advantage of new voice-mail and cellular phone technology, allowing people to call and leave messages at a central voice-mail bank and to handle appointments on their own. A typical route in the mid-1990s was the *dengon daiyaru* (message dial), in which people paid to leave messages leading to dates, compensated or otherwise.[66] By essentially ensuring that these telephone clubs are not physically located anywhere near schools, the clubs have managed to circumvent the restrictions regarding operations near children.

These media were rapidly successful and fed into a growing trend toward a kind of part-time sex work in which women could make contact with men and then choose to date or have sex with them for money. In honor of the thirtieth anniversary of the Anti-Prostitution Law, the Japanese government's Management and Coordination Agency carried out a study of 676 women investigated for prostitution. The largest group of women, more than a quarter of the total, met clients "by arrangement," while the rest met them at the more traditional sites such as soaplands, cabarets, and clubs.[67] By the early 1990s, it had become apparent what the new telephone clubs were allowing people to do: to engage in sex work part time, as "amateurs," rather than as "professionals" employed by the standard sex-oriented businesses.

What distinguished the prostitution scandals of the early 1990s from most previous arrests was the amateur status of the women involved. In one particularly questionable analysis two out of three women involved in prostitution were argued to be housewives.[68] The 1991 prosecution of a "date club" (similar to an escort agency) in the Tokyo suburb of Shin-Matsudō revealed that of the forty-three women working there, thirty were housewives. Clients paid ¥25,000 (at the time, about $200) for a ninety-minute session, with ¥15,000 yen going to the woman and the other ¥10,000 going to the club. Reporting on the story, the British news digest the *Economist* speculated that the housewives' boredom probably contributed to their choices. In doing so, it also took the opportunity to take a potshot at Japanese men, calling the women's salaryman husbands "male chauvinists to a man—[who] hardly spend any time at home."[69]

Leaving aside the ghastly (and, to my mind, inexcusable) generalization about Japanese men, the reference to boredom unexpectedly captures something important about enjo kōsai: that it is difficult to reduce the phenomenon to strict notions of prostitution. In one recent collection of pieces on enjo kōsai, a housewife writing under the pen name of Yoshida Sawako describes her own introduction to the liberating world of compensated dating. Having heard about "message dial" lines, she decides to call and—after initial disappointment because most of the men are looking for younger women—hooks up with a married man. They meet once for coffee before connecting again later at a hotel. They have sex, but she asks for money only because she needs to take a taxi back to her house to arrive at a reasonably early hour. Money is at first only incidental, and she prides herself on never demanding it directly.[70] The story is perhaps fabricated, though it certainly provides a vicarious thrill; perhaps this is the point of having it in the collection. The editors of the collection in which "Yoshida's" piece appears claim, in her biographical note, that she is preaching the "enjo kōsai *fukuin* [gospel])" to other housewives. In any case, her story highlights one notable aspect of the debate surrounding enjo kōsai: whether or not it is a simple clear transaction. At least in some accounts, it involves a courtship of sorts.

Telephone clubs, enjo kōsai, and the like have now been firmly established as *fūzoku* phenomena, and are at least as recognizable as soaplands, "fashion health" clubs, and porno videos. Enjo kōsai has typically relied on the development of the *dengon daiyaru* systems and telephone dating clubs that keep clients away from the women until there has been some agreement about the extent and cost of the liaison. It was perhaps only a matter of time before teenage girls began to use these systems; they can generally command much higher prices than housewives or twenty-something office ladies, and uniformed schoolgirls in Japan had been seen as sex objects for at least a decade.[71] The privacy and ease of these new technologies offered women and girls the possibility of earning thousands of dollars quickly,[72] making the potential financial benefits of enjo kōsai extremely seductive. As feminist scholar Ueno Chizuko writes:

It was really a question of the accidental access [by the girls] to this market (through being picked up, through oral communication, through telephone clubs and cellular phones allowing them to speak with potential clients). This accident . . . was not a matter of ethics; it was nothing more than a matter of probability.[73]

The Varied Constructions of Enjo Kōsai

In a thoughtful epilogue to her study of eros and love in early twentieth-century Japanese literature, Saeki reports that she is often asked about the difference between enjo kōsai and the *yūjo,* or brothel occupants described in pre-Meiji novels. For her, the difference is obvious. Before being displaced by increasingly "modern" conceptions of nearly platonic love, the *yūjo* characters had been participants in complex emotional relationships, involving sex that was often noble and merciful. Enjo kōsai, however, is another "cup of tea entirely" (*nitehinaru mono*), because it involves nothing but a transaction of flesh for money.[74] Many would disagree. Although enjo kōsai, particularly as practiced by the kogals, ultimately became the linchpin in the debate over Japan's acquiescence to the norm against the commercial sexual exploitation of children, it was never as simple an activity as its many critics would have it.

Growing Panic about an Ambiguous Problem

As a matter of law, it is not entirely clear why enjo kōsai had to be a problem. The national age of sexual consent in Japan is thirteen, though the local obscenity regulations effectively raise this in many prefectures; as noted, the Anti-Prostitution Law is silent on sex-for-cash transactions. Moreover, it is sometimes difficult to identify precisely where the crime in an enjo kōsai liaison takes place. Even if prostitution itself were criminal, enjo kōsai is often ambiguous enough as a phenomenon that it would be difficult to stipulate whether it too would be prohibited. One news report featured a schoolgirl who said:

High school girls don't really sell their bodies for just 20,000 yen or 30,000, yen. . . . People misuse the phrase *enjo kōsai.* Real enjo kōsai is when a girl plays the role of a lover to a rich man in exchange for 200,000 yen to 400,000 yen a month. We do not consider one-night relationships enjo kōsai.[75]

Referring to a local initiative to crack down on enjo kōsai, one young
commentator and journalist, Fujii Yoshiki, said in a 1998 interview:

In Osaka, the government set up the "Enjo kōsai is prostitution"
[*baishun*] campaign. But enjo kōsai is not that simple a problem. It
absolutely doesn't just equal prostitution. Let's say that a sixteen-year-
old schoolgirl goes out for a dinner date with a thirty-three-year-old
man, and he gives her ¥10,000 [about $80]. Is that prostitution? How
about going to a karaoke box [private karaoke room] and letting him
touch her breasts, and then getting ¥20,000? What if it's not her
breasts, but her genitals, and no money changes hands, but he buys
her some clothes? This is about the diversity of sexual activity, so it's
a really complex problem. Anyway, the "Enjo kōsai is prostitution"
campaign should just be called "Anyway, whatever it is, it's bad, so
stop it!" campaign.[76]

Fujii errs not in failing to show the complexity of enjo kōsai but in
oversimplifying prostitution, which he portrays as the simple exchange
of sex for cash. He does, however, make a crucial point: the unease about
enjo kōsai was about more than the issue of high school girls having sex
with adult men. This concern did, however, largely drive the enjo kōsai
media phenomenon, which by the late 1990s was out of proportion to
the size of the problem. With some polls in 1995 and 1996 indicating that
as many as 30 percent of Tokyo high school girls had contacted the telephone club dating systems that have been central to enjo kōsai, newer
research indicates that this was a gross exaggeration.[77] A 1998 study com-
missioned by the Asian Women's Fund found that fewer than 10 percent
of schoolgirls had engaged in enjo kōsai, with only a small number of that
group actually trading sexual services for money. Over 90 percent of interviewed schoolgirls felt uncomfortable with the sale or purchase of sexual services, and 60 percent were uneasy about enjo kōsai itself; for
respondents and analysts alike, the distinction mattered.[78]

Of course, in a country of over 120 million people, this is still a significant number of potential participants, particularly if one were to
compare it with the likely percentage of middle-class American or European high school girls involved in part-time sex work. Moreover, if one
takes a less than charitable view of enjo kōsai—which at least a few, if not
most, Japanese observers consider to be the sexual exploitation of children—this is an alarmingly large number of teenagers to have engaged
in compensated dating. Yet the hype about it—which ranged from the

nearly envious and respectful television profiles of those "independent-minded" girls to apocalyptic prognostications of social conservatives worried about what a generation of amateur sex workers meant for the future of Japan—rarely evinced genuine concern for the girls.

Indeed, most of the public discourse about enjo kōsai appears to be motivated by a fundamental fear of the ostentatious sexuality of the high school girls involved. A new "type" of Japanese high school girl—the kogal—had emerged as the symbol of enjo kōsai. The kogal style—discussed below—is visually distinctive and noticeable. And unlike the debates over child pornography and prostitution in Asia that fuelled the creation of the international anti–child porn movement, the enjo kōsai discourses focus only minimally on the consequences of enjo kōsai for the girls themselves. Instead, the essential debate is over what the emergence of the kogals—symbols of materialism, or a decline in traditional values, or gender equality, or moral relativism—says about Japan and Japan's future.

At first, the number of high school girls involved in enjo kōsai was relatively low, with the schoolgirl market something of a nonissue during the housewife-prostitute scare of the early 1990s.[79] By 1994, however, virtually all of Japan's newspapers carried stories about high school girl prostitution, increasingly popularizing the term "enjo kōsai," with the *Yomiuri Shimbun,* one of Japan's most widely read dailies, reporting that one in four high school girls claimed to have contacted a telephone club, and the *Nikkei* (similar to the *Wall Street Journal* or the *Financial Times*) saying that 7 percent of junior high school girls had done so.[80] Even if these figures were accurate, calls to telephone clubs probably correlated no more closely to actual dates, let alone sex, than do the numbers of American high school students who giggle over personal ads in local newspapers or the Internet. But the attention helped to inspire growing curiosity about the girls.

The initial curiosity was largely salacious, including stories in major men's magazines that offered titillating details about the number of trysts or johns girls were likely to have each month. Throughout 1996 and 1997, magazines like *Spa!* and *Friday* offered garish stories implying that these girls were having far more fun than were the male readers. At the same time, women's gossip weeklies found space between stories about purportedly promiscuous female celebrities like Matsuda Seiko to heap invective on the shocking behavior of these girls. Perhaps most bizarrely, in July 1997, the relatively serious TV-Asahi program *Asa made nama terebi*[81] featured the topic "Gekiron: Joshi kōsei to nippon" (Shocking! High School Girls and Japan), whose panelists included sociologist Miyadai Shinji, journalist Fujii Seiji, and porn-actress-turned-talk-show-panelist Iijima Ai, presumably to speak from the girls' perspective. In a poll, the show found that 70 percent of respondents opposed enjo kōsai, while 30 percent approved of it, though the tone of the comments suggests that it was a referendum on the girls rather than the activity.

Starting in the mid-1990s, an increasing number of high school girls began to adopt the kogal appearance, one that set them apart from earlier idealizations of the orthodox, uniformed schoolgirl. Although they still wore uniforms, many girls began to dye their hair brown or blonde (*chappatsu*), generally in violation of school rules, and to wear "loose socks" (similar to leg warmers) with their skirts, which they would hike up to nearly miniskirt levels. In addition to their unusual hair color, their short skirts, and baggy socks, the kogals had a penchant for wearing expensive accessories. Topping off their image, many of these girls spoke in casual jargon that many adults said, quite histrionically, that they could not understand at all. By October 1997, the kogal costumes one could purchase for Halloween reflected the kogals' place as scary monsters menacing modern Japan.

Miyadai's and Iijima's joint appearance on the late-night show captures perfectly the dueling impulses at the heart of the enjo kōsai debate. On the one hand, the issue was regarded not just as a concern but also as a large-scale social problem, one affecting Japan as a whole, and desperately in need of serious thought. On the other hand, it was always so rich with the possibility of sordid and scandalous details of the lives of beautiful high school girls that to analyze it one might as well have as a guest a TV celebrity whose basic claim to fame was her earlier career in porn.

Conflicting Explanations

For many moderates and conservatives, enjo kōsai displayed contemporary Japan at its decadent, hedonistic worst. Cultural critic Katō Norio wrote that although Japan's postwar democracy affords individual freedom, it does little to offer principles and norms constraining what people can do: people think "the most important thing is to have fun, as long as one is not bothering anyone else." He added that this kind of behavior would be "unthinkable" (*kangaerarenai*) outside of Japan.[82]

The head of the influential International Research Center for Japanese Studies, Kawai Hayao, made a similar distinction between decadent

Japan and the principled West in a 1998 essay on enjo kōsai. According to Kawai, European schoolgirls do not engage in an equivalent of enjo kōsai because in Europe, the "cradle of modernity," a Christian normative order maintains social control even in the face of major change. In contrast, the coming of modernity to Japan was accompanied by a European value system that shredded the ties binding the Japanese together. Under such conditions, it is no wonder that it is impossible to tell these girls not to engage in prostitution.[83] One Buddhist priest and writer, Sawada Kantoku, however, saw no reason to extol the West in comparison, saying that enjo kōsai represents a Japan insecure about its status and the constancy of its moral beliefs. He went so far as to link enjo kōsai to Japanese funding of U.S. bases, saying that Japan sells a bit of itself in catering to U.S. wishes: "Isn't Japan America's enjo kōsai partner?"[84]

For many of the conservatives, the great risk of enjo kōsai was not to the participants themselves, but rather to Japan. After all, these kogals would grow up and be wives and mothers:

When [the kogals] grow up and get married, for a little bit of spending money they will probably return with no compunction to prostitution. With their easily earning tens of thousands of yen, money that has been stained by the taste of pleasure [*kairaku no aji*], there will be left behind only a weak remnant of humanity. Ultimately, only money will matter in this world.[85]

Even if they do not become housewife-prostitutes, they cannot possibly be good mothers. As Ito Kazuyoshi of the Tokyo Private Junior and Senior High Schools Association pointed out:

Many of the girls will become mothers in the not-so-distant future. . . . [The results] certainly will not be favorable ones. . . . Many parents are unable to keep an eye on their children and supervise them properly. Only parents can control their daughters' activities from the time they leave school until they reach home. If they can do that, there will be a large drop in the number of schoolgirls roaming around in entertainment districts late at night.[86]

Like the conservatives, a number of academic and liberal authors have expressed concern about what enjo kōsai means for Japan's future— though they shift blame away from the girls and toward the materialistic society that produced their mad drive for Versace bags. The most important of these observers, Miyadai, began to publish on the topic in 1994, when his book *Seifuku shōjotachi no sentaku* (The Choice of the Little Girls in Uniform) first appeared. Taking on the new enjo kōsai issue as well as the popular trend of selling used uniforms and underwear to sex stores, Miyadai was interested in examining how the sexual behavior of these girls would likely be socially judged. In his analysis, the growing public outcry about enjo kōsai demonstrated uneasiness about these girls for two reasons. First, Japan's nearly fetishistic obsession with "cuteness" (*kawaii*, a term embodied by such icons as "Hello Kitty")—in which social life and other people are rendered harmless and almost cuddly—not only encourages adult attraction to children and teens but also enables these girls to do things they might otherwise consider distasteful. After all, it is just for fun. Second, any effort to condemn enjo kōsai would have to rely on some form of "moral absolutism" (*zettaiteki dōtoku*), and its history was extremely "shallow" in Japan, going back no further than the universal educational reforms of the Meiji Era. In other words, Japanese critics of enjo kōsai were largely arguing from a moral position that they themselves thought to be precarious.[87]

In chapter 6 of his book, Miyadai specifically identifies the growth of Japanese materialism as the culprit, singling out the *shinjinrui* ("new race," "yuppies") who were purportedly self-absorbed and obsessed with accumulation.[88] One young novelist, Sagisawa Megumu, added that the excesses of the bubble era in Japan promoted the idea that high-priced fashion goods were "absolutely must-have" items for schoolgirls.[89] In Murakami Ryū's novel *Rabu & Poppu* (Love & Pop), which focuses specifically on enjo kōsai, there are entire chapters that consist of nothing but lists of brand names. This is presumably Murakami's way of allowing the reader to inhabit the mind of a high school girl who is willing to have sex with strangers to earn the money for a ring. So bombarded is she by the materialism of contemporary Japan that she simply cannot understand anything beyond the glittering merchandise that Tokyo's department stores dangle before young people, especially girls.

Murakami's novel (which later became a film) reflects liberals' concern for the schoolgirls, though it is mixed with some respect for their independence (perhaps because the novel would be marketed to them). Though not exactly adopting a "child welfarist" position that posits the defenselessness and vulnerability of enjo kōsai participants, Murakami expresses concern about their safety. To earn enough money to buy her trinket, Murakami's schoolgirl heroine goes on three dates in one day.

On the first, she and other girls are asked to chew and spit out pieces of food so the obviously insane customer can get DNA from their saliva and clone innocent, beautiful playmates. She next goes to the adult section of a video store with a young man who has an illness that gives him terrible body odor, making it impossible to find a girlfriend through conventional means. In the final episode, she meets a strikingly handsome and funny young man who calls himself Captain EO, who lures her to a love hotel, then turns on her in a rage and tells her she is a prostitute and doing something very dangerous. He concludes his informative and intelligent lecture by giving her four yen, which he says is what she would earn if she were a child prostitute in India.[90] A literary critic might forgive Murakami for introducing his garrulous doppelgänger into a rather straightforward morality tale, though perhaps not for his Bret Easton Ellis-esque touches, such as hammering away at the intense materialism of life in contemporary Tokyo. *Rabu & Poppu* ends with a postscript that says, "Schoolgirls, I'm on your side."

Journalist Kuronuma Katsushi's widely read book *Enjo kōsai* features relatively unsensationalized interviews with schoolgirls, in which he points out the dangers in enjo kōsai, such as running afoul of organized crime.[91] Probably the best—and weirdest—film about enjo kōsai, Harada Masato's *Bounce Kogals*, takes on the issue of the girls' safety in Japan's sexual underworld. The hard-boiled leader of a group of girls learns a lesson when she is briefly abducted by a yakuza leader who is upset about the girls' cutting into his prostitution business. Fortunately for her, this particular gangster, played by redoubtable everyman Yakusho Kōji, is a former student radical who operates a karaoke club decked out with kitschy references to global socialist movements. After scaring her for a few minutes, he cements an agreement with her by having her join him in a karaoke version of "The Internationale."

The real-life dangers for girls involved in enjo kōsai are, of course, less baroque and more viscerally upsetting. In July 2001, two years after the practice had essentially been outlawed, Kamiie Noriko, a twelve-year-old girl, apparently ran away from home, having told her family that she would spend the night at a friend's home; she fled when spotted by her father at a train station near her home in Kobe. At nine the next night, she called her parents and said she was at a train station in Osaka. Less than two hours later, Kamiie was found barefoot and handcuffed, bleeding heavily, by the side of the highway. She was rushed to the hospital but was pronounced dead at 3 a.m. A few days later, police arrested Fukumoto Ken, a thirty-four-year-old former schoolteacher, who had apparently met Kamiie through a dating website. He allegedly had met other juveniles the same way and had beaten one seventeen-year-old and stolen ¥30,000 from her. In this case, Fukumoto evidently handcuffed the girl and took her shoes to prevent her from escaping while he drove. Presumably terrified, Kamiie managed to open the door to the car and leap from it while Fukumoto raced along the Chūgoku Highway near Kobe; she was almost immediately struck by a truck, which then sped away.

In October, the police questioned the fifty-three-year-old trucker who apparently struck Kamiie Noriko. After offering vague reasons for fleeing the scene, the trucker left the police station and apparently hanged himself from a steel tower in the vicinity.[92] Fukumoto was later convicted of illegally confining the girl, though not of murder, as she apparently had thrown herself from the car. The prosecution appealed his six-year-sentence, arguing it was too light for the gravity of the incident. Upholding the sentence, Osaka High Court judge Shirai Kazuhisa said that Fukumoto's position as a teacher had led people to demand an unfairly heavy sentence, saying, "Public criticism of the defendant has naturally been severe as the case is regarded as a crime by a teacher, but considering the criminal liability, it is not fair to give a sentence much heavier than for an average person." He also pointed out that Kamiie was herself partly responsible because of her willingness to engage in this kind of indecent liaison with an adult.[93]

This case differs dramatically from the prevailing representations of schoolgirls involved in enjo kōsai, even in the novelistic accounts written by those sympathetic to the girls. By using fiction to treat the girls as real but endangered moral agents, Murakami and Harada align themselves with an academic observer like Miyadai. All of them are worried about the risks to the girls involved in enjo kōsai, and all take the girls seriously in some sense as agents. Unlike the conservatives, none places moral responsibility for their behavior on the girls themselves; it is instead the fault of a capitalist economy saturated with advertisements and the omnipresent demand for consumption. Murakami even takes society's unwillingness to focus on protecting the girls as emblematic of contemporary Japan's soullessness and selfishness. In a 1997 interview on the topic, he argued that no one felt a sense of social responsibility to stop enjo kōsai, provided it was not their own daughters who were involved.[94]

While not disagreeing with the basic premise that enjo kōsai's existence suggests that there is something terribly wrong with Japanese society, a number of feminist scholars have gone further than Miyadai's and Murakami's reluctance to criticize the girls' decision to engage in the

practice. Instead, they see the girls' choices as acts of resistance. Ueno
Chizuko, for example, acknowledges the potential dangers of enjo kōsai
as well as the rather blatantly materialist impulses of the participants, but
argues that the schoolgirls derive from it a sense of power and of control
over themselves and their bodies.[95] Another writer, Hayami Yukiko, suggests that the behavior of these girls has to be, if not lauded, understood
as a rejection of control that is exerted on girls and women in Japan.[96]

From this perspective, if enjo kōsai is to be understood as a problem
(and Ueno and other feminists are highly alert to the dangers faced by
the girls involved), it should be handled differently than would-be regulators on all sides would have it. Rather than taking legal steps to ban enjo
kōsai, whether for the sake of the girls involved or for Japan's future, people ought to be concerned with providing children with the knowledge
necessary to make informed decisions. For many liberal and feminist authors, the real solution would have to be sex education that could allow
juveniles to avoid sexual abuse while still exercising autonomy over their
own bodies.[97] As opposed to earlier sex education rules that had focused
primarily on "moral behavior," and on recent revisions that stigmatize
"deviant sexual behavior,"[98] one male sexual education specialist, Murase
Yukihiro, argues that Japan must teach schoolgirls the value of their own
bodies and that in sex, one should *meiku rabu* ("make love," written in a
syllabary for foreign words).[99] In this view, education, rather than coercion or punishment, should be the key. Indeed, among many writers the
issue has been framed as one of *sei no jiko ketteiken* (sexual self-determination) rather than one of violence or of ethics. Responding angrily to
a 1997 *New York Times* article that described enjo kōsai and the "Lolita
complex" among Japanese men, Yuriko Yamaki wrote:

> No one should approve of schoolgirls who engage in prostitution due
> to their materialistic desires. However, I suppose this incident might
> also represent the manipulation conducted by these defiant Japanese
> girls who have grown up humiliated in a society which has no respect
> for being a woman. . . . One cannot draw a line between teenage girls
> and women, when it comes to sexuality. Only individual differences
> exist.[100]

The point here is not that the feminists are right and the conservatives
wrong, or vice versa, though my sympathies are probably clear. Rather,
what the arguments described above suggest is that within a short period
of time, something that need not have been interpreted as a problem at

all (given both the legal age of sexual consent and the tacit legal acceptance of prostitution) was understood as a *social* problem. In other words, in the minds of most observers, enjo kōsai was so striking (perhaps troubling, perhaps encouraging) that it had to say something about contemporary Japanese society. Like most Americans following the shootings at Columbine High School, where most liberals blamed guns and most conservatives blamed moral breakdown, nearly everyone in Japan agreed that *something* was wrong. Ultimately, however, the kogals were exploitable as symbols. They represented a Japan that had lost its traditional values; a Japan that had not had central values before the Meiji Restoration; a Japan of male dominance; a Japan of greed and mendacity; or even a Japan that acted as a "compensated date" of the United States. Of course, what the kogals represented depended primarily on the social views of the observers, and the discursive struggle over enjo kōsai is rather less indicative of the activities of the schoolgirls than it is of public intellectuals' handling of the "vague sense of insecurity" (*aimai na fūan*) described in chapter 2.

Why did the kogals have to represent anything? As the photos on page after gaudy page of the book *Enjo kōsai dokuhon* (Readings on Enjo Kōsai) demonstrate, kogals were in the late 1990s extraordinarily visible. The kogals, in their modified school uniforms (traditional sailor tops, blue miniskirts, and loose socks), with their Versace handbags and chappatsu hairstyles, simply stood out in a way that uniformed schoolchildren generally have not. That most of the thousands of girls with such appearances were not in fact schoolgirl prostitutes was less important than the fact that they *could* have been. Having developed a particular look, one that signified sexual awareness, schoolgirls with cell phones, with dyed blonde or light brown hair, or with loose socks were all potentially sexually active. They always had been, of course, but the creation in the 1990s of a singularly striking appearance fueled a voracious public appetite for stories about them, about why they looked like that, about how they could afford to look like that. For the most part, the kogals looked too active, too willfully licentious, and too dismissive of social censure to be considered real victims.

In fact, what makes a small number of educational booklets, mostly written by teachers and school counselors and published since 1997, so interesting is that they *do* see enjo kōsai as being a crime with victims, and they press strongly for sex education programs designed to keep girls out of the practice.[101] In these texts, lurid stories of elementary, junior high school, and high school girls serve as cautionary tales regarding what might happen to girls in these compensated relationships.[102] This is not to say that the other commentators on enjo kōsai were completely uninterested in the consequences of enjo kōsai for the girls themselves. But most articles on enjo kōsai seemed to take it as axiomatic that there is something wrong with prostitution—in spite of its long existence in Japan and the only half-hearted efforts to ban it—and therefore something wrong with any girl that would voluntarily choose to trade sex for cash or presents. The consequences need not be enumerated: they are simply understood to be bad. If the girls themselves do not feel the effects, Japan as a nation surely will. And this is something to fear.

The Exploitable World of the Kogals

In his 2000 book about the rise in juvenile crime, one of Japan's foremost conservative criminologists, Maeda Masahide, includes a chapter called "Increasing Female Crime." Deploying a large but unsophisticated collection of graphs—they make no distinctions between types of crimes and the level of danger involved—Maeda argues that crimes by teenage girls have increased far more rapidly than have crimes by adult women or by teenage boys. Alongside the alarming charts, Maeda includes one photograph, provided by the *Mainichi Shimbun*. It shows, from behind, the legs of two high school girls wearing their school uniform skirts and their loose socks, the baggy white socks nearly ubiquitous in late 1990s Tokyo. One carries a large handbag. The caption, "High School Girls with Loose Socks," hints at what makes them so scary. Because they are not self-evidently involved in any crimes, we are instead asked to note them as archetypes of a generation of style-obsessed high school girls whose intimated activities constitute a threat to Japan's public order. The photo shows only two girls wearing loose socks, but that is enough— when juxtaposed with the statistics—to make the point. These are *not* victims, or at least not only the victims; these are the offenders.[103] For Maeda, as for many other observers, the kogal is notable not as a possibly vulnerable juvenile, but as a symbol of something gone terribly wrong in modern Japan.

No one, of course, was accusing the kogals of committing the kinds of brutal murders that provoked the intense media scrutiny leading to revision of the Juvenile Law. But the kogals did not exist in a vacuum; they were highly visible emblems of a larger anxiety in 1990s Japan over the collapse of public order. As intellectuals like Maeda and institutions like the National Police Agency pushed to enact tighter controls on teens, the kogals were useful examples: disrespectful to adults, easily identified, and probably up to no good, even if they were doing nothing as obvious as trying to clock their gym teachers with broom handles. Their media-fueled recognizability meant that just a pair of legs in loose socks could represent something deviant and criminal. For officials seeking to expand the coercive role of the state in the service of solving an apparent rise in violent juvenile crime, the kogals were like the gift of an ad campaign.

Of course, the revision of the Juvenile Law could not and would not engage the kogals unless they actually committed the kinds of brutalities associated with the Sakakibara Seitō case; it would do very little to eradicate the kogals or their most famous activity, enjo kōsai. Indeed, the kogals remained, mutating with the warp speed in which fashion changes for Tokyo's teens: some shifted back to a more deceptively orthodox schoolgirl appearance, while others adopted the *ganguro* look (nearly blackened skin with blonde hair and white eyeliner and lipstick, virtually rendering them photographic negatives). Some went so far in that direction that they were called *yamamba* (crazy old witch from the hillside). Magazines like *Egg* and *Cawaii* still catered to their reading tastes, and by all accounts the enjo kōsai market itself remained virtually unchanged. In chapter 4, I turn to the role the kogals—still a source of social anxiety—came to play when left-leaning activists began to criticize the Japanese government to get it to crack down on sex tourism for pedophiles in Southeast Asia. Surprisingly, the global effort to abolish the sexual exploitation of children became a political tool at home, one aimed as much at bringing Japanese teens in line with local expectations as at bringing Japanese laws into line with global ones.

A genuinely friendly conversation between high school girls and police at the Shibuya Station Hachikō *kōban.*

CHAPTER FOUR

GUIDANCE, PROTECTION, AND PUNISHMENT IN JAPAN'S CHILD SEX LAWS

Few things bring people together like opposition to the sexual abuse of children. Child pornography, for example, has emerged as one of the unqualified crimes in international politics, one that can be defended no more easily or comfortably than "ethnic cleansing," slavery, or apartheid. Indeed, the May 1999 passage of legislation to ban child pornography and child prostitution in Japan would seem to be curious only in its tardiness. The fundamental wrongness of sexually exploiting children in this manner has, in this logic, entered the common sense of global politics. And so in much of the media scrutiny of the issue, one gets the impression that only in what is generally categorized as a patriarchal, atavistic society like Japan's could its practice have been this widespread until now. Indeed, American and European press reports focusing on the schoolgirl fetish purportedly common among Japanese salarymen has painted the new legislation as, in effect, dragging Japan kicking and screaming into the twenty-first century, or perhaps even the twentieth.

In this chapter, we turn to the ways in which the developing international norm against the sexual exploitation of children became a complex instrument in Japanese politics. On the one hand, it did what norms are supposed to do: it encouraged policymakers to move toward standardized policies designed to solve a commonly understood problem. The 1999 law—which establishes new punishments for adult offenders and provides additional tools for investigators seeking evidence of sex tourists' misdeeds overseas—is unimaginable without consideration of the way that a transnational movement and its domestic networks effected change. But by the same token, the story neither starts nor ends with the law, because the law became a key element in a larger and longer debate over the proper place of children, especially girls, in the sex industry and in sexual relationships. As discussed in chapter 3, this had become a nettlesome political issue, particularly as it related to the emergence of the kogal style among teenage girls. The movement activists who sought to encourage the Japanese government to sign onto and to abide by international agreements against child pornography and child prostitution encountered a domestic argument in which, more often than not, schoolgirls were seen to be the villains rather than the victims.

The International Norm against the Sexual Exploitation of Children

The international regulation of sex has always been a special kind of problem, drawing together uncomfortable and unstable configurations of race, gender, and power. Ethan Nadelmann's analysis of prohibitionist regimes provides a helpful glimpse at one that helped to codify a link between nationality and sexuality. In the early twentieth century, activists against the "white slavery" trade aimed not only at the protection of women but also at the reassertion of traditional gender roles, using racist iconography to make the case. After all, it was presumed, no white woman would choose to have sex with a brown- or black-skinned man; anyone who did had to be a "slave." The campaign did leave in its wake a number of rules regarding what women could or should be expected to do, but probably had only a minimal effect on the incidence of prostitution. It did, however, begin to unify an international movement against sexual commerce. Because this effort at prohibition was inextricably linked to conservative attempts to protect patterns of social order, it has not been remembered fondly by either gender theorists or historians.[1]

This criticism owes at least something to the collapse of the old feminist consensus regarding the harm inflicted by prostitution. Until fairly recently, the dominant line of feminist thought held that prostitution reflected pure gender domination. Additionally, the unequal gender relations involved had clear implications for the economic, political, and social well-being of women. Although many liberal and Marxist feminists in the 1970s took a more permissive tone toward prostitution, most radical feminists continued to deplore it, suggesting that it not only harmed the women involved but all women, as it promoted a view of women as commodifiable sex objects. Only with the development of a libertarian feminism emphasizing the issue of choice, combined with the sex trade workers' movement of the 1990s (such as the organization COYOTE— Call Off Your Old Tired Ethics), did a sustained defense of prostitution, often conceptualized as "sex work," take place within feminism and gender studies, fields that are now deeply divided over the issue.[2]

Yet this disagreement collapses when the issue involves children. Whether it is against "child prostitution," "child pornography," or "child sex tourism" (especially "Asian child sex tourism," which has a notorious reputation in this regard), the growing momentum of an international movement has been unmistakable. To some degree, the fervor arises from moralistic campaigns to regulate sexuality, especially that of women and children, but there is little doubt that a commitment to "child welfare" now features prominently in these efforts.[3] In 1979, dubbed "The International Year of the Child" by the United Nations, UNICEF and member nation delegates began to write the Convention on the Rights of the Child, which was adopted in 1989 and, within two years, broke nearly every applicable international record for the speed of its almost universal ratification. Among the convention's many stipulations is that states must not allow the sexual exploitation of children, including in pornography and prostitution; children are defined as those under the age of eighteen, unless individual states set for themselves a lower age of majority.

That children continue to be sexually exploited for commercial gain, however, is hardly in doubt. Even when governments decry it, all too often officials can be persuaded by sex traffickers to turn a blind eye to the use of children in the sex industry, a sector that can be particularly important in developing countries dependent on international tourism. As the voluminous literature on sex tourism suggests,[4] sex trafficking remains a contemporary scourge. Moreover, with the AIDS crisis, sex tourists have sought child partners more strenuously than before, in part because of the false belief that they are less likely to be HIV-positive. Although reliable figures are impossible to obtain, there are estimates that millions of children worldwide are involved in the child sex trade, from street children to those directly employed by and held in brothels. The World Tourism Organization estimated in 1996 that at least one million children under the age of sixteen work in the sex trade in Asia, with especially high numbers in Thailand and the Philippines.[5] Even in newer tourist destinations such as Mongolia, the numbers of children in the sex trade and children with HIV has risen dramatically.[6] Although children over the age of twelve constitute the bulk of the child sex trade, traffickers can earn extra money for bringing children as young as six to brothels in major cities in developing countries in Asia. Foreign men are not by any means the only customers at these sex businesses, but their economic importance can be far greater than that of local patrons.[7]

To push the child welfare line more effectively and to put the spotlight on children employed in the sex trade, activists created a bona fide transnational movement aimed at child protection. Leading the child sex crusade has been End Child Prostitution in Asian Tourism (ECPAT), an international NGO with its world headquarters in Bangkok. ECPAT was founded in 1991 primarily by three Asian Christian groups—the Christian Conference of Asia, the Asia Catholic Bishops' Conference, and the Ecumenical Coalition on Third World Tourism[8]—and chose a child sex trade activist and Disciples of Christ pastor from New Zealand, Ron O'Grady, as the group's coordinator.[9] A few years later, the declaration of the UN International Conference on Population and Development prominently featured language on children's rights, including freedom from trafficking and sexual abuse.[10]

ECPAT also managed to put the sexual exploitation of children on the agenda of UNICEF, which had not yet backed up its support of ECPAT's goals with concrete action. And so in August 1996, UNICEF, in cooperation with ECPAT and the Swedish government, sponsored the World Congress against Commercial Sexual Exploitation of Children in Stockholm. Focusing primarily on child prostitution in such countries as the Philippines, India, and Thailand, the conference's participants discussed how sex tourists might be punished, how governments could combat the trafficking in children, and how policymakers could more effectively prohibit child prostitution and child pornography.[11] Although member nations differed on important details, such as the appropriate age of consent (which was as low as twelve in some developing nations), congress participants passed a nonbinding "agenda for action" that inveighed against the sexual exploitation of children.[12]

The movement had achieved some success even before the Stockholm conference. By the time of the congress, several developed nations, including the United States, Germany, and France, had already passed extraterritoriality laws permitting authorities to arrest citizens of these countries for having sex with children, even in countries where such transactions are legal; several other nations made similar moves shortly thereafter. The congress, however, focused on the responsibility of all advanced industrial states to prohibit overseas child exploitation by their own citizens. In so doing, it implicitly acknowledged the difficulty of implementing reforms only in the developing countries themselves, which were in need of foreign income and benefited from the sex tourists.[13]

This emphasis quickly began to draw attention to Japan. Japanese sex tourists had been notorious throughout Asia, in part because of their numbers and in part because of the willingness, until the mid-1980s, of Japanese travel firms to describe in explicit detail the attractions their packaged sex tours provided. Even though Japanese men are hardly the only offenders in sex markets, the proximity of Japan to regions with large sex industries, combined with the amount of mostly male business travel, has made Japan a symbol of wealthy men exploiting poor women and children. Compounding this was the government's tardiness in cracking down on child pornography and sex tourism.

In the developing international movement against the sexual exploitation of children, child pornography in Japan has been a lightning rod for global criticism. The relationship between child pornography and the child prostitution campaign is complex, centering on the victimization of children in photographs and videos and the idea that viewers find sex with children morally acceptable. The growth of the Internet has ensured that what is legally distributed in Japan is available overseas, if illegally, to anyone with a web browser. Before 1999, Japan's child pornography legislation was permissive regarding distribution, and critics claimed (with questionable accuracy) that by the late 1990s as much as 80 percent of the world's child pornography originated in Japan. As Carol Smolenski, head of ECPAT's U.S. office, argued, "We are affected by Japan's laws. The Internet has changed the field. . . . We're absolutely outraged by how easy it is to get."[14] At a May 1998 Interpol conference in Lyon on international child pornography, Japanese National Police Agency representative Gotō Keiji was hit with criticism so stinging that several representatives of other national police agencies, presumably no shrinking violets themselves, felt the need to assure him later that the attacks were not meant personally. Gotō said later that year in Tokyo, "I became aware that Japan's approach to child pornography is not acceptable internationally. . . . Our standards of decency have been seriously questioned by the international community."[15] At a later conference in Tokyo, twenty countries displayed their action plans for dealing with child prostitution and pornography, with Japan, the conference's host, having nothing to show.[16]

Of course, "standards of decency" have long existed in Japan, though these standards are embedded within a legal system that has permitted teenage sexuality. The national legal age of sexual consent in Japan was and remains thirteen, though local obscenity regulations effectively raise this in many prefectures, and the principle of the sexual self-determination of teens is at least debated if not completely accepted as a legal standard in Japan.[17] Even so, the combination of the Child Welfare Law and local obscenity (*inkō jōrei*) regulations made commercial sex with or the sexual display of children under the age of eighteen legally risky. Even before the passage of the 1999 law, a child or his or her family could launch a complaint with the potential for serious penalties for the producer, distributor, or customer of child pornography.

Consequently, sex-oriented businesses had established ways to circumvent the fearsome punishments one might face if a child victim or her family pursued litigation. Before the 1999 laws, child fetish magazines, for example, generally walked a tightrope, featuring models eighteen years of age or older suggestively stripping off school uniforms, or models under that age wearing different types of "blue sailor" school uniforms or gym clothes. When independent or gray market magazines and videos displayed nudity of or sex with young children, they frequently used Southeast Asian children, who were filmed overseas and were by and large incapable of filing the necessary complaints to prosecute the photographers. Japanese child-pornography producers claimed to be mindful of this important distinction between foreign children and Japanese children.[18] Thus, in spite of the criticism in Lyon, it is not exactly true that Japan was completely open to child pornography. Rather, the insufficient national laws and stricter but hodge-podge local regulations together framed a difficult environment for the prosecution of those involved in the sexual exploitation of children. Japanese child pornography inspired international contempt not because there was no regulatory system to prevent it but because Japanese law skewed outcomes and made it safer to use poor children from other Asian nations. Its fully international character meant that virtually anything produced in Japan could be seen elsewhere, potentially inspiring pedophiles of all nationalities, and the children most clearly victimized were from the Southeast Asian nations where much of the work of the movement to stop child prostitution was concentrated.

This made Japanese participation in the movement all the more relevant. In the years leading up to the law, ECPAT had two affiliated offices in Japan. The Tokyo office, also known as STOP, was headed by

Miyamoto Junko, a long-time antipornography activist and a staff member of the Women's Christian Temperance Union (WCTU).[19] The WCTU has had a somewhat unusual history in this non-Christian nation. It escaped official persecution in the prewar era, and in the postwar era, it continued to campaign to outlaw prostitution and pressed for gender equality, while maintaining special roles for women as wives and mothers.[20] These positions have at times made it an effective social control partner for the government. STOP has pushed an unusual hybrid of Christian and radical feminist taboos against pornography and prostitution, which made it a logical partner for the international ECPAT activists when they established their regional office, which is now named ECPAT/STOP.

In contrast, the Kansai (western Japan) chapter of ECPAT, based in Osaka, had a stronger liberal activist stance, and focused more closely on the question of the sexual abuse of Southeast Asian children. Although not entirely mute on the issues of prostitution or pornography as such, the Osaka activist organizers have stressed the need to prohibit *seiteki gyaku-tai* (sexual mistreatment or abuse). They pushed heavily to strengthen existing legislation to ensure that Japanese who were sexually abusing children in Japan or overseas would be punished. Because of their different emphases on sexual abuse versus sexual commerce, the two ECPAT groups had different judgments regarding the proper shape of legislation to halt child prostitution.

Although it would be going too far to suggest that Japan had been uniquely guilty of promoting sex tourism or child exploitation, little doubt existed by the late 1990s that it was a pariah among the advanced industrial countries. The Law for Punishing Acts Related to Child Prostitution and Child Pornography and for Protecting Children (CPCPL, or Child Prostitution/Child Pornography Law) passed by unanimous vote in the Diet in 1999, which would seem to be a natural reaction and clear evidence that the international norm had spread. The story of child prostitution in Japan appears to follow the usual narrative of the adoption of international norms: A transnational movement—made up of earnest and hard-working activist groups in the industrialized and developing world—forces an issue onto the global agenda. Its connections to domestic social movements (in this case, Japanese representatives of ECPAT and other organizations) localize this pressure and force the government to adopt and implement the norm. Viewed both from above, focusing on the transnational actors, and from below, looking more closely at the domestic networks of activists,[21] we see an international norm doing exactly what the theories suggest—aligning practices around a core set of globally accepted principles, buttressed by the legitimacy of international organizations.

Yet some of these same activists were among the only public critics of the 1999 legislation. ECPAT-Kansai, for example, claimed that it was not a law about sexual abuse but a "bill to eradicate enjo kōsai."[22] These activists thought the proposed legislation had been hijacked by lawmakers hoping to use it as an opportunity to ban compensated dating. As we observed in chapter 3 enjo kōsai had evolved in a regulatory environment that constrained other portions of the sex trade. In the late 1990s, however, the National Police Agency had despaired of cracking down on schoolgirls' practice of enjo kōsai, given the extent of the debates over juvenile rights, the appropriate role of the state in controlling moral issues, and the relative accountability of the girls and their customers for their actions. For the police and their supporters in the Diet, the international norm was a crucial political opportunity.

Policing Enjo Kōsai

Few symbols allowed adults to visualize the breakdown in mores and values among teens better than the rise of the kogals. Japanese high schools provided the first front where adults other than the girls' family members faced enjo kōsai and kogals. After all, Japanese schools have strict dress codes and have cracked down in the past on violations ranging from rebellious hairstyles to elaborate makeup. And yet the kogals continued to multiply, in spite of their clear violation of school appearance regulations. The most popularly held view was that so many girls rapidly adopted the style that it was impractical to try to discipline them. Other interpretations had it that male teachers were themselves intimidated by the girls, an explanation I find plausible, judging from my own reactions.

Japanese police had largely handled the earlier waves of teenagers entering sex markets by clamping down on the firms employing them and by reprimanding the girls, rather than by arresting customers. But the rise of enjo kōsai and the difficulty of using the law on sex-oriented businesses against the telephone clubs at the core of the trade increased the pressure on the girls. Police mostly relied on local obscenity regulations when they scolded the schoolgirls involved. These rules generally proscribe four categories of activity: (a) sexual activities outside of marriage creating "impure desires" in society; (b) activities outside of marriage (particularly adultery) that violate community standards; (c) sexual activity that tears away at interpersonal bonds; and (d) sexual activities that threaten the spiritual or moral development of, or that create spiritual instability among, youth under the age of eighteen.[23]

Generally charged with *itsudatsu kōi* (indecent behavior), the girls have primarily been reprimanded by local police in an informal, noncompulsory procedure known as *hodō* (guidance).[24] Police tend to use hodō for moral violations by "vulnerable" people, including children and prostitutes.[25] Hodō is an especially unwelcome term to human rights activists because its informal nature means that it can be applied, depending on the situation, in radically different ways, and there is only minimal oversight. Police can, for example, contact the parents of a girl if they feel it is appropriate; the coercive nature of this tactic, however, does not sit well with those interested in protecting the rights of children, especially if the result may be child abuse by the angry parent. At the other end of the spectrum are hodō efforts that seem like mere formalities, with neither the officers nor the kids paying much attention. In one case—about which I have heard only as an anecdote, though it fits the image Japan's hodō experts have independently given me—a local police officer gave a sermon about sexual morals to a group of bored high school girls who sat sullenly, waiting for him to shut up.

The local obscenity laws tend to take a sweeping approach to the sexuality of teenagers. These regulations in effect override Japan's national age of consent (thirteen) by stressing that sexual commerce with anyone under the age of eighteen—even if not prohibited by national law— violates community standards as well as the "wholesome upbringing" (*kenzen ikusei*) of children. Notably, police have been able to use these regulations informally against the children through hodō, even though the punishments have been minimal and embedded in a paternalistic environment of "advice" to the vulnerable. By the mid-1990s, police and other officials argued that these rules simply could not provide enough of a legal framework to halt the growing enjo kōsai trade. Across the nation, local governments began to take different steps to stop the practice. By creating a patchwork quilt of rules regarding sexual commerce with children, these governments produced remarkably uneven handling of enjo kōsai, with some cities and prefectures far stricter than others. In some areas, local governments built on the National Police Agency's experience, described in chapter 3, in regulating sex-oriented businesses or *fūzoku*. In 1995, for example, the Gifu prefectural government responded to pressure from local PTAs and other groups by placing addi-

tional restrictions on telephone clubs, the enterprises allowing women
to meet men via telephone to arrange liaisons. The Gifu telephone club
law dramatically enhanced penalties on those telephone clubs allowing
participation by those under the age of eighteen.[26]

The Osaka prefectural government, like a number of others, took the
more dramatic and punitive step of announcing that enjo kōsai amounted
to prostitution (the "enjo kōsai wa baishun" campaign). Agreeing with
the police interest in a crackdown, the prefectural board of education
authorized the display of anti–enjo kōsai posters in Osaka's high schools.
Referring specifically to Japan's Anti-Prostitution Law (and thus implying that the girls would be arrested in accordance with the law), the
posters featured a photo of two sets of legs—a man in a suit and a schoolgirl in her uniform—walking together.[27] Notably, the campaign aimed
at deterring the youngsters rather than their adult customers, though
these men too might have been arrested, particularly if the juvenile were
to make a complaint. Local police officers detained and questioned
thirty-two schoolgirls in connection with violations of the Anti-Prostitution Law in 1996, roughly double the number of the previous year.[28]
With the Juvenile Law preventing full criminal prosecution of schoolgirls, conservative law enforcement authorities were frustrated by their
inability to halt the trade.

Whether through enhanced "guidance" of the girls involved, tightened restrictions on sex-oriented businesses, or zealous use of obscenity
regulations, most of Japan's prefectures had adopted specific anti–enjo
kōsai measures by 1997. By this time, almost any sexual activity between
an adult and a child under the age of eighteen could be prosecuted, in
one way or another, in any prefecture of Japan, with the exceptions of
Tokyo and Nagano.[29] Tokyo's more liberal standards relating to sex markets almost certainly increased enjo kōsai–related activity at key entertainment spots in the city, especially those conveniently located within
commuting distance of Japan's more conservative areas. In chapter 1, I
described the moment on a Japanese subway when two schoolgirls
changed clothes in front of me. That train's terminus was Ikebukuro, a
major transportation hub, serving (among others) commuters coming
from Saitama Prefecture north of Tokyo. Ikebukuro was by this time a
renowned assignation place, reputedly because both the girls and the
men found the police environment in Saitama too strict.

It was with much fanfare, then, that the Tokyo metropolitan government—often criticized for being too permissive of teen sex markets—
passed new regulations to deal with enjo kōsai in late 1997. These new

rules targeted primarily customers and intermediaries, not the children themselves, and authorized fines for up to ¥5 million with a one-year prison sentence for a conviction. Health and social workers were muted in their praise of the rules, arguing that they were not tough enough on offenders and that they did not deal with the underlying causes of enjo kōsai.[30] Even so, the focus on customers rather than on the schoolgirls was in many ways a welcome and desirable shift for child welfare advocates. Interestingly, the two prefectural assembly members voting against the bill were both women; one, Fujita Aiko, argued that "adults should teach youth properly how to judge on their own whether or not to buy or sell sex, before making regulations."[31]

Fujita did not win the day, and doubts about government regulation of child sexuality fell away in the Diet's 1999 vote as well. Yet it is fascinating that Fujita's statement could have been made at all. The space for legitimate political discourse differs from country to country, and it is not always in the outcomes of struggles that we catch the most pristine glimpses of political or social life. It would be unthinkable in Japan for anyone in government to argue seriously that weapons sold at gun shows should be relatively unregulated. Conversely, it would be nearly unthinkable for a U.S. legislator to argue that prostitution involving sixteen-year-olds should be legally protected, even as the government tried to "teach youth properly how to judge whether or not to buy or sell sex." Fujita's point is in this way instructive, displaying the contours of prevailing debates in Japan: about what enjo kōsai is, whether it is good or evil, or whether it ought to be legal or not.

The uncoordinated and now radically conflicting legal responses to enjo kōsai mirrored the larger social discomfort with the phenomenon. Were schoolgirls the victims of sexual exploitation by adults, as the Tokyo regulations implied? Were they willing participants who were too easily lured by businesses like the telephone clubs, as the Gifu restrictions suggested? Or where they young prostitutes, guilty of moral as well as legal transgressions, as the Osaka had it? Lost in almost all of the extraordinary media attention to the phenomenon was that enjo kōsai was highly uncommon, practiced by, at most, a tiny percentage of Japan's schoolgirls. The kogals—with their crude and incomprehensible vernacular, their shockingly frank sexuality, their unorthodox hairstyles, and their gaudy display of their physical charms—were a great deal more common. At least some (and perhaps most) of the political impetus behind the various enjo kōsai crackdowns reflected a discomfort with the appearance and behavior of Japan's girls and young women, concerns that sat uneasily alongside those efforts to protect juveniles from sexual exploitation.

The Limits of "Guidance"

The heart of the police handling of juvenile crime lies in *hodō*, the softly coercive form of "guidance" that theoretically does not rise to the level of "punishment." In more severe cases, such as when a police official finds himself or herself dealing with the same juvenile a number of times, the guidance will likely take place at a police station or in a police-run juvenile center.[32] The center that I visited in spring 2004 is a plain, somewhat forbidding building in a suburban neighborhood. Among the approximately seven hundred contacts that it handles in a given year, most are from parents, often repeat callers. Parents whose children have run away from home or who have been treated violently by their sons or daughters frequently ask for advice. Girls rarely come in to discuss enjo kōsai; more common are children who are social outsiders and the victims of Japan's sometimes intense bullying (*ijime*) at school. In spite of the best efforts of the staff, this is not a happy place to visit; people go there because they feel powerless to prevent the breakdown of their families.

The center's personnel take their role as counselors very seriously, and have made the facilities as accommodating as possible for those family members intrepid enough to come directly to them. I noticed this most clearly when one counselor showed me a small "therapy room," with a sand tray, maybe a meter square, and a bookcase filled with small figurines. People could deal with stress and express their feelings by using the dolls and set pieces to create a scene in the sand tray. At the time of my visit, the box's contents were the handiwork of a ten-year-old fifth-grade girl who was traumatized by bullying and ostracism at her school.[33] She had created a wilderness scene: a mélange of animals, including a lion that was stalking a herd of zebra, and a family of cheetahs. There was a moose—seemingly unaware of the hunt taking place immediately to its right—wandering near a forest that she had built on the side of the box. In the back left corner she had set a plastic waterfall, the large, thundering, American or African kind, not the delicate and narrow type idealized in Japanese art. A crab, impossibly outsized in this setting, stood on its short legs, raising its large red claw in greeting or defiance—it is hard to tell with a plastic crab. This counselor's job was, I realized, another in an extremely long list of those that I would be emotionally incapable of doing; I felt heartbroken after three minutes in the room, and I never even met the child.

Because few juveniles engaged in delinquency or enjo kōsai voluntarily report for guidance, most of the Metropolitan Police Department's activities take place out on the streets in areas popular with Japanese youth. Anyone can engage in hodō: as one police officer told me, if a shopkeeper lectures some kids to stop loitering around his or her store, that is, in a sense, guidance for the children. Special volunteers can serve as *hodōin* (guidance personnel), though only police officers can engage in the formal guidance activities that are reported in the local and national police statistics on juvenile delinquency. In my various interviews and site checks, all of the guidance I witnessed was carried out by police officers.

They were not, however, wearing uniforms. Some were in casual clothes, and others wore suits, which seemed not to fool the children. The first sense I had of this came when I walked with a suit-wearing police officer into a train station to ride to a neighborhood patrolled by hodōin. Three schoolgirls were chatting with one another behind us as we were starting to come down the steps. One appeared to spot the police officer and suddenly grabbed her friend and said, "Wait a second, hold on" and pulled her back upstairs. There was no particular fear in her voice (in fact, she was giggling when warning her friend), but she seemed intent on taking the next train to avoid the officer. The police officer told me later that the youths in this area all recognized him.

EXCERPTS FROM A GUIDE FOR HODŌIN (APRIL 2004)

PURPOSE:
- Finding and administering guidance quickly is extremely important for stopping juvenile delinquency and also for building a wholesome environment. When kids are becoming delinquents, it is important to move as quickly as possible to nip it in the bud and move them in a better direction; when it appears that they might be at risk of delinquency, we should use guidance as initial steps toward making sure they stay on the right path. Also, when you see a juvenile behaving well, you should take the opportunity to praise that behavior—this is another way to discourage crime.

IDENTIFYING YOUTH FOR GUIDANCE:
- Wearing pants low (low-rider)
- Wearing fashionable clothes (*yōfuku*) or makeup from famous brands, or carrying a purse or bag from a famous designer, particularly if the ju-

venile is treating the item as precious no matter how old or beaten up it is. Girls sitting on the ground, operating their cell phones, and who seem to be waiting to be "picked up" (*nanpa*)

CONFIRMING AGE:
- Are they carrying school ID, driver's license, medical ID card, or something else that can help confirm their identities?
- Confirm their birth date (using the imperial system, Western system, or Chinese zodiac)
- Do they have transportation passes, membership cards, or the like? Usually check at least two or three per person.

POSSESSIONS:
- Get permission to touch their pockets [to check what they are holding]. Also have the juvenile himself or herself open their bags or backpacks for you. Advise them that they should not smoke.
- In cases in which one person in a group is smoking, there is a good chance that others in the group are also carrying tobacco.
- Take a good look at pockets and tote bags while they are walking (you can actually see tobacco in shirt pockets if the youth is wearing a school uniform).

ENCOURAGING WORDS IN CLOSING:
- If you hear, during the conversation, about something that they plan to really work on (like entrance exams, sports, etc.) encourage them in that direction.
- Think of something good about the child (appearance, personality, seems cheerful, etc.), take a moment to praise him or her.

WHAT NOT TO SAY:
- Don't talk down to the juvenile pompously.
- Don't indicate at the start that you don't believe them—they'll clam up.
- Don't call them childish.

OTHER POINTS:
- If you ask someone's age and it takes awhile for them to respond (or no answer comes at all), it almost certainly means that she or he is underage.
- If a juvenile is lying to you, ask as many questions as possible so that you can record the contradictions.

Source: ZZ-Ward Shōnen Sentā, *Shōnen hodō katsudō no jūyōsei to pointo (wakamono to no sesshikata)* [The Importance of and Tips for Youth Guidance (Getting through to Young People)], April 2004.

Guidance follows a well-established pattern in Tokyo and in other parts of Japan.[34] I received a copy of a manual (see excerpts in box) for people doing hodō, and it captures the basic thrust of at least the inter-actions I witnessed and others described to me. Police officers and guid-ance volunteers can approach anyone, of course; the entire process is ostensibly noncompulsory, and so there is no legal prohibition against it. Ideally, police officers on "guidance patrol" should approach not only the potential troublemakers but also those kids who seem serious and ac-tive, taking the opportunity to praise and encourage them. It reflects the notion that community policing is about more than just intimidation but about building networks of trust. My sense, however, was that praise was uncommon. More often, police concentrate on teenagers they believe are up to no good. In some cases, simply wearing a school uniform is likely to invite police attention, particularly if it is after 11 p.m. or during normal school hours. The combination of a school uniform and tobacco (illegal for those under twenty) is one of the most common ways for po-lice to identify someone who needs a lecture.

The training manual also encourages police to look at the fashions and appearance of the teens to determine who might be at risk of delin-quency. A friend of mine, himself no stranger to the receiving end of police guidance, looked at the list of suspicious clothing in the "hodō guide" excerpted above and told me that it simply reflected the "police's prejudices" (keisatsu no henken). If someone is wearing regular clothing (shifuku) but looks suspiciously young to be smoking or out after 11 p.m., the hodōin can approach him or her. Because this contact is informal and noncompulsory, police generally have to rely on the juvenile's good will and his or her uncertainty about police authority to elicit answers and get evidence.

The police are aware that the noncompulsory nature of hodō means that the juvenile can, in essence, simply choose not to answer or can run off. In part for this reason, the guidance officials are told to identify themselves right away to the juvenile, establishing authority immediately. After that, the hodōin will probably exchange pleasantries with the teenager and will try to praise something about him or her in order to establish a smooth conversation. Because teens, especially those with cig-arettes, will frequently lie about their age, a typical police question is "What is your Chinese zodiac sign?" (Eto wa nan desu ka). A child who knows to say "twenty" for age, or "1984" for year of birth, may stumble before saying "Year of the Rat." Catching the juvenile in a lie allows the police officer to operate a bit more freely, to make more demands and apply more pressure.

On one site visit, I realized that there were at least five or six police officers, all within a few meters of one another, approaching teens when they deemed necessary or appropriate. I watched one speak with two attractive schoolgirls after a young man, possibly a talent scout for a sex-oriented business, had approached them and chatted with them for a few minutes. During her conversation with the girls, she listened intently but did not seem to take notes in her memo pad, as there was no evidence that the girls had done anything wrong. Her next target, only a few minutes later, was a lanky boy wearing hip-hop clothes; he had been smoking and she had correctly surmised that he was underage. He looked down at his shoes, sheepishly nodding his head, while she filled up her memo pad. In a surreal moment, she talked to two teenage girls in bear costumes, though without heads or masks; they were part of a four-person group of *ganguro* girls who had been filming some kind of advertisement or television segment at the end of the street. While the hodōin held up these two to ask about their activities, their two friends watched warily from a nearby alley, attempting neither to flee nor to intervene. To be sure, watching a plainclothes police officer lecture two *ganguro* Japanese girls in bear outfits was not quite what I had expected when I was given permission to watch hodō patrol, but I was encouraged to see that some patterns are universal. Treating the police officer with the same degree of deference that my undergraduates ordinarily display to me, one of the girls continued to speak on her cell phone throughout the conversation.

Although it was probably not a comfort to the hodōin at this particular moment, the ubiquity of the cell phone can be a benefit to police who try to use guidance in cases of enjo kōsai and child prostitution. There are few telltale signs that can be used to justify a police officer's asking girls about possible sexual misconduct. If one is seen walking with an adult in a shady part of town at the wrong time of day, that may be enough, but often the police are stuck with the problem of relying on other offenses (tobacco, most commonly) as leverage for asking the girls about enjo kōsai. If they are wearing expensive accessories or carrying bags from expensive boutiques, the hodōin might praise the girls' fashion sense before asking about their patterns of conspicuous consumption. A police officer with a particularly disarming manner can sometimes induce the teens to turn over their cell phones for a quick inspection, often by lightly saying, "Come on, let me see it" (*misete, misete ne*). If there are a number of suspicious-looking e-mails from one address to another, police can use the opportunity to ask the teen more about her boyfriends or, in some instances, about a sugar daddy. The most graphic evidence I saw of this came in a visit to one youth center, where I was shown (but not given) a printout of the e-mail conversations recorded on one anonymous teenager's cell phone.[35] She had been in touch with adult men, evidently through an Internet dating club. The conversations were remarkably blunt, with the men asking her breast size or whether she would have sex for ¥25,000. The transcript went on for about seven pages and involved at least four different men.

In a situation like this, or when the teen is caught in a lie, or police discover tobacco, they can bring the teen to a nearby police box, the police station, or a juvenile center to proceed with formal guidance. This is the level at which young people enter police databases and statistics. My friend, himself a hodō target in his youth, informed me that in terms of the actual encounter with the police, there is little difference between formal guidance and an arrest. The main difference lies in the secrecy of the files. He indicated that his hodō record had remained confidential and that it could not have been used against him in determining college or work acceptance. An arrest record becomes a permanent blight. But he surprised me when I asked him about being praised by police officers; my guess had been that most teens would rather drink hemlock than be praised for obeying the law. Instead, he said, "No, that would be nice. Who doesn't like being praised?"

The police with whom I spoke thought that hodō is an imperfect system but the best one available at the moment. They uniformly said that delinquents need to be reformed and rehabilitated; and the process itself relies on a view of the juveniles as misguided but correctible, which may even extend to those prosecuted under the revised Juvenile Law.[36] At the same time, most police officers I talked with seemed somewhat jaded about the social environment they confront. The constant refrain is that Japanese families are failing and that, as a result, Japanese teens are now out of control. As noted, statistically this is a difficult case to make, at least when compared to the long sweep of Japan's postwar history. By any standards, Japanese streets are at least as safe as those of other advanced industrial nations. But now, the problem feels different; the apparent collapse of order—whether construed as discipline or as "traditional values"—among Japanese youth seems both emblematic of and responsible for larger social problems facing the society. And so the police carry out their patrols, trying both to protect teens and to keep them in line, all the while aware of the limits of their authority and of juveniles' ability to ignore them. The legislation responding to the international norm against the sexual exploitation of children ultimately bore the imprint of those wanting tougher police measures against the teens themselves.

The Child Prostitution/Child Pornography Law

The Legislative Climate

With so much attention going to the enjo kōsai problem, local representatives of ECPAT and their supporters faced an uphill battle in establishing children as the victims of prostitution. Even as activists sought to align Japanese policies with those of the nation's advanced industrial counterparts, they confronted longer and larger debates over the rights of children to engage in sex, over sexual commerce itself, and over the meaning of enjo kōsai in a nation nervous about its future.

Indeed, initial comments in the Diet about enjo kōsai reflected concerns not about the damage potentially being done to the schoolgirls but rather about the immoral nature of the girls' choices. In a January 24, 1997, upper house session, female LDP member Ono Kiyoko made a lengthy statement about social problems facing the nation, specifically linking compensated dating to drug abuse and the absence of a "wholesome" (*kenzen*) environment for Japanese teenagers.[37] Four days later, in the budget committee, Tasso Takuya of the New Frontier Party, one of the LDP's rivals, used the term metaphorically to lambaste corrupt policymakers. Referring to financial scandals that had engulfed Japan's ministries, Takuya in essence called the bureaucrats whores, asking whether it was a "good message to send young people, that you can do whatever horrible things you want to earn money."[38] Subsequent references to enjo kōsai in 1997 linked it to educational issues or to the growing menace of juvenile crime, a theme that became even more prevalent after the arrest of a fourteen-year-old in the Sakakibara Seito murder case in Kobe.

A meeting in June 1997 of the lower house Subcommittee on Regional Affairs addressed the patchwork of local regulations on enjo kōsai and, in doing so, called two of the scholars discussing the issue to testify. Miyadai Shinji, the liberal sociologist discussed in chapter 3, gave a lengthy description of compensated dating, arguing that the problem was more widespread than some statistics suggested. He also argued that regulations had shifted the nature of enjo kōsai, encouraging the participants involved to stick with known partners in "long-term contracts" (*chōki keiyakuka*). In alerting the subcommittee members to the complexity of enjo kōsai, Miyadai made a telling point comparing the traditional Japa-

nese word for prostitution, *baishun,* which combines the characters for
"sell" and "sex," with the neologism *kaishun,* which replaces "sell" with
"buy." Users of the new term shift the responsibility for the crime away
from the women providing sexual services to their male customers. Faced
with following Miyadai's extremely lengthy and detailed (though not
carefully substantiated) testimony, the next speaker, renowned social psychologist Kawai Hayao, praised Miyadai for his "concrete" and detailed
testimony, and said sheepishly that he would speak "from the heart" about
enjo kōsai. Hayao, the more conservative scholar who, as reported in
chapter 3, had described compensated dating as a function of Japan's
loss of traditional ethics, carefully adopted some of Miyadai's progressive
language (such as *kaishun*), placing blame on the adults. But he also
emphasized that Japan needed to teach its children right from wrong
("yappari ikenai koto wa ikenai to iu koto wa hakkiri yatte itadakitai").[39]

    With enjo kōsai appearing as a topic in committees on regional affairs,
crime, education, the budget, and other Diet discussions, ECPAT's Diet
supporters faced the difficult task of shifting the conversation about
child prostitution toward the issue of Japanese victimization of children
overseas. Cooperating with ECPAT, in 1997 Japanese upper house coalition legislators Owaki Masako and Shimizu Sumiko[40] agreed to submit a
package of bills dealing with the problem. The previous year, Owaki had
taken a fact-finding tour to Thailand, where she was reported to have
been shocked by the stories told to her by local young girls—in fluent
Japanese—and was thus convinced that Japan needed to take a stronger
stand.[41] Under the leadership of former education minister Moriyama
Mayumi, a group of lawmakers from the then-ruling coalition—the Liberal Democratic Party, Japan Socialist Party, and New Harbinger Party–
Sakigake—introduced the Child Pornography/Prostitution Bill.[42]

    The initial proposal put forward in spring 1998 by the coalition par-
ties made a number of relatively bold legal proposals. The law's purpose
would be to "protect the rights of children" and it defined "child" as anyone under the age of eighteen. It stipulated that prostitution or pornography involving children would be illegal and that perpetrators could
face heavy fines and prison sentences of up to five years. Moreover, in the
case of prostitution, those prosecuted would be the customers, a major
departure from the focus on sex-oriented businesses and the girls or
women involved. In contrast with the Child Welfare Law, children would
not need to file complaints in order for the police to arrest and prosecute for prostitution or pornography, nor would the accused need to be
apprehended in flagrante delicto. Ignorance of the child's age would not

be an excuse, and any Japanese violating this law overseas could be prosecuted at home even without a complaint from the victim.[43] Across the board, this proposal was a radical break from the legal traditions surrounding sex and child protection in postwar Japan, owing much to the work of international NGOs such as ECPAT that informed lawmakers as to how these kinds of regulations were written elsewhere.

Members of the bureaucracy typically take a muscular role in drafting the legislation passed by the Japanese Diet. Indeed, one of the common critiques of Japanese politics is that the Diet largely debates laws given to them by bureaucrats, calling into question who actually wields power.[44] In the case of the Child Prostitution/Pornography Law, legislators themselves provided the initial draft, prompting some to suggest that the NPA had no real stake in the law. To some degree, this is probably true, as the NPA's expressed interest during that era was in enhancing its ability to punish juveniles for their crimes, rather than to pursue sex tourists. The NPA agreed to participate in a study council established by Moriyama to redraft the law, although it found itself hemmed in by the child welfarist orientation of the activists who had pushed for it.[45]

Moriyama, a formidable intellect and political talent, managed to merge the issues into a bill that linked the international movement's major concerns with the growing national interest in halting enjo kōsai. Owaki, like other JSP members, adopted a distinctly humanistic, moralistic approach to the problem; Japanese exploitation of Asian children sat as badly with these leftists as the "comfort woman" problem and the sexual exploitation in Japan of women trafficked from Asia.[46] Moriyama discussed the national shame of child pornography, saying, "No nation that values democracy and freedom should condone child pornography. . . . We must pass the law for the honor of Japan."[47] But her party, the LDP, was interested in more than the exploitation of Asian children, the crux of the international pressure on Japan.

Instead, LDP members sold the bill partly as a cure for enjo kōsai, especially to their socially conservative supporters. In their judgment, the law was not only designed to respond to "harsh international criticism" of Japan but also to promote the "wholesome upbringing" (kenzen ikusei) of Japanese youth.[48] The Japanese National Parent-Teacher Association, a conservative counterpart to the leftist teachers' union, also praised Moriyama for her efforts toward providing a wholesome upbringing for Japanese children, and even chose to describe the law as banning baishun, which makes women and girls accountable, rather than the customer-focused kaishun.[49]

The Development and Collapse of Opposition

LDP efforts to link the issues, however, prompted criticism from the Left. In order to ensure the unanimous vote that she wanted for this internationally visible legislation, Moriyama's study group sought to gather as many opinions as possible and to reach out to different constituencies. To the strongest proponents of the international norm with its focus on the human rights of children, the law's inclusion of enjo kōsai symbolized its having been hijacked by conservatives. Fearing that an overly wide net would result in few prosecutions and in only limited implementation, ECPAT-Kansai argued that the specter of enjo kōsai was being used to undermine the real purpose of the bill—to protect children around Asia from genuine human rights violations. By discussing the proposed law in terms of the "wholesome upbringing" of Japanese children, it appeared that its purpose was to reestablish a moral order based on traditional gender roles rather than to recognize. Notably, feminist and activist attorney Tsuboi Setsuko's complaint that the law was more about enjo kōsai than about child abuse captured the sense of betrayal felt by ECPAT-Kansai members.[50]

Similarly, the Japan Federation of Bar Associations (Nichibenren) objected not only to the possible violations of civil liberties in antipornography legislation, such as freedom of speech and freedom of expression, but also to the setting of the age of a "child" at eighteen. Nichibenren proposed that there be some kind of distinction made between the crimes of Japanese overseas, where the victims were children forced into prostitution in often gruesome conditions, and enjo kōsai at home. Arguing that the best way to make this distinction would be to set an age limit that would differentiate twelve- to thirteen-year-olds being exploited in sex markets in Thailand, India, the Philippines, and the like from Japanese high school girls engaging in enjo kōsai, the federation proposed that a child be defined as a person under the age of sixteen. It furthermore urged that one of the core elements of the new law—that the victim not be required to file a complaint—be stricken, as it could be used to violate the rights of a defendant.[51]

The wreckage of Japan's other new parties coalesced in 1998 as the Democratic Party of Japan (DPJ), which became the largest and most important opposition force. With a number of former socialists among its ranks, the DPJ challenged the law from a perspective partly resembling ECPAT Kansai's. They argued that the purpose of the law should be to protect children's rights, not to create an ideal of wholesomeness; it should stress preventing the sexual abuse (*seiteki gyakutai*) of children, rather than placing limits on the sexual freedom of teenagers. Additionally, the DPJ sought to protect freedom of expression by trying to limit the bans on child pornography to the production, sale, and purchase of videos and photographs, with punishment for neither mere possession nor for drawings or otherwise artificial representations of children in sexual situations.[52]

The Left saw the proposed law as more than an effort to crack down on sex tourism and pornography; it was yet another example of creeping authoritarianism endangering individual rights. For them, the conservatives' stance on the law reflected a manipulative step away from international norms. In April 1999 testimony to the lower house's Special Committee on Juvenile Problems, where he had been asked to discuss education problems, Miyadai argued that the conservative impact on the law had done more than turn it from a law about the sexual exploitation of children into a law about enjo kōsai. It had, in defining the basic age of consent to sexual commerce as eighteen, deprived teenagers of their right to autonomy (*jiko ketteiken*). It also displayed an antiprostitution zeal that had nothing to do with human rights and everything to do with public order (*chitsujō*). Turning to education, Miyadai argued that it was now "common sense in advanced industrial nations" (*senshinkoku no jōshiki*) that teenagers need to be taught to think independently and critically. To have children develop a "public mind" (*paburikku maindo*), Japan would need an educational system that encouraged independence and creativity. Concluding with a flourish, he argued that greater juvenile autonomy would facilitate real communication between parents and children, which had been lacking because it had been crushed by a community mentality that obstructed Japan's full maturity as a society.[53]

Although the final version of the bill reflected a few of the DPJ's proposals (particularly with regard to pornography rules), it maintained the bulk of its original framework. In so doing, it referred to the goal of banning sexual abuse but specifically targeted acts of child prostitution and child pornography.[54] The 1999 law furthermore maintained the age limit of eighteen, against the suggestions of the bar federation, Miyadai, and some of the ECPAT-Kansai members. Its passage, however, could be counted, and often has been, as a success for child welfare and human rights advocates on both terminological and substantive counts. By replacing *baishun* with *kaishun*, the law genuinely posits the customer as the criminal party, and it punishes only the adult offenders. The decision, moreover, of the relevant NGOs to support the bill, even if delayed, would seem to cement the sense that Japan had unproblematically signed onto the international norm.

Reactions and Consequences

But, of course, the story does not end with the vote, its unanimity notwithstanding. The law's implementation and effects invite scrutiny as well. By most accounts the NPA has pursued child pornographers with some verve,[55] making nearly two hundred arrests per year, starting in 2000 (see table), and apparently forcing some child erotica magazines to rethink their strategies.[56] The corresponding arrest rates for the prostitution statute began with 613 in 2000, then grew to 900–1,200 per year in 2001–2003. For the cop on the streets of Shibuya, Ueno, or Ikebukuro, the law may have made it marginally easier to get cooperation from teenagers on the street. One "guidance veteran" told me that it was easier to approach the schoolgirls and get their attention, because enjo kōsai had been rendered a real crime; other police officials disagreed. One said, however, that in certain cases, the 1999 law allowed them to question schoolgirls more easily if they could get them to a police station or youth guidance center. Because the penalties are focused on adults, the girls may tell their side of the story, knowing they will not be penalized.

Of course, even this depends on what one considers to be a real penalty. Japanese police officials do not consider "guidance," as a girl's trip to the police station would likely be categorized, to be punishment. As noted above, however, for the teens involved, the difference between arrest and hodō might be largely nominal. For many girls, the questioning at the station clearly feels like discipline, and the encounter may involve the girl's parents, leading to dire consequences at home even if, in the formal eyes of the law, they are now merely victims. Feminists and child welfare advocates had long argued that police do not concern themselves with parental abuse that may result when the family is called in. For the police, the more troubling outcome was that, by most official assessments, the 1999 law may have done little to discourage enjo kōsai or child prostitution; like the sex industry regulations described in chapter 3, it may have shifted the nature of the facilities involved. Telephone clubs can now be punished for aiding and abetting enjo kōsai between adults and juveniles, but people may have moved to Internet dating sites and other venues to replace them.

The NPA's statistics suggest, however, a distinctive take on the problem. Although the police report on arrests related to the 1999 law refers to an "incident" in which a Japanese man was arrested for paying a child for sex in Thailand in August 2003,[57] the statistics provide no additional breakdown on the number of men arrested for sex tourism. Indeed, there is good reason to believe that this may have been one of only a small handful involving a non-Japanese child. In a 2001 report about the progress of the law, ECPAT-Tokyo's director, Miyamoto Junko, pointed out that the government had made a significant arrest involving child pornography produced overseas, but the suspect was given a suspended sentence. And by 2001, only one person had been charged with child sex tourism.[58] To be sure, arrests for crimes overseas are more difficult to prosecute than are those for crimes committed in Japan, but the imbalance in NPA interest in sex tourism versus enjo kōsai, and the proposed remedies, indicates a real discrepancy between the international norm behind the law and the domestic implementation of it.

In the 2003 Police White Paper (*Keisatsu Hakusho*), the agency's annual report, the NPA's own figures suggest a conservative bent that has led them to focus on enjo kōsai rather than sex tourism or prostitution involving Asian children. The paper traces the number of children involved in some kind of sexual offense, drawing no clear distinction between those listed as victims and those seen as offenders. These offenses constitute only a small number of overall cases of police "guidance" to juveniles, and the police include a subcategory of girls who engaged in sex because they wanted "money to have fun" (*asobu kane hoshisa*). Although the overall number of juveniles provided with guidance or "protection" (hogo) had dropped from a high of 5,481 in 1995, the 2002 figure of 4,615 reflected the highest number in five years, and included 1,903 juveniles who had admitted to having sex for the money.[59] The NPA seemed especially alarmed at the number of cases involving new online dating sites (*deaikei saito*), easily available on cell phone web networks. By 2003, the online sites were involved in over three times as many cases as were the telephone clubs that had been so crucial in the development of enjo kōsai in the first place.[60]

In October 2002, the NPA created a research group called the Shōnen Yūgai Kankyō Taisaku Kenkyūkai (Council on Measures against Unhealthy Environments for Youth), which focused largely on the dating sites as problematic institutions for Japan's youth. By the time of its midterm report in early 2003, the group had not only identified the Internet dating sites as the locus of concern but had also drafted a bill to

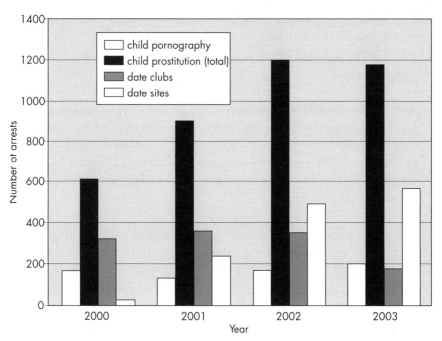

Shift to dating websites in enjo kōsai as shown by arrests. Note: These numbers are for cases "cleared" (*kenkyō*) rather than for actual arrests. In some cases, police can "clear" a case by passing it to prosecutors even without taking a suspect into custody. *Source:* Keisatsuchō Seikatsu Anzen Kyoku Shōnenka (National Police Agency, Lifestyle Safety Bureau, Juvenile Division), *Shōnen hikō nado no gaiyō* [Overview of Juvenile Delinquency and Related Matters, 2003] (Tokyo: NPA, 2004).

halt teenagers from meeting adults through dating sites; the bill virtually rocketed through the Diet, with final approval on June 6.[61] The NPA trumpeted their proposal's extraordinary popularity, with a poll showing that about 80 percent of voters favored its passage.[62] In pushing the law, the NPA pointed out that in their investigation of dating site–related child prostitution cases, 90 percent of the contacts were initiated by the children.[63] The NPA's law not only provided for fines and potential imprisonment for customers and the dating sites but also for fines of up to ¥1 million (about $10,000) for the juveniles involved.[64]

The shift is largely symbolic, but crucially so. Because the girls' cases must be handled in family court, they cannot technically be punished, but only "protected" (hogo). For this reason, it is unclear who could levy fines on the girls and the conditions under which fines might be considered. In other words, the fine seems to be as much a moral statement as a coercive instrument that police can use when giving "guidance" to wayward teens.

But the theoretical possibility of a fine against the girls at least allows police to express clearly that the girls are largely responsible for the increase in teen prostitution, and might become tactically useful as a threat in discouraging teens from seeking enjo kōsai partners through their mobile phone networks. As an NPA spokesperson said in 2002:

> We are fully aware of the argument that underage sex-seeking adults are solely responsible for child prostitution. . . . However, in reality, children are no angels, so we have reached the conclusion that online soliciting [including by minors] needs to be regulated just like pimping on the streets.[65]

The interest in and methods for putting a stop to the dating sites should tell us something crucial about the application of the international norm against the sexual exploitation of children to Japan. The 1999 law's initial authors and supporters had been motivated primarily by a desire to put an end to the scourge of sex tourism involving young children. But rather than tackling this continuing crisis—and, by virtually any measure, it continues to be a very serious problem—the NPA has maintained its focus on the continued existence of enjo kōsai (which had not been at the heart of the original proposal for legislative action). Indeed, the new law against dating sites specifically sidesteps the 1999 law's emphasis on the girls as victims, instead implicating them in the sex trade as culprits. I do not mean to suggest that the NPA and its allies are wrong to punish the operators of websites that allow teen prostitution, or are uninterested in the welfare of the girls. Instead, I hope to draw attention to the mixed motives and complex environment that the norm has met since the 1990s, and the qualified results it has thus far achieved.

The Mixed Outcomes of the Norm

When the 1999 bill outlawing child pornography and child prostitution passed in the Diet, several observers immediately heralded Japan's adherence to international standards on the sexual exploitation of children, referring specifically to Japan's place as an honored member of the international community. A March 1999 editorial in northern Japan's *Kahoku Shimpō* that appeared at the time of the bill's reintroduction in the Diet opened with a reference to international criticism and later detailed how the law would be effective:

Child pornography and prostitution, which are internationally criticized, will be caught up in a new regulatory net. . . . Three years ago
Japan was heavily criticized at the conference in Stockholm for sending many sex tourists to Asia as well as for producing and exporting
child pornography. . . . Laws against child prostitution and pornography are already fixed in the countries of Europe and North America. In most countries, offenders face harsh penalties. *It was only
natural that Japan would have to make laws it could be proud of.*[66] (emphasis added)

Central Japan's *Ehime Shimbun* made the issue of national pride even
more apparent in a May editorial, coinciding with the final (and unanimous) passage of the law:

In 1549, [an early Christian missionary] wrote in a letter that he sent
to his native Spain, "Among the newly discovered peoples, the Japanese are probably the finest race." Because of the integrity and the
high principles of the Japanese, we were well-liked. But three years
ago at the international conference [in Stockholm], the Japanese
were virtually called "the world's most disgraceful nationality." And
this law has been inspired by this criticism.[67]

In another reading, the law not only responded to the international
norm but also played a role in the expansion of children's rights in Japan. Indeed, the foremost Western student of Japanese child welfare
rules, Roger Goodman, argues that the 1999 law almost certainly established a precedent that was critical to the subsequent passage, in 2000,
of wider legislation banning child abuse.[68]

A closer look at the debates behind the law, however, reveals intellectual and political fault lines that shaped the terrain not only for the law's
passage but also for its subsequent implementation. Because the law did
not in itself end all child prostitution—an impossible goal—conservatives have had the qualified and constrained ability to reframe the problem as one of wayward youth in need of discipline. Again, at a certain
level determining whether the norm was a "success" comes down to a
glass-half-empty-or-half-full proposition, and I have no real quarrel with
those, like Goodman, who point to its positive outcomes. Those wishing
to argue that the international norm was successful can point to the
unanimity of the vote for the 1999 law, as well as its straightforward construction of the girls as victims, echoing the 1997 Tokyo regulations as

well as the demands of international movement activists. Critics of Japanese sexual mores might point to the continued fetishization of schoolgirl uniforms and the sprawling openness of a sex industry that seems to be exceptionally visible in almost any urban area, arguing that Japan remains fundamentally unchanged in its patterns of sexual commerce and gender inequality.

My view is more ambivalent because I believe that events since 1999 reveal the norm's diverse legacies, which may become more apparent as more time passes. The controversy continues, and the legislative outcomes—both the 1999 law and the 2003 law that largely built upon it—are unintelligible without attention to the domestic networks of the international movement against the sexual exploitation of children. Even the more punitive 2003 law has seemed to be symbolic rather than substantive, at least with regard to its placement of moral blame for child prostitution on the teens themselves. But then, the whole national debate about child prostitution has largely been about symbols: about teens, particularly girls, running wild and violating the social values that ostensibly bind Japanese together. Japan is changing, and more than a few analysts believe that women and girls are at the epicenter of these seismic cultural shifts. The fights surrounding the 1999 and 2003 laws can no more easily be separated from national debates about the culpability of schoolgirls than they can from the international norms themselves. The anger and anxiety that the kogals produced had provided an especially rocky terrain for the landing of a global norm premised on juvenile vulnerability and adult culpability. For the time being we should expect to see Japan's implementation of the norm targeting ostentatiously sexual teens, through amplified "guidance" and arrest, just as it does their potential and actual customers.

But the norm may now be used more emphatically in the continuing debates. On March 18, 2004, officials from the National Police Agency and the Ministry of Foreign Affairs testified in front of the lower house's Foreign Affairs Committee about, among other things, the NPA's release of its report on juvenile delinquency. The New Komeitō Party's Maruya Kaori began the committee session by pointing out that international estimates suggested that the problem of sex tourism involving children was, if anything, becoming worse. Turning to NPA Juvenile Section official Hishikawa Yūji, she asked what steps the NPA had taken. Hishikawa responded that it was "kind of difficult to determine" (*nakanaka chotto haakaku shizurai mono*) the number of child victims of Japanese sexual exploitation overseas. But he confirmed that the NPA had, apparently over the four years since the passage of the 1999 law, proceeded with five cases involving children overseas, producing eleven suspects (eight suspects in two pornography cases, and three in three separate prostitution busts). Maruya then commented sardonically on the government's eagerness to pass punitive legislation related to dating clubs even as it had accomplished so little on the Asian sex tourism front, which had been critical to the signing onto the norm.[69]

Could the arrests cited by Hishikawa serve as serious deterrents and thus play a significant role in reducing sexual exploitation by Japanese of children overseas? Possibly, but the NPA's post-1999 activities, as well as the strong popular support for its dating club regulations, suggest that something besides strict adherence to a child welfare norm is at work. Instead, the government's stance indicates continuing battles over the proper role of the state in policing innocence and moral behavior in Japan. For advocates on both sides, this is about far more than whether children should enjoy a "wholesome" environment or greater autonomy. It is about what kind of country Japan is supposed to be: a Japan in which future mothers and wives are unsullied by the stain of compensated dating, or a Japan free from a paternalistic and even predatory state. The 1999 law hardly ended the debate. It did, however, create an environment in which people like Maruya could raise these questions.

作戦コード

Tokyo

Watch or Die!

見るか。死ぬか。あなたはこのままでは生き残れない！

海外安全対策アニメーションビデオ

製作 財団法人 警察協会

Cover art from the animated video *Sakusen kōdo Tokyo* (Battle Code: Tokyo). The slogan on the right says, "Will you watch it? Or will you die? You can't survive the way you are now!" Used with permission of the Keisatsu Kyōkai and the Council for Public Policy.

CHAPTER FIVE

TRUST IN JAPAN, NOT IN COUNTERTERRORISM

In the satirical animated short *Sakusen kōdo Tokyo* (Battle Code: Tokyo), Japanese businessman Okamura-san wakes up to what seems like just another day in Tokyo before being confronted with a number of perplexing incidents. His wife makes him sushi for breakfast and humbly bows as he leaves the apartment; Mount Fuji appears to be only a mile or so outside the city limits; rickshaws, geisha, and samurai mingle in the streets with Hondas and Toyotas. It turns out, in this "overseas safety film" created in 1996 by the Kōkyō Seisaku Chōsakai (Council for Public Policy, or CPP), that this is a simulacrum of Tokyo, which is run by a foreign government for the purpose of kidnapping Japanese businessmen and making them believe that they are in fact at home in Tokyo. In an expository sequence that seems anachronistic because the film was made at the nadir of Japan's longest postwar recession, the viewers learn that the captors' purpose is to study the businessmen's everyday behavior in order to learn the keys to Japanese economic success. The plan fails—in scenes intended to be both humorous and instructive—because the foreign designers of this virtual Tokyo are unable to grasp one of the central differences between Japan and the rest of the world: Japan is safe, and its people are protected. Without warning signs, safety measures, and a society made up of authentic (and peaceful) Japanese, the Japanese guests keep getting killed.[1] On the video's cover, an English-language slogan—"Watch or Die!"—comically takes a more direct approach than even the most bombastic Hollywood previews would dare for a would-be summer blockbuster.

During a trip in late 1999 to the Ministry of Foreign Affairs Overseas Security Information Center, I saw posters for the CPP's video series on the wall and was informed that one could borrow these videos at neighborhood libraries. I have no sense of how many people watched them, though I suspect the number was probably quite small. But *Battle Code: Tokyo* and other videos sharply display the ways in which Japanese policymakers viewed the seemingly hopeless mission of protecting their citizens overseas. Unlike secure and well-protected Japan, the outside world was dangerous, and the government had virtually no tools—particularly not military tools—to maintain its people's safety. The best bet, in this view, was to make Japanese smarter about risks overseas specifically so that Japanese officials would not need to get involved.

The frustration of counterterrorism policymakers—who are expected to protect the public from shadowy and often unknown threats but who face all manner of political, diplomatic, and constitutional constraints—is now legendary.[2] But the animated video series (there were three more in the following years) was a distinctive kind of stopgap measure, one strongly affected by an especially restrictive legal environment. Just as Japanese police officers felt that they were unduly prevented from taking proper measures against the wayward teenagers described in chapters 3 and 4, so too have other officials felt that they are often placed in an untenable position in protecting Japanese overseas from terrorist or other violence. Several officials told me that somehow they were supposed to rescue Japanese imperiled by terrorism, even as the Japanese political landscape denied them virtually all the instruments necessary for doing so. Additionally, Japan's increasing participation in international agreements on counterterrorism created even greater expectations as to what the government would have to do in terrorist crises, placing further constraints on policy without necessarily guaranteeing any real success.

In chapter 6 I address the effects of post-9/11 maneuvers on Japanese politics, but even before the attacks on Washington and New York, Japan had been enmeshed in an increasingly dense web of global norms relating to counterterrorism. In this chapter, I examine the political environment that made the creation of the security videos a fairly logical decision. The tools the police used to arrest or expel domestic left-wing militants—including relentless if narrowly targeted surveillance—were not particularly useful for dealing with international terrorism, and they were controversial enough to limit the police's acquisition of new powers. Constitutional restrictions virtually ensured that Japan's Self-Defense

Forces could not serve any counterterrorism role either at home or abroad. Additionally, although international counterterrorism agreements largely supported many of the law-enforcement techniques preferred by Japanese policymakers at home, they explicitly rejected the kind of negotiations that Japanese officials had occasionally used to defuse crises overseas. Intense public pressure during terrorist crises in the 1970s and the 1980s, discussed below, had furthermore convinced Japanese policymakers that allowing Japanese to perish in attacks was not an option. And so the three obvious options for dealing with terrorism—using force, negotiating, or simply doing nothing—were especially problematic for Japan. In this context, officials focused instead on imploring Japanese citizens to take good care of themselves overseas, because their government would be nearly helpless to save them.

Japanese Counterterrorism at Home

In his 1996 examination of Japanese security politics, Peter Katzenstein argued that the Japanese police face tough limits on their methods for dealing with internal security, similar to the constitutional and political constraints on the exercise of Japanese military force overseas.[3] These restrictions had long shaped the government's handling of terrorism, which was itself seen as a relatively straightforward matter of left-wing or Communist groups dedicated to overthrowing the regime through the use of violence. As noted in chapter 3, one of the U.S. Occupation's central goals had been demolition of the powerful Japanese Home Ministry (Naimushō), which had included police functions. In the creation of the National Police Agency, SCAP had aimed at limiting power over prefectural police while maintaining a crucial coordinating role for the national agency. But after an initial period of openness, Occupation forces took a hard line against Japanese leftists under the shadow of the looming cold war. And so as the Occupation era ended in 1952, the Japanese government moved to establish laws, some based on prewar methods of control, to police those organizations suspected of disloyalty or subversion. Building on the existing anti-leftist bias of the police, the Diet passed the Antisubversive Activities Law (Hakai Katsudō Bōshihō) in 1952, to be implemented largely by two bodies in the Ministry of Justice: the Public Security Investigation Agency (PSIA), which carries out investigations, and the Public Security Examination Committee, which legally authorizes them. Much of the PSIA's clout has come from its long-term ability to engage in surveillance of Communist and other left-wing organizations, though it has generally steered clear of recommending either restriction of a group's activities or an organization's outright abolition.[4] The simple act of surveillance plays a coercive role that has consequences for groups, even when they are not formally charged or disbanded. Indeed, the Anti-Subversive Activities Law has been formally used only eight times, and always against individuals rather than organizations.[5]

The Public Security Investigation Agency, the National Police Agency, and Tokyo's Metropolitan Police (the most elite of the prefectural police) had their hands full in the late 1960s. As they did in other advanced industrial nations, student protest movements in Japan produced radical splinter groups eager to use violence to achieve their often unclear goals. The Red Army Faction (Sekigunha) emerged as a result of a struggle within the leading leftist student organization in 1969, with hundreds of members breaking away to take part in the Faction's "revolutionary" activities against the government. Consistently harassed by the Japanese police (who surrounded the building where the group held its first meeting), the Red Army Faction quickly splintered into smaller factions that took various approaches to violence over the next two decades.[6]

Two of the groups came to play significant international roles. One, led by Tamiya Takamaro, decided to hijack a Japanese airliner to Cuba; once on board the group realized that the craft could not make it all the way to Havana, so they opted to go to North Korea instead. This was a pivotal choice, for the group remained there for decades, absorbing North Korean ideology and supporting the anti-Japanese activities of the North Korean intelligence agencies. They also participated in at least some of the kidnappings of Japanese citizens to North Korea,[7] a topic to which I will return in chapter 6. Another group, led by Shigenobu Fusako, traveled for revolutionary training to Lebanon, where they created the Japanese Red Army (Nihon Sekigun). They were later responsible for one of the most shocking attacks of the 1970s: the 1972 Lod Airport Massacre in Tel Aviv.[8] The group also hijacked a Japan Airlines flight in the Netherlands and laid siege to the French embassy in the Hague, ultimately securing the release of one of their jailed colleagues.

Those radicals left behind in Japan largely secluded themselves in order to skirt surveillance as well as to straighten out continuing factional disputes. These came to a head in February 1972, during the hostage crisis at the Asama mountain cottage (Asama Sansō) in Nagano Prefecture. Chased by local police, a small group of Red Army members took hostage the wife of the mountain resort's owner, provoking the NPA to send members of the elite anti-riot units of the Metropolitan Police Department to resolve the crisis peacefully but without letting the hostage-takers escape. In his memoir former NPA official Sassa Atsuyuki paints the crisis as one of almost absurd constraints on the police. Sassa and his men were not allowed to use firearms and had strict orders to protect the lives of the Red Army members and their hostage. Intense media coverage— which almost certainly contributed to the NPA determination to prevent bloodshed—and the cold Nagano winter further complicated matters.[9] After the siege, the NPA discovered that the hostage-takers had themselves been the survivors of a violent internecine Red Army struggle that had claimed the lives of twelve members.[10]

Although the foreign branches of the Red Army continued to carry out attacks through the 1970s and even into the 1980s, the Asama Sansō incident essentially ended the group's activities in Japan. The ferocity of the killings inside the organization discredited it with young Japanese leftists, while the hostage situation renewed the vigor with which Japan's security forces harassed organizations that might even consider insurrection. The only other violent leftist threat operating in Japan through the remainder of the 1970s was the Chūkakuha (Middle Core Faction), which aligned itself with Japanese farmers protesting the government seizure of land in Chiba Prefecture to build Narita airport.[11]

And yet even as the Narita problem tapered off and the Red Army was primarily defunct inside Japan, Japan's internal security organizations continued to follow an anachronistic anti-leftist ideology. By the 1970s, the Japanese Communist Party had embraced "democratic revolution" as the only real path for advanced industrial nations, in essence becoming an unusually dedicated and voluble but otherwise normal political party.[12] Even so, the PSIA, even in the late 1980s, continued to film the party's headquarters and keep notes on who came and went.[13]

Long-standing divisions between Right and Left thus defined the nature of Japanese domestic counterterrorism policy. Governments headed by the Liberal Democratic Party suggested that restrictions on the police had permitted almost absurd levels of political violence, and that the only reasonable response was tight and constant monitoring of dangerous organizations to ensure their inability to pose a threat to public order. In this vein, informal intelligence networks centered around *kōban* (police boxes) became critical components of public security, fostering a cooperative public spirit against potential menaces. In the kōban system police officers are assigned to small neighborhood offices (police boxes), where ideally they cultivate ties to residents; this is supposed to create trust as well as link the police to social networks they can mine for information.[14] Those on the Left—radical student groups, labor activists, left-wing journalists, and the like—understood that this system was being used against them. Left-leaning commentators promoted public distrust of the police, claiming that Japan's counterterrorism policies typified a conservative state apparatus deployed specifically against progressive movements and ideas.

The anti-left bias of the police helps to explain the catastrophic intelligence failures that allowed the millenarian cult Aum Shinrikyo to carry out their 1995 attack on the Tokyo subway. The group had been involved in the murder of cult critics, the stockpiling of weapons and even helicopters in Russia, and the development of a biological weapons program larger than those of some "rogue states," and even a similar attack using sarin gas a year earlier in Matsumoto City.[15] As Katzenstein notes, the focus on leftists coupled with reliance on a substantial amount of Japanese "self-policing" (particularly by the yakuza) had left Japan's police and security forces unprepared to deal with organizations outside of those already on their agendas. By concentrating intelligence resources on known leftist networks, the police had not cultivated sources among other communities in Japan, making it extremely difficult to gather information about potential threats and challenges emanating from other groups.[16] And so on March 20, 1995, when Aum members released sarin gas on commuter trains converging on Tokyo's Kasumigaseki Station, they not only killed twelve people and injured over five thousand (some permanently) but also punctured the myth of Japanese security and the fundamental logic of Japanese counterterrorism policy.[17] Had the attackers been more competent in making the chemical compound, the incident could easily have claimed thousands of lives.

The subsequent legislative and investigative countermeasures of the government reflect the weird plasticity of terrorist attacks, which play on culturally inscribed fears and produce institutionally delimited responses. To give a comparative example, in the United States the Aum incident provoked intense policy concentration on the possibility of chemical and other "unconventional" terrorist methods.[18] U.S. counterterrorism experts had long considered the possibility of unconventional terrorist attacks—such as those with nuclear weapons—though most considered it unlikely because of terrorists' need for support communities, and because their goal was usually presumed to be achieving concessions of one sort or another. In the oft-quoted (1985) view of RAND

Corporation terrorism expert Brian Jenkins, "Terrorists want a lot of people watching, not a lot of people dead."[19] But the Aum affair was a crossing of the Rubicon, indicating that religious cults or movements were willing to pursue cataclysmic violence to achieve social transformation or political retaliation. In a 2000 report to Congress from the National Commission on Terrorism, former director of the Central Intelligence Agency R. James Woolsey was quoted, somewhat hyperbolically, as saying, "Terrorists don't want a seat at the table; they want to destroy the table and everyone at it."[20]

After the Aum attack, U.S. counterterrorism circles focused on risks of WMD or CBRN (Chemical, Biological, Radiological, Nuclear) terrorism so extensively that the government even held a "top officials" (TOPOFF) exercise simulating a biological attack. The wave of books by top U.S, terrorism specialists in the late 1990s focused almost exclusively on the idea of a "new terrorism," largely based on the Aum case, though with heavy references to Islamist networks that were posing a special threat to U.S. interests.[21]

In Japan, the Aum attack had a profoundly different effect. Coming, as it did, in the midst of extraordinary policy failures in the financial sector, and right on the heels of the government's distressingly ineffective response to the Kobe earthquake, the subway attack signaled the basic ineffectiveness of the government in dealing with crises and, more specifically, the social menace of cults preying on Japan's young people. The resulting response, therefore, aimed at centralizing government authority over decision making and curtailing Japan's new religious movements. Crucially, none of the initiatives undertaken was described at the time as a "counterterrorism" measure. They were instead "crisis management" rules meant to streamline government aid efforts in the event of trouble, or they were narrowly crafted responses to an ostensibly unique religious cult, geared to avoiding political opposition from other groups concerned about the government's casting too wide a net.

Until the September 11 attacks, the vast majority of Japanese counterterrorism work dealt with crisis management, a topic largely associated with Sassa Atsuyuki, the NPA's hero from the Asama Sansō crisis. In his 1997 book *Kiki Kanri* (Crisis Management), Sassa emphasized that in crises, Japanese leaders need to take definitive and decisive action. Hampered by fears of accountability (he argues that for Japanese, taking responsibility for failure still psychologically means seppuku, or ritual suicide), Japanese leaders design decision-making systems specifically to avoid individual responsibility. This brings crisis decision making to a halt; Sassa's implication is that Japanese leaders, by dint of their psychological makeup, are ill-suited to handle terrorist crises.[22] In a suggestive chronology of crises, Sassa includes hijackings and sarin attacks alongside the Bay of Pigs debacle and the Kobe earthquake disaster as emblematic challenges facing decision makers.[23] In his analysis, terrorism appears to be one more type of exogenously produced crisis, an act of God that is especially troublesome in Japan due to a culture of caution.

Along these lines, the first response of the government after the Aum attack was to centralize crisis-response measures under the prime minister and the cabinet. By most accounts, the government's response to the attacks was disjointed, reflecting poor coordination between security, transportation, medical, and other units. In 1998, Japan established the new Cabinet Office for National Security and Crisis Management, which provides support to a deputy chief cabinet secretary responsible for handling national emergencies.[24] The office has no regular employees and acts only on an ad hoc basis.[25]

The second response reflected a distinctive take on the nature of the threat. In the years following the Aum attacks, LDP-led coalitions passed two bills authorizing increased surveillance of religious movements. One, a revision of the Religious Corporations Law, requires religious organizations to provide the government with information about finances and other organizational matters; it also provides the state with the still-unused authority to track and restrict religious groups suspected of crimes. The LDP's ulterior motive in this law had been to discredit a major opposition party, New Komeitō (Clean Government Party), which is closely tied to the Sōka Gakkai lay Buddhist sect that many Japanese consider to be a cult.[26] The second bill, produced in 1999 after the New Komeitō had joined an LDP-led coalition, is the Law to Control Organizations that Have Committed Acts of Indiscriminate Mass Murder. Although the law provides the government the technical ability to restrict "all" such organizations, it targets only Aum.[27] Crucially, this law gives the badly embarrassed PSIA the ability to investigate Aum, an authority it used to enter Aum premises over thirty times in the first year of the law's existence.[28]

The Development of International Norms on Terrorism

In its focus on police tools, the Japanese government appears to adhere to international norms of counterterrorism, though this has evolved primarily out of the local political decisions detailed above rather than from conscious adoption of global standards. Indeed, international agreements on terrorism have increasingly encoded certain law enforcement tools as the proper responses to terrorism, usually with reference to their supposed effectiveness. Analysts, however, have paid little attention paid to the construction of global counterterrorism rules and methods, in spite of their remarkable diffusion and their social scientific indefensibility. I do not mean to imply that counterterrorism policies do not work, but rather that methods for testing their effectiveness are deeply flawed. What countries' policies should be considered "successful" against terrorism? On September 10, 2001, U.S. counterterrorism policy seemed so effective that the Justice Department planned to reduce counterterrorism outlays to the FBI and to shift to other crime-fighting priorities.[29] As I admitted in chapter 1, I had made an essentially similar claim, suggesting that terrorism was not a serious enough threat to the United States to justify crackdowns on civil liberties or alliances with human rights abusers. I still believe that the threat of terrorism does not justify these reactions, but I am glad—particularly after September 11—that I had not dismissed the threat of terrorism in public.

There are few explanatory accounts of counterterrorism policy. Much of the literature on counterterrorism has been prescriptive, aimed at policy audiences.[30] One exception has been former deputy homeland security adviser to President Bush Richard Falkenrath, who has written persuasively on how U.S. counterterrorist capabilities have been responses to the immediate concerns of U.S. policymakers, ultimately yielding a patchwork of inconsistent powers and tactics. For example, President Nixon's foray into the establishment of dedicated counterterrorist units followed the attack by Black September, a radical Palestinian group, at the 1972 Munich Olympics act of terrorism, when they took hostage nine members of the Israeli Olympic team, killing two others in the abduction; it was followed by a botched siege resulting in the deaths of all the athletes and most of their captors. Although Falkenrath does not use the term, he shows the "historical institutional" logic underscoring the evolution of U.S. counterterrorist capabilities, as these units grew, shifted, and expanded in the face of new concerns.[31]

Peter Katzenstein and Yutaka Tsujinaka have examined the domestic normative environment of Japanese counterterrorism,[32] but the international normative background has been largely unexplored. Indeed, most of the transnational action on terrorism occurs at the level of law enforcement, because it adheres to prevailing norms of sovereignty and state monopolization of the use of force. One might categorize two other broad approaches to handling terrorism—military engagement and political negotiation—that have both been frozen out of most international agreements because of the ways in which they violate industrialized states' interests in limiting conflict and criminalizing transgressions. European governments, building on various European Union institutions of police cooperation, have tended to fold terrorism into larger issues of regional law enforcement, sometimes angering the United States by refusing to elevate it to a realm that could lead to military intervention.[33] Sovereignty concerns have also shaped related EU legal agreements (for example, on immigration),[34] further suggesting that cross-border military engagements to deal with terrorism were nearly unthinkable[35] before the 9/11 attacks.

The focus on law enforcement likely owes something to the interests of the democracies of the advanced industrial West in creating constitutionally valid tools for handling terrorism, while robbing it of any political legitimacy. This effort to depoliticize terrorism, rendering it a criminal rather than political matter, lay at the heart, for example, of the British response to the famous prison hunger strike by Irish Republican Army member Bobby Sands and nine of his colleagues. The British government had imprisoned them as ordinary criminals, not as political prisoners; Sands and his colleagues aimed, in vain, for the British government to recognize them formally as political actors.[36] In considering the evolution of counterterrorism norms, we need to consider not only the counterterrorism tools that leaders consider to be effective but also the ways in which the international agreements dictate who can use violence and what kind of violence is permitted.

From Prevention to Policing

The international legal regime on terrorism began primarily as a preventionist one, targeting certain acts of violence for elimination. During the cold war, the United Nations created a number of international conventions, usually negotiated first at the level of the G5 or G7 or in consultation with the Soviet Union, and these emphasized specific activities to be banned. For example, the major powers could agree for the most part on the need to forbid airliner hijackings (1970), the murder of diplomatic agents (1973), and the taking of hostages (1979), and these became the core of various cold war–era counterterrorism conventions.[37] In spite of their signatures on the documents, both the United

States and the Soviet Union turned a blind eye to violations of these rules by their allies in various proxy conflicts in Latin American, Africa, and Asia.[38] Even so, the two superpower adversaries agreed, at least nominally, on the need to limit "asymmetric"[39] tactics that would benefit primarily nonstate actors and others too weak to challenge either of them directly.

That there is a norm against state support for terrorism, even if it has been violated frequently, seems indisputable. Few will admit to believing that terrorism can be legitimate. Although Russian revolutionaries in the late nineteenth century proudly described themselves as terrorists, as had some of their French predecessors,[40] the term has, in the latter half of the twentieth century, been thoroughly delegitimated. Aside from straightforward problems of defining what terrorism is, states and organizations will vehemently argue that their own tactics are nonterroristic. The bromide that "one man's terrorist is another man's freedom fighter" is less profound than those uttering it would like, but it neatly captures the extent to which groups will deny outright that they have committed acts of terror. At one level, broad condemnation of terrorism seems thoroughly obvious. After all, states may agree on few things, but one of them would likely be the belief that states should have a monopoly on the use of violence. To be sure, states have often violated strict rules on support for terrorist groups. But when states have supported terrorist groups, they have generally had to deny doing so and have also argued secondarily that the group's tactics cannot be defined as terroristic. And even when some states have been reluctant to sign and ratify specific counterterrorism conventions—as has been the case with some Arab states, particularly Syria—they have been willing to sign onto broad condemnations of terrorism designed to leave some latitude for the continuation of key policy priorities.[41]

The legal and political content of counterterrorism norms has increasingly emphasized depoliticization, criminalization, and non-negotiation with terrorists,[42] and this orientation is perpetuated both by international law and through specialized training programs focused on law enforcement. International law has played a role in defining state responsibilities and proscribed activities alike. There are twelve UN conventions that deal in some form with terrorism, most of them enjoying wide support from governments. The post–cold war agreements—for example, the Convention on the Marking of Plastic Explosives for the Purpose of Detection (1991), the International Convention for the Suppression of Terrorist Bombings (1998), and the International Convention for the Suppression of Terrorist Financing (1999)—display an interest not just in prohibiting certain tactics but in providing greater investigative tools to law enforcement authorities. In these conventions, terrorists are clandestine actors whose acts require more than formal prohibition; they mandate extensive state tools for surveillance and interdiction.[43]

The most recent counterterrorism convention is instructive. Even before the September 11 attacks, the French government had, in consultation with its European neighbors, proposed international rules designed to increase financial transparency to more easily track the spread of funds among terrorist movements. First at the G8 level, and then at the United Nations, France, the United States, and other governments pushed for universal accession to the International Convention for the Suppression of the Financing of Terrorism. The convention's primary concrete goal is the standardization of financial reporting rules and government monitoring techniques in order to allow easier surveillance of the flow of resources to terrorist organizations.[44] For a number of terrorism specialists, this convention has been considered indispensable for constraining terrorism. Much of the blame has been placed on *hawalas*, the Islamic remittance systems that have, for many Muslims, replaced banks because of strict Koranic edicts prohibiting interest and usury.[45] The clear U.S. and European hope is that adherence to the convention will disrupt murky *hawala* funding. By standardizing rules and techniques for surveillance, authorities should be able to challenge the support infrastructure of terrorist groups. The assumption behind the convention is that if states cooperate to police these potential spots of financial disorder more effectively there will be less terrorism. It is a logical assumption, provided that one believes that levels of political violence are tied primarily to the existence of specific terrorist groups that can be policed and eliminated. But the tightening web of financial monitoring—which might yet turn out to be crucial in limiting terrorism—has not yet resulted in the reduction either in the number or severity of attacks.

Besides diplomatic pressure for uniform international legal standards, the best institutionalized efforts to spread counterterrorism practices lie in the field of development assistance and training. Since the mid-1980s, the U.S. State Department's Bureau of Diplomatic Security (formerly Diplomatic Security Service) has operated the Antiterrorism Assistance (ATA) program, training hundreds of counterterrorism personnel from other nations each year, primarily in law enforcement tech-

niques.[46] The FBI has also developed several counterterrorism courses
as part of its overall international police assistance efforts.[47] And after
the 2001 attacks, federal support for ATA courses jumped dramatically,
with the number of trainees rising from nearly one thousand per year in
the late 1990s to nearly five thousand in 2002.[48] These programs—as do
a limited number sponsored by other governments, including Israel,[49]
the United Kingdom,[50] and Japan[51]—aim at spreading a shared reper-
toire of tools designed to enhance law enforcement capabilities and, in
theory, to limit the ability of terrorist groups to act. Among the U.S.
courses are those that focus on the detection of explosives, protection of
VIPs, tactics in hostage situations, and investigative techniques.[52]

Remarkably, counterterrorism norms do not include the military and
political tools that governments actually have used, sometimes successfully, against terrorism. As I discuss in chapter 6, the United States has
increasingly emphasized military force, but it has not aimed yet at insti-
tutionalizing global military responses to terrorism, reserving these tools
for extraordinary circumstances, carried out entirely under U.S. leadership. More conventionally, political and diplomatic negotiations have
been crucial in draining support from terrorist movements and have
been prominent in reducing terrorist violence in a number of disparate
cases, from the negotiations to end the Tamil campaign in Sri Lanka to
the Good Friday accords in Northern Ireland. One might credibly categorize the withdrawal of most U.S. troops from Saudi Arabia after the
9/11 attacks as a concession to Islamist militants. But when such matters
are discussed as policy, they are part of "strategic shifts" or "peace agreements," not negotiations with terrorists.

Moreover, the "no concessions to terrorists" pledge now represents
such an important part of the counterterrorism canon that advanced industrial states claim to adhere to it even when their actual behavior is suspect. The rescue of over a dozen Europeans taken hostage by the Abu
Sayyaf group of the Philippines in 2000 occurred because of a ransom
payment by the government of Libya, reportedly originating from European governments but laundered in Tripoli.[53] These European governments, of course, condemn negotiations with terrorists in general, but
have kept mum as to what resolved this specific crisis. States will, on oc-
casion, negotiate with terrorists to save lives or end campaigns but they
are above all concerned with avoiding the legitimization of terrorist
groups as political actors. And these negotiations never become part of
the codified standards of responding to terrorism.

Resistance to using military force or political negotiation characterizes this view of dealing with terrorism. Terrorism, from this perspective, is not a series of basically dissimilar attacks or an indicator of social unrest. It is not the predictable result of the dispersion of weaponry around the globe, nor is it the consequence of a nearly understandable desire to be noticed, to make a point in a mass media–saturated world.[54] It is instead the work of roughly similar quasi-criminal organizations that can best be handled through surveillance, investigation, extradition, and punishment. The solution to terrorism therefore becomes the arrest and imprisonment of identifiable terrorists. It is not the use of military force to crush entire communities—whether national minorities or governments that support terrorist tactics—and not political negotiations that might reduce support or lessen the "need" for violence. Counterterrorism norms exist, but they exclude some of the tools that might, in a different world, be understood as crucial to ending terrorist campaigns, because endorsement of these very tools might legitimize the use of terrorism as a tactic. Military or negotiation interventions remain ad hoc, controversial, and unelaborated in ways that law enforcement tools presumably cannot be.

Rationalizing Counterterrorism

Counterterrorism norms based on law enforcement have, largely unconsciously and ex post facto, been rationalized as the most effective manner of handling terrorism. Since the 1970s, a number of terrorism specialists—most notably Paul Wilkinson—have turned their gaze toward the establishment of counterterrorism policies that are consistent with democratic political institutions and civil liberties.[55] For the most part, these scholars have emphasized the importance of treating terrorism as a crime, though one that takes a particularly political form. In this view, the erosion of democratic liberties in the effort to eradicate terrorist movements could increase popular support for these groups. Moreover, on a strictly ideological level, destroying the democracy in order to save it has been unacceptable to most liberal analysts. These studies have proved to be a durable cornerstone for generations of research and conventional wisdom on terrorism.

By the 1990s, a small set of researchers began to question the efficacy of antiterrorism techniques in general. One study used statistical analyses to demonstrate that many measures simply convinced terrorists to change tactics,[56] and another employed rational choice methods to argue that terrorists could factor expected retaliation into their plans, thus undermining the utility of state responses.[57] These approaches, however, have been outliers; the most common approach in research on counterterrorism has been the controlled comparison of a few cases to determine what policies are effective. In the foreword to one such study, former CIA director Woolsey provides his view of the purposes of cross-national comparisons:

> [The authors] have assembled an extremely useful collection of do's and don'ts of fighting terrorism. There is no better way to tell if a perception about terrorism is sound or if a counterterrorist strategy or tactic is likely to be successful than to examine with care the various responses that have been made by serious people. All the rest is hunches and arm-waving.[58]

These studies of the "do's and don'ts" of counterterrorism have stressed that the law enforcement experiences of one state can be translated across borders and contexts, and that they will work effectively against "terrorism" elsewhere. In so doing, these studies have defined terrorism as a discrete phenomenon, one that can be evaluated and understood in universal and theoretical terms, divorced from the precise political contexts in which terrorist attacks take place.[59]

The problem, however, is that we simply do not know what works against terrorism. If there is a terrorist attack, does this mean that counterterrorism policy is ineffective, or rather that this was the one strike that got through in spite of many others that failed? And does the absence of attack mean that policies are succeeding, as U.S. Attorney General John Ashcroft apparently believed on September 10, 2001? This is not a new problem in evaluating security policy; it underlay some of the cold war debates on deterrence policy. After all, under what conditions does the absence of war suggest that a policy of deterrence—as opposed to other potential causes—itself is "working"?[60] International terrorism poses an even more daunting challenge because terrorist groups are, by nature, clandestine. In order to survive over the medium to long term, terrorist organizations must be able to gather resources, recruit members, plan attacks, and maintain control over financial flows, all in secret. Some of the U.S. efforts in late 2001 and early 2002—such as its strong push for a United Nations convention on the financing of terrorism—reflect the perception that the fight against terrorism is a "smart war," based primarily on knowledge and on the ability to take on what is hidden, secretive, and quiet. One concern here is obvious: it may be difficult even for intelligence analysts to assess in rigorous terms whether a given policy is having its desired effect on any terrorist organization, let alone terrorism in general, especially in such clandestine matters as recruiting and financing.[61]

Even so, UN and other international efforts at more effective counterterrorism have centered around enhanced law enforcement and investigative abilities, reflecting institutionalized beliefs about what works and what does not against terrorism. Like religious faith, beliefs about counterterrorism often display hope and desire rather than empirically grounded observation. For example, most believers in the "no concessions" pledge will refer to the logically sound assumption that if one makes concessions (e.g., paying ransoms for hostages) to terrorists, one will encourage more terrorism. But the evidence on this is cloudy at best, and the judgment relies in part on shaky reasoning regarding the lessons that terrorist organizations draw from their own and one another's campaigns.[62] The frequent calls for adherence to international agreements on terrorism, however, rest not on the argument that this is all that states can do, or that these provisions are the only legitimate tools available, but rather that by cooperating in these key areas, states can and will stop or reduce terrorism, by tracking the terrorists more carefully in a unified, consistent manner.

This emphasis in essence depoliticizes terrorism. Even as all observers generally regard terrorist organizations as having political goals, the focus on law enforcement treats the problem as breaches of law and order, not as one involving conflicts over governance and power. Terrorism thus appears to be symptomatic not of political conflict but rather of disorder.[63] When counterterrorism specialists and writers discuss "politics," they frequently use the term to explain the limits on state capacity, where competing groups seek to expand or constrain the right of the state to investigate, prosecute, and punish. Different states' handling of terrorism thus reflects the balance of forces regarding the proper behavior of the government, and the prescription is always the same: more police and intelligence authority, though within the framework of democratic liberties. Through law enforcement cooperation, states can overcome disorder, or so one might conclude by listening to the requests for accession to UN conventions on terrorism. And because of terrorist organizations' secrecy, it is a difficult claim to disprove.

The existence of these norms should not imply that counterterrorism policies are identical. Even before the September 11 attacks, the United States was known as the "hardliner" among the G7 nations, at least until

Russia joined the G8. Ideally resting on extraordinary levels of inter-agency cooperation as well as the national designation of "foreign ter-rorist organizations" to be pursued and constrained, U.S. policy has been extraordinarily aggressive. Some hawks had viewed European nations as insufficiently tough on militant groups, especially those connected to Iran.[64] Between European efforts to unify legal standards, U.S. pressure for more proactive global policing, and Russian efforts to justify tough treatment of Chechens as counterterrorism, there has been some flexi-bility for interpreting the demands of handling terrorism as a criminal threat. But the efforts to align practices have invariably focused on this construction of terrorism as crime.

Even among these different approaches, however, Japan was some-thing of an outlier, as it viewed international terrorism as a minor diplo-matic issue. Concerned, for example, that it might endanger Japan's relations with oil-producing Arab states, the Nakasone cabinet only re-luctantly agreed with the other G7 nations to condemn Libya in 1986 for its presumed role in terrorist attacks, including the bombing of a dis-cotheque in Berlin.[65] Although Japan's handling of domestic terrorism as a criminal justice matter was a central issue for the government's in-ternal security system, officials treated international terrorism as of little national urgency. While expressing support for international norms against terrorism, they adopted a position meant to minimize govern-ment risk while maximizing flexibility in given hostage crises.

Constraints on Japanese Policy against International Terrorism

Maintaining flexibility in international crises has been critically important to Japanese counterterrorism policymakers because of strict constraints on government action. Japan's constitutional limits on the Self-Defense Forces generally have not allowed for the extensive use of special forces (such as the United States and Britain have) for counterterrorism mis-sions overseas. Force has largely been "off the table" as a policy option. Additionally, international agreements against concessions to terrorists have raised the cost of (though probably not entirely prohibited) nego-tiation and compromise to end terrorist crises. At the same time Japan's policymakers believe that principled inaction—refusing either to fight against or to negotiate with terrorists on the grounds that it is better to sacrifice a few lives in one incident than to alter other policy priorities—is politically unacceptable. Japan's policies against international terrorist threats have therefore been less consistent and more fractious than its relatively steady approach toward homegrown leftist militants.

Before the codification of international norms against negotiating with terrorist groups, Japan had earned a reputation as a "bargainer" in international terrorist crises because of deals with the Red Army in the mid-1970s. In 1974, it released five Red Army prisoners to end a hostage situation at the Japanese embassy in Kuala Lumpur. Three years later, Red Army members hijacked a Japan Air Lines flight from Paris to Tokyo via Bombay. Forcing it to land in Dhaka, Bangladesh, they demanded that the Japanese government release JRA comrades from prison and pay a ransom. Memorably saying that "a human life is heavier than the earth" (*jinmei wa chikyū yori omoi*) Prime Minister Fukuda Takeo agreed, and the Japanese government paid approximately $6 million for the release of the 151 passengers and crew. When the justice minister, Fukuda Hajime, took responsibility for the crisis and resigned, his successor, Setoyama Mitsuo, said that the government would hold firm in the face of future attacks:

> It is regrettable that our constitutional, law-abiding system, which has been established only with the enormous efforts of the Japanese people, would be destroyed by violent acts of small terrorist groups. We have to show our determination to protect our society at any cost in such cases.[66]

This principled stand, however, was not the popular choice, with most citizens supporting the prime minister's comments about life. A poll carried out by the Prime Minister's Office in the aftermath of the Dhaka crisis found that most respondents believed that concessions were preferable to the death of the hostages. Sixty-two percent of respondents agreed with the statement "the government should make the lives of hostages its priority," and only 24 percent agreed that "the government should take a stern approach to protect law and order, even though lives may be lost."[67]

The growing web of international norms began to ensnare the Japanese government, forcing a politically unpopular and theoretically inflexible stand on terrorist crises. Under pressure from its advanced industrial allies, the government signed a crucial G7 agreement at the Venice summit in 1987, stipulating that governments must not negotiate with terrorist groups. Even in the mid-1990s, however, the description of the policy by the Ministry of Foreign Affairs (MOFA) reflected the striking ambivalence at the heart of the government's stance. The 1996 edition of the *Gaikō seisho* (Diplomatic Bluebook) includes a special section called "Terrorism and Japan's Standpoint." Its central passage reads:

> In the event that Japanese are taken hostage overseas and that illegal demands are placed on the Japanese government, the government will work with the government of the foreign country in its unambiguous responsibility to resolve the situation. It is naturally our highest priority to ensure the safe return of the hostages, but this must be done in a manner consistent with the international legal order. In order to prevent the same kind of crisis from occurring again, successive summits have confirmed that we must stand on the principle that we will not compromise with terrorists. It is crucial that we resolutely maintain this stance.[68]

The element of international responsibility—codified through G5, G7, G8, and UN agreements—therefore weighs heavily on the Japanese government's understanding and presentation of its stance toward terrorism. Unlike the U.S. State Department's *Patterns of Global Terrorism*—in which the "make no concessions to terrorists and strike no deals" policy is simply stated as a principle, without any justification supplied[69]—MOFA's public document explains that it has been decided (elsewhere, outside of Japan) that deals are unacceptable. Therefore, keeping this premise in mind, the Japanese government ostensibly will work to bring Japanese home safely, but not by making concessions. But norms regarding Japan's responsibility in the realm of international security clashed with prevailing local norms regarding the state's responsibility to its own citizens: How could the state eschew all negotiations if they might save lives?

Nothing displayed the disagreements within pre-9/11 Japan about counterterrorism policy better than the response to the 1996–1997 siege of the Japanese ambassador's residence in Lima, Peru. On December 17, 1996, Tupac Amaru Revolutionary Movement (MRTA) rebels attacked the Japanese ambassador's residence in Lima during a party to celebrate the Emperor's birthday. After the 1990 election of President Alberto Fujimori, a Peruvian of Japanese descent, Japan's ties to Peru had grown substantially closer, and the party was attended by a large number of high-ranking Peruvian officials. All evidence suggests that the residence was chosen because it was relatively unprotected and offered a target-rich environment for any group seeking hostages, as the MRTA did, in order to bargain for the release of MRTA members held in Peruvian prisons. After a 127-day standoff, during which most non-Japanese, non-Peruvian hostages were released (often followed by rumors of ransom deals), a Peruvian military raid led to the rescue of the hostages and the deaths (execution-style, according to many accounts) of all of the MRTA rebels.[70]

The crisis and its sudden resolution gripped Japan. Immediately after the siege, Japanese newspapers and articles focused on two of the more "scandalous" features of the crisis: the odd composure of the Japanese ambassador in his statements after the rescue, and Prime Minister Hashimoto Ryūtarō's anger that Fujimori had not warned him in advance of the takedown.[71] But among policymakers and Japanese terrorism specialists, the focus was on the orientation of the government toward security, crises, and future protection from terrorism. In June 1996, a committee in the Ministry of Foreign Affairs produced a confidential report on the crisis that identified physical security problems in Peru and at other MOFA installations. As a policy issue, however, the MOFA report primarily argued that its options were limited by the nature of the demands (on the Peruvian rather than Japanese government); that MOFA would need to work more effectively with the media, the Red Cross, and hostages' families in the future; and that cooperation with the host government would be essential for the safe return of the hostages in the event of future crises.[72] It concluded with an almost wistful statement about the possibility of having Japanese armed guards at embassies and foreign residences—the equivalent of U.S. Marines—while tactfully avoiding any specific discussion beyond a general claim that "there are many points to investigate in connection with our country's legal framework."[73]

Other Japanese organizations working on counterterrorism and overseas security took divergent positions on what Japan should do to ensure the safety of Japanese abroad. The CPP, the quasi-public think tank that produced the animated video mentioned at this chapter's beginning, emphasized a hard-line approach for Japanese security. Quoting virtually all of the UN and G8 statements in recent years on international terrorism, the CPP's report on the crisis reminded the Japanese government of its international responsibilities, especially its promise not to make concessions to terrorists. It also included as an appendix the text of a 1996 CPP report on a Japanese businessman held hostage in Mexico, who was released only when his firm paid a heavy ransom:

Because paying ransoms puts financial resources into the hands of criminals, and therefore enables their subsequent crimes, firms bear a heavy responsibility. Consequently, to ensure that this kind of event does not happen again, we hope that firms will take the responsibility for taking actions to ensure that these kinds of events do not happen in the future.[74]

In contrast, the organization representing many such firms—the Japan Overseas Enterprises Association—released a longer report that suggested better information and intelligence sharing between MOFA and Japanese firms overseas, establishment of private risk-management offices within firms, and more effective counseling for families and hostages after their release. Notably, it avoided any mention of concessions.[75]

Both the Peru case—in which there were rumors that the government encouraged Japanese firms to pay ransom to have the MRTA release their employees from the ambassador's compound—and a subsequent case in Kyrgyzstan tested the government's stance on concessions. In 1999, four Japanese geologists working for the Japan International Cooperation Agency were taken hostage by the Islamic Movement of Uzbekistan (IMU) in Kyrgyzstan. When they were released after two months, rumors of a ransom deal ran rampant through Japanese newspapers. With ransom payment estimates of ranging from $2 million[76] to $5 million,[77] Japanese journalists hinted that the negotiations were over the size of the payoff and how it would be made. When the hostages were released, one Japanese government spokesperson adamantly denied that any ransom had been paid, saying only that the release was a "delicate" matter and that he could not reveal any of the conditions involved.[78] Some Japanese observers have speculated that the government paid ransom through Tajikistani government intermediaries,[79] which seems plausible, given the complex web of religious factions across Central Asia's notoriously porous national boundaries. The *Yomiuri Shimbun*, the newspaper with the largest daily circulation in Japan, pointed out that the November 1999 MOFA report on the crisis avoided the ransom question entirely.[80] While not disclosing any elements of the negotiations, one Japanese official told me that "this wasn't about Japan; the terrorists wanted things from the Kyrgyz, not us."[81] I find the comment unpersuasive; the IMU members taking the hostages were no doubt aware that the Japanese government has deeper pockets than the Kyrgyzstani, and, in the absence of compelling evidence to the contrary, it seems unlikely that the late Juma

Namangani and other IMU warlords would have released the hostages
without some kind of compensation.

Whether or not the Japanese government paid a ransom, two relevant
points stand out. First, the Japanese government could not *publicly* make
concessions, a stand that certainly complicated negotiations, if any, that
Japanese representatives had with the IMU. Second, virtually all Japanese
observers believe that a ransom was paid. Although journalists have failed
to obtain proof, there has been little doubt about the possibility of such
a deal. Equally important, virtually no one criticized the government for
having possibly paid off of the kidnappers. After all, the four geologists
all returned uninjured to Japan, and the clandestine nature of the deal—
if there indeed was one—shielded Japan from international condemnation. Even if the Japanese government did pay, the international norm
against concessions to terrorists placed an important constraint on the
maneuver, making the negotiations more time-consuming, complicated,
and furtive. It also made it difficult for the Japanese government to make
any claims of success in bringing the unlucky scientists home.

Officials admitted that with the virtual impossibility of using military force, the "no concessions" pledge, and the expectation that the
government would protect the lives of Japanese overseas, they had to
approach terrorism entirely on a "case-by-case" basis.[82] From this perspective, the trouble with international norms on terrorism was not that
they were wrong; virtually all of my colleagues in Japan's counterterrorism world seemed to believe that the international agreements had the
right idea. Instead, the problem was that they ran against the grain of
domestic demands for saving Japanese lives. Japan's basic law enforcement stance on terrorism had corresponded to prevailing international
standards on the problem, but this had emerged more from Japanese
practices than from a clear goal of adherence to global norms. MOFA's
stance on international terrorism before 2001 was neatly exemplified by
the structure of counterterrorism units. Unlike the United States, where
the Office of the Coordinator for Counterterrorism operates as an independent section within the State Department, the Japanese counterpart
organization was nested in the Consular and Migration Affairs Division—
the division chiefly responsible for the protection of Japanese citizens
overseas. Although known in English as the Anti-Terrorism Office, the
Japanese name—*hōjin tokubetsu taisakushitsu*—is better translated as "Office for Special Measures for Our Citizens Overseas." Its principal goal
was not the eradication of terrorism or terrorist organizations per se but
the protection of Japanese in specific terrorist crises.

After the Aum incident and the Peru crisis, the Japanese government made a small number of tactical adjustments. The NPA's Foreign Affairs Division, for example, established a new counterterrorism office responsible for intelligence,[83] though its capabilities were limited. And the tight controls on the government's international security activities included restrictions on and limitations to the gathering of intelligence. Although the government now has a surveillance satellite that provides optical intelligence on proximate threats such as North Korea, Japan's ability to gather intelligence on foreign military threats is surprisingly shallow. The SDF's intelligence-gathering staff numbered only around one hundred in the late 1990s, and their primary source of information was newspaper clippings.[84]

Fixing the Problem by Fixing the Japanese

I was in Tokyo for the U.S.-Japan Counterterrorism Talks in spring 2000 when news came that the Abu Sayyaf group had taken hostage twenty-one people, including a number of foreign tourists, on the coast of Sipadan in Malaysia. My first question, of course, was whether there were any Americans in the group. Hostage crises are particularly difficult for policymakers.[85] Having spent three months at the State Department's counterterrorism office as the regional affairs officer responsible for Southeast Asia, I had a fairly clear sense of what would happen if there were any captured Americans. I would have been on the job twenty-four hours a day, sifting through daily intelligence updates and news articles for clues and leads regarding the hostages, and dealing with concerned and possibly irate family members (and possibly their congressional representatives). While reassuring their loved ones that we had the hostages' welfare in mind, I would also have been responsible for maintaining policies against negotiations and concessions. As luck had it, an American couple escaped capture in this instance because the husband reported that his wife was unable to swim and that they would not go on the captors' boats. And for reasons that I do not fully understand, the gunmen left them there unharmed, apparently because they were too busy rounding up the other vacationers to have time for an argument.[86] Because of this lucky break, the American couple was spared the five-month-long hostage crisis that ended for some of the European hostages with the payment of a ransom by the Libyan government.[87]

In spite of ample evidence of other countries' extraordinary struggles with hostage crises, my Japanese counterparts evidently believed that they faced special, unusually intense pressure to ensure the safe return of their citizens taken overseas. MOFA officials involved in the handling of recent terrorist events told me that one of the most acute sources of stress in their work was the overbearing pressure from family members of victims of terrorism,[88] who would often be able to work with their representatives in the Diet to publicize the cases dramatically.[89] In explaining the different burden on Japanese decision makers, one Japanese security expert spoke enviously of Britain and the United States. In those countries, human connections are "dry," whereas in Japan, they are "wet"[90] (sticky and dense), a conclusion seconded by many others. Like other claims that Japanese are "collectivistic" while Westerners are "individualistic," or that Japanese adhere to "situational ethics" whereas Europeans and Americans adhere to principled moral reasoning, this generalization obscures more than it clarifies. In this judgment, Japanese are more sentimental about human life, while Americans and Britons can more easily write off even family members as losses in a greater public struggle.

Needless to say, these interpretations overstated the willingness of other governments to take a gamble on their citizens' lives. After all, President Reagan risked impeachment in sanctioning an arms deal with Iran meant to free U.S. hostages. He was forced to apologize for violating the "no deals" policy, but he had clearly done so because of the enormous pressure on the government to bring home U.S. hostages in Lebanon safely. The apparent European payment, via Tripoli, to the Abu Sayyaf Group to release hostages suggests that these pressures are relatively common. These cases are hardly enough to dispel a theory, but the Japanese policymakers' belief that they face special pressure to bring all citizens home safely was based on a combination of anecdote and ideological constructions of the "national character" of the Japanese. As with the effectiveness of the "no concessions" policy, there is simply no way to test easily whether Japanese counterterrorism policymakers are held more responsible than are U.S., British, or others for the lives of their citizens overseas. But this is less important than the fundamental and seemingly unshakable belief in Japanese policy circles that there was as a difference, a belief that had shaped views of appropriate policy options.

That Japanese are especially vulnerable overseas has been taken for granted, institutionalized both in discursive conceptions of Japanese uniqueness and in government approaches to terrorist crises. After the Persian Gulf War (during which two hundred Japanese were used as "human shields" by Saddam Hussein's regime), MOFA established the Overseas Security Information Center, a tiny division with a ground floor office and special entrance in the MOFA building, offering information to Japanese on how to behave more safely overseas. One official there informed me that Japanese are particularly susceptible to all manner of dangers overseas—crime, con artists, swindlers, terrorism, accidents—because unlike Americans and Europeans, they are inexperienced travelers and are not sufficiently suspicious and cautious. The office responds to the problem not only by keeping a record of incidents involving Japanese overseas (categorized by region, rather than country, in order to avoid criticism from countries that they are being unfairly stigmatized as dangerous) and by offering a variety of public relations material designed to teach *jiko sekinin* (self-responsibility).[91] Notably, when I visited in 2000, the office had no evidence that Japanese were in special danger, and the staff there seemed surprised that I would even ask. The office held no comparative statistics and had attempted no cross-national research on the dangers faced by Americans, Europeans, or anyone else. And this guiding sense of Japanese uniqueness, which underscored much of their public relations literature, seemed to be out of step with the "human shields" crisis in the Persian Gulf War; after all, Americans and Europeans were held in large numbers too, and the taking of the Japanese hostages seems to be poorly correlated with their putative lack of self-responsibility.

Yet this fundamental conceit—that the Japanese are especially vulnerable overseas because they do not understand the world outside of the Japanese cocoon—was as broadly and unproblematically accepted in Japanese policy circles as is the "no concessions" philosophy in the United States. It was, after all, a logical corollary of the deeply institutionalized view of the Japanese national character as insular, inept in interacting with outsiders, and indulged both by parents and by a village-style society.[92] In fact, virtually every person I interviewed in Japanese policy, quasi-public, and private circles on the topic argued that Japanese faced special problems when traveling because of their lack of "security consciousness" (*sekyūriti ishiki*). Unlike U.S. citizens, for example, who might be specially targeted for political reasons, Japanese were likely to be victimized by those groups more interested in cash than politics. After all, which active terrorist groups had an anti-Japan grudge? The problem was that terrorists seeking financial gain would be able to take advantage of the Japanese, the traveling moneybags who trusted the rest of the world to treat them as they are in their pampered and secure lives at home. Indeed, the comments from my Japanese informants frequently complained about Japanese not being smarter about their safety abroad, though they sometimes expressed an almost parental concern about the safety of their compatriots overseas. The common thread remained that the Japanese faced distinct peril abroad, and that those in jeopardy would be highly troublesome for policymakers at home.

Hampered by the difficulties inherent in fundamentally shifting Japanese counterterrorism policy toward a more military stance or away from international agreements on concessions, Japanese policymakers and other actors created security initiatives that relied on this belief in the particular defenselessness of the Japanese. The Overseas Security Information Center office, in addition to producing its own literature, videotapes, and statistics, prominently displays posters of the CPP's animated films, such as *Tāgetto: Nihon Kigyō* (discussed below), suggesting that visitors watch them before they go overseas.

The planning for the CPP's video series began in the early 1990s, when CPP staff—who primarily focus on providing superb comparative studies of counterterrorism and police policy—lobbied for financial support from the NPA, which in turn requested financial backing from the Japan Lottery Association (Nihon Takarakuji Kyōkai). Determining that the videos should be more than simple "how-to" videos, which they felt would be boring, the CPP members decided that they could most economically produce creative, entertaining public relations films by turning to animation, which is far more popular as a television and film form in Japan than in it is in the United States. Employing a team of writers and a director, the CPP drew up a schedule for four animated shorts, which were to be distributed to firms, travel companies, and public libraries around Japan. Most important to the CPP planners was that the series be watchable; after all, if they were to be effective, the videos would have to be sufficiently entertaining to entice people to check them out of a library or to view them at a travel office.[93] The writers and the director were thus charged with the task of putting together short cartoons that would be amusing and informative; they would, by design, have to play on prevailing ideas of Japanese overseas that the audience would find recognizable, meaningful, and engaging.

The first video, the 1996 video discussed at the beginning of the chapter, *Battle Code: Tokyo*, follows the misadventures of Mr. Okamura, as he stumbles through the simulacrum of modern Tokyo, built by two shadowy, white foreigners, one of whom speaks (cartoonishly accented) Japanese. Okamura-san is the eighth "experiment," and like the others, he meets his maker because of his inability to take responsibility for his own safety. The earlier deaths remain a mystery, but Okamura-san is killed when he struggles for help after an auto accident, banging on the door of a startled resident in the neighborhood. The resident, a typical American (though clad in a slumber cap), sleepily opens the door, is stunned to see this incoherent, Japanese-spouting man pounding away at the door, and then fires point blank at Okamura-san with a double-barreled shotgun. Most likely, the 1992 killing of a Japanese exchange student, Hattori Yoshi, in Baton Rouge, Louisiana, had inspired this scene. Hattori, having had incorrect directions for a Halloween party, had walked up to the wrong house, apparently frightening the residents, Bonnie and Rodney Wayne Peairs. Perhaps misunderstanding the husband's command—"Freeze!"—Hattori continued to walk toward the house, at which point Mr. Peairs fatally shot him. The narration helpfully points out that the message of the video is that Japanese have to take responsibility for their own safety overseas and cannot rely on warning signs or guides to protect them when abroad. Japan may be safe, but the rest of the world is not, and in the absence of warnings, Japanese must assume the worst rather than the best.

A 1997 sequel of sorts, *Battle Code: Paradise* (*Sakusen kōdo: Paradaisu*), finds the same two white characters in the employment of an island paradise government or perhaps its colonial rulers. Their job is to protect a group of stereotypical Japanese tourists—three young, shopping-oriented "office ladies"; three middle-aged, unattractive, coarse, and stingy women from Osaka; a young honeymooning couple featuring a know-it-all husband; and an elderly couple, in which the husband is a cantankerous veteran of the Imperial Army in World War II—from the many dangers facing them overseas. The Japanese simply have no idea how many hazards face them on this tropical island; they are menaced by thieves, con artists, terrorists, and (in one moment that comes close to the truly unsavory) a would-be rapist. In fact, the only Japanese tourists who get through the event unscathed (at least without the help of a bizarre deus ex machina that saves the others) are the elderly couple, and only because of the husband's cagey and belligerent xenophobia. The tone in this video, as in *Battle Code: Tokyo*, is decidedly ironic, and it plays entirely (and successfully, judging by the reactions of Japanese friends with whom I have watched them) for laughs. The message, however, is both clear and serious: Japanese simply are too trusting and have to be far more careful when they are abroad.

In 1998, the tone of the videos turns somewhat darker, and *Kidnap* traces a hostage crisis involving the head of a Japanese joint venture in Southeast Asia, presumably the Philippines, though this is never stated directly. In this longer (thirty as opposed to twenty minutes) and more complex animated video, the action focuses almost entirely on the second-in-command at the joint venture, who is faced with a tremendous number of difficult decisions. How can he effect the release of his boss? Can he acquire the ransom money himself if the firm's financial rules require that the boss, currently held hostage, has to sign for all large transactions? Should he tell the boss's wife? Two features of the narrative invite particular scrutiny. First, the Japanese firm, often represented both in Japan and abroad as a model of efficiency and cooperation, is presented in the video as nasty, dysfunctional, ineffective, and venal. When the nervous second-in-command reaches Tokyo colleagues by phone, he receives neither sympathy nor help and is told simply to solve the problem and even called stupid for not knowing how to handle this kind of crisis. Second, when he contacts the Japanese embassy for help, the embassy representative puts him in touch with a representative of an international private security firm, presumably similar to Control Risk (a British firm) or Kroll Associates (a U.S. company). The firm representative is white, and he proceeds to tell the hapless second-in-command about what kind of security help he can supply.[94] Finally, he points toward the viewer and says, "I can only provide advice. The decision of how to proceed . . . is yours." The world's top security firms are indeed located in the United States and western Europe. But the white character in *Kidnap* is as striking as the two foreigners are in the earlier comedies, and the message is clear: if Japanese want to be safe overseas, they will have to learn from Westerners. And the white character is hardly an unambiguously heroic one. He is tough-minded and clear on what kind of help he is willing to provide, but his behavior is neither sympathetic nor understanding toward the besieged Japanese employee.

In the fourth animated video, 1999's *Tāgetto: Nihon kigyō* (*Target: Japanese Enterprises*), a Latin American terrorist group plots the kidnapping of the president of the local operation of a Japanese firm. Using, as its central character, a female member of the group, the film shows that although the group probably views "U.S. imperialism" in the region as the real enemy, it has selected a Japanese target because of the deep pockets of the Japanese company and because of the deepening foreign aid ties between Japan and the unnamed country's repressive government. The rest of the film shows the group capitalizing on the many security errors of the Japanese company: using a predictable route home from work, not having a bodyguard for the firm president, and the like. Much more a specific corporate instruction film than its siblings, *Target: Japanese Enterprises* advances the simple message that Japanese firms are being selected for attack overseas and that they must take stricter security measures.

These four films together display a unified vision of the Japanese as having special difficulty in comprehending and handling the dangers posed by life overseas. Because of their trusting nature, and their reliance on a protective relationship with a benevolent state, Japanese abroad simply make more hazardous mistakes than do citizens of other countries. After all, in this view, Americans and Europeans more or less built the world and therefore understand it when they have to travel; citizens of lesser-developed countries live in those lesser-developed countries, meaning that they are either part of the problem or close enough to it to be relatively safe. The Japanese, in contrast to both, lack experience with danger, and trust that no one is out to hurt them. The theme song of the series, "Trust," which plays over the closing credits of all the films (except for *Battle Code: Tokyo*), is an English-language love song that closes with the words "I will never let you down / Trust that I will be around / Believe that I will be your guide / That I always will be by your side."[95]

Public education messages on overseas safety are not unique to Japan, but this message is distinctive. In the United States, for example, public relations efforts by private security firms, as well as the Overseas Security Advisory Council run by the State Department, aim at teaching Americans how to behave overseas. These are, however, at best peripheral efforts that take a decided back seat to the government's comprehensive counterterrorism strategy. Moreover, the U.S. versions are more akin to "how-to" books that assume that the danger to Americans flows from the prominent international role of the United States, rather than from the specifically naive or other behavior of Americans as Americans.[96] In the case of Japan before September 11, overseas safety instruction was among the most consistent and programmatic elements of the government's efforts to deal with the threat of terrorism overseas, because public relations campaigns managed to negotiate the tiny space allowed by tight constraints on other approaches.

Whose Fault?

All of my on- and off-the-record conversations with Japan's policymakers before September 11 have left me with the strong impression that virtually all who talked with me would have preferred the Japanese government to adhere more closely to international norms on counterterrorism. Most argued that Japan's case-by-case approach had been a poor substitute for a forward-looking strategy for the eradication of terrorism, which is what the United States has had (in one form or another) since the 1980s. The problem, in their judgment, was that the Japanese public is not ready to pay the price necessary to become a full member of the international counterterrorism team, to put the principled goal of eradicating terrorism ahead of the need to protect Japanese lives. Lacking the security consciousness of their counterparts in other advanced nations, Japanese presumably got themselves into trouble more frequently than did other people, and were more likely to demand government assistance. The fault was not with the norms, which seemed both commonsensical and practical for "dry" nations like the United States and Great Britain. Instead, the Japanese people had let down the government.

This speaks to the power of the norms, which in many ways have been as convincing to Japan's counterterrorism specialists as they are to the Americans and Europeans who have largely pushed them. Japan's counterterrorism officials have needed to rationalize the government's apparent deviation from global standards, even to themselves. It also reminds us of enduring notions of Japanese uniqueness, which come into play as explanations for Japan's special vulnerability to international terrorism. Most important, however, it reflects the political place of terrorism in the Japanese popular imagination of the late 1990s: as one more type of trouble or crisis that could befall the nation, and for which the government was unprepared. Without significant "antiterror" forces in the bureaucracy or the Diet, many Japanese observers placed the issue in a larger basket of emergencies and threats to public order. In so doing, they aimed at limited responses and tried to avoid danger rather than proactively trying to eradicate terrorist groups in the manner of the United States. Unannounced dangers lurk around every corner in the outside world, so Japanese who trust their society and the state that governs them must accept responsibility for protecting themselves when they venture abroad. Warning signs at home symbolize the presence of a benevolent government that recognizes how much protection the Japanese really need. Overseas, all bets are off.

Visitors gathering to see the *kōsakusen* (operations boat) exhibit at the Japanese Museum of Maritime Science, September 2003.

CHAPTER SIX

THE SELF-FULFILLING AFTERTHOUGHT

Even in Japan's rapidly changing employment scene, eighteen-year-old Imai Noriaki's career choice on graduating from high school in 2004 was an odd one. Rather than entering college, joining an established firm, or taking the *furiitaa* (part-timer) route while planning a career or preparing for college entrance exams, Imai decided to create a picture book. He had been raised in a left-wing household, and having already made a name for himself in Japan's nonprofit organizations as a dedicated critic of the government,[1] Imai chose to write a book about warfare, specifically about the effects of U.S. depleted-uranium rounds on people in war zones. And so Imai traveled to U.S.-occupied Iraq to get first-hand experience.

Within a few days of crossing the border from Jordan into Iraq, Imai—along with his travel companions, NGO worker Takato Nahoko and photojournalist Kōriyama Sōichirō—was taken hostage by a group of militants calling themselves the Saraya al-Mujahideen. Releasing videos of the Japanese hostages with knives at their throats, the previously unknown terrorists called at first for the withdrawal of Japanese troops from Iraq and then, hearing that Prime Minister Koizumi would not comply, demanded U.S. withdrawal from the besieged city of Fallujah. During the odd and deeply dispiriting hostage crisis that followed, Imai was accused at home of cooperating with his abductors, of being stupid, of having strange-looking (*san-paku-gan*) eyes, and of being profoundly irresponsible. On his release, Imai learned that he and the other two were expected to reimburse the government for some of the expenses involved in the government's rescue efforts.

The three hostages were fortunate, certainly more so than Kōda Shōsei, a Japanese tourist who was beheaded by militants in Iraq later in October 2004. In May 2005, Saitō Akihiko, a Japanese employee of a British security firm, also perished while held hostage in Iraq, though evidently from wounds suffered from the firefight that had precipitated his capture. But this earlier case invites special consideration because it focused attention on the political fights between Left and Right over the dispatch of Japanese troops, the responsibility of individual Japanese, and the changing role of the government in international terrorism. Throughout the incident, Koizumi and other government spokesmen, particularly Chief Cabinet Secretary Fukuda Yasuo, stressed the importance of Japan's international commitments and argued that the government could not back down in the face of terrorist threats. On the one hand, this tough-minded response seemed entirely to coincide with the no concessions pledge that has stood at the heart of international norms on terrorism since the 1980s.[2] To be sure, the recriminations against Japan had the government withdrawn from the coalition because of three hostages would have been even more severe than the U.S. invective heaped on the Spanish government for pulling out after the devastating Madrid train bombings of March 2004, which contributed to Prime Minister José Maria Aznar's losing his job in subsequent parliamentary elections. But Japan then experienced wide-ranging criticism for the seemingly vindictive treatment of its three unfortunates. U.S. Secretary of State Colin Powell quickly praised the hostages on Japanese television, saying, "If nobody was willing to take a risk, then we would never move forward. . . . The Japanese people should be very proud that they have citizens like this willing to do that and very proud of the soldiers that you are sending to Iraq that they are willing to take that risk."[3] A front-page story in the *New York Times* chalked up the Japanese handling of the hostages to cultural peculiarities, particularly the nation's putative group orientation, almost entirely neglecting the political context that shaped the debate.[4]

Has Japan become "normal" in its handling of international terrorism? In the previous chapter, I argued that the Japanese stance on terrorism had differed from that of other advanced industrial nations, in spite of the Japanese government's accession to most international conventions on terrorism. Rather than viewing terrorism as the threat of transnational networks of interchangeable militants against whom states could usefully pool law enforcement resources, the Japanese government had long seen it as fundamentally disconnected political battles with little direct relevance to Japan. Where Japanese terrorists have been involved, the primary government interest had been in pushing the militants out of Japan while maintaining steady if very low-level pressure for their arrest or detention overseas. Otherwise, the Japanese government viewed terrorist events outside of the country as crises that, like any other acts of God, would need to be handled with the strict goal of protecting the lives of Japanese abroad. This view, I hasten to add, is no more selfish than are the policies of most other nations, and it is in many ways more intellectually defensible than many of the counterterrorism strategies on the global stage.

Since the September 11 attacks, Japan has moved somewhat closer to global norms on counterterrorism, though more as an afterthought than by initial design. Because the attacks were followed by U.S. demands for Japanese cooperation in U.S.-led actions in Afghanistan and Iraq, they served in Japan primarily as a catalyst for amplified security cooperation with U.S. forces. By moving toward the more assertive military role overseas that many hawks have publicly supported for years, the Japanese government has justified its decision as part of a strategy against global terrorism—though this has been more commonly associated in Japan with North Korea. In effecting this realignment, officials have realized somewhat belatedly that Japanese abroad may now be targets rather than victimized innocent bystanders in future campaigns by transnational terrorist groups, an ironic and unwelcome consequence of Japan's entry into the war on terror.

Japanese conservatives have now connected a broad conception of terrorism to fears that many citizens already had, particularly of North Korea and of foreign criminals. Unsurprisingly, it has been the intention of many of those pushing for "tougher" measures to exploit these fears and to legitimate their proposals by referring to international norms and responsibilities. But, as with the child prostitution and pornography norm discussed in chapters 3 and 4, Japan's adoption of international standards of counterterrorism reflects choices made by key policymakers operating in a tense and uncertain political environment. As noted in chapter 5, Japanese counterterrorism policymakers had for years taken a cautious approach on international norms of counterterrorism, emphasizing law enforcement—as most G8 nations continue to do. The George W. Bush administration's decision to militarize counterterrorism, to treat it as a war, provided an opportunity for Japanese conservative leaders to recalibrate a more expansive role both at home and abroad for the Self-Defense Forces, as a crucial tool against terrorism, whether manifested as al Qaeda's attacks in New York and Washington or, more problematically but more relevantly, North Korea's kidnapping of Japanese citizens. This framing was crucial in justifying Japan's changing security stance.

In making this argument, I have to enter the long-standing debate over Japan's external security policy, though I do so tentatively and from an angle that prevents me from choosing one of the prevailing explanations for Japanese strategy. Because Japan's complex stance on security—including a pacifist clause in its constitution and a sizable and credible fighting force that has faced strict political limits on its deployment and use—seems so unusual, it has provoked a wide variety of causal accounts. In 2004, for example, one realist scholar, Jennifer Lind, argued that Japan's approach to postwar security has amounted to a "buck-passing" strategy that takes advantage of U.S. willingness and ability to provide the lion's share of Japanese security.[5] Others have pointed to Japan's postwar "culture of antimilitarism," or the development of a hard political constraint on remilitarization.[6] Peter Katzenstein argues that domestic decision-making norms mandating respect for strongly held minority views have prevented ruling conservative coalitions from overwhelming JSP opposition to an expanded military role for Japan.[7] My point here is not to choose among these or other approaches but to suggest that the local representation of threat matters, regardless of where we draw the causal arrow connecting something global or something local to Japan's uncommon defense posture.

The U.S. invasion of Iraq in 2003 offers an illustrative example. I do not know precisely why the Bush administration made the decision to go to war; most analysts seem to agree that the interest among those who became administration officials in toppling Saddam Hussein long predated Bush's becoming president in 2001. As a political matter, the explanations have ranged—with predictable divergence among supporters and opponents of the administration—from the intellectual history of the "neoconservatism" associated with Richard Perle and Paul Wolfowitz to the need to secure access to Iraqi oil fields to the desire to reshape the Middle East to the vexed family history of powerful families in the United States, Iraq, and Saudi Arabia. In the long term, scholars of international relations will provide explanations that fit the war into larger theories of national interest, bureaucratic politics, or psychological miscalculation. Virtually all observers agree, however, that the administration's decision was politically sustainable in large part because of the willingness of most Americans to connect Iraq in some meaningful sense to the September 11 attacks, a connection that administration officials drew (often elliptically) in the months leading up to the attack. Without taking a position as to why the U.S. government took its position on Iraq, or even as to whether it was a good or bad decision, I believe it uncontroversial to state that any genuine account of the war is incomplete without attention to the construction of Iraq as a "terrorist" threat, one with political meanings associated with the videotaped images of airplanes crashing into U.S. skyscrapers.

And so my goal in this chapter is to explore how similar processes took place in Japan. I cannot provide a definitive account of the Koizumi cabinet's decision to dispatch troops to Iraq or for the expansion of Japan's regional security role. These outcomes were probably overdetermined by factors as wide-ranging as increased security demands from the United States, the collapse of the Socialist opposition in the Japanese Diet, the rise to power of a prime minister from a historically security-minded faction, and the saber rattling of Kim Jong Il in North Korea. But the construction of North Korean activities as "terrorism" is hardly an obvious choice. After all, terrorism is generally understood to be largely symbolic violence aimed at attracting (and terrorizing) an audience, and North Korea's kidnapping of Japanese citizens—to name the most obvious example—was carried out in secret: nearly the antithesis of terrorism. In this context, the construction made sense in part because of the Koizumi cabinet's use of shifting counterterrorism norms that now stipulated military force to be a crucial component in an overall strategy against terrorism. Crucially, the decision to deploy the term "counterterrorism" as a label for long-desired shifts in Japan's overall security stance provoked the belated recognition that Japanese, as citizens of an increasingly "normal" nation, might themselves start to become more common targets of terrorist attacks, and by groups—like those in Iraq—that had previously ignored them.

The United States Leads, Japan Follows

In one of those small paperbacks (*shinsho*) that can usually be read with one hand while standing aboard a train, one of Japan's top international relations scholars, Fujiwara Kiichi, in 2002 offered a number of critiques of the position of the United States as a virtually unchallenged global leader. Though clearly outraged by U.S. strategic decisions after the September 11 attacks, Fujiwara is anything but a simple America-basher; the book ranges widely from detailed discussions of U.S. colonialist behavior in the Philippines to the orientalism expressed in popular Hollywood films. He is also an uncommonly excellent writer, who weaves different permutations of the phrase "America leads and other countries obey" (*amerika ga shudō shi, kakkoku ga shitagau*) into his preface, each time emphasizing different aspects of American power.[8] From Japan, the U.S. role in shaping global security relations looks especially intense. Wherever one places the causal weight for Japan's changing military policies— the end of the cold war, an altered domestic political environment, the personal predilections of Prime Minister Koizumi—the United States has been a consistent and crucial voice for the expansion of Japanese capabilities. Americans exasperated with Japan's willingness to allow them to shoulder the burden of Japan's defense would likely draw attention to the many Japanese rejections of U.S. demands, and I myself believe that Japanese leaders have made crucial choices that have not always pleased their U.S. counterparts. But U.S. policies have dramatically shaped the context in which those choices have been made.

By stipulating that "the Japanese people forever renounce war as a sovereign right of the nation and the threat or use of force as a mean of settling international disputes," Article IX of the Constitution of Japan puts the nation in the remarkable position of embracing pacifism as a core value. But like America's stand for freedom of expression, the idea has been far more controversial and complex than its enshrined constitutional spot might suggest. Japan has long maintained the SDF, a remarkably capable, substantial, and well-equipped fighting force that would, by most accounts, be capable of defending Japan from most conventional threats, particularly since the collapse of the Soviet Union.

And pacifism has always been part of a political struggle, not a universally accepted orientation. The U.S. officials who pushed for Japan's pacification after World War II soon became among the most vocal cheerleaders of remilitarization. With the outbreak of the Korean War, U.S. officials hoped for a larger Japanese security commitment, potentially involving Japanese troops fighting alongside their new U.S. allies against the Communist menace. Prime Minister Yoshida Shigeru, for reasons having nothing to do with innate pacifism, held off on the U.S. request, believing that Japan's postwar economic recovery would be threatened if the government were forced to pay more for national defense.[9] Struggles between the LDP and the JSP typified the long postwar struggle over Japan's proper role; in 1960, the Socialists even blockaded the Diet in an unsuccessful bid to prevent Prime Minister Kishi Nobusuke from pushing through the extension of the U.S.-Japan Security Treaty. From a personal standpoint, the prime minister's victory was Pyrrhic, provoking the largest protests in Japanese history and costing him his job, but he had sealed the deal. A dozen years later, the announcement of the "Nixon doctrine," demanding that the Asian allies of the United States take greater responsibility for regional security, convinced the LDP to revise its defense plans and prepare for heavier spending. The resulting National Defense Policy Outline, passed in 1976 over the objections of the JSP, extended guarantees regarding Japanese participation in U.S.-led security efforts.[10]

The end of the cold war might have been expected to initiate dramatic shifts in U.S.-Japan security relations, with the disappearance of the United States's most important rival. If anything, however, the pattern of U.S. demands for greater Japanese participation in the alliance—followed by political fights in Japan that ended up limiting the extent of Japanese contributions—became even more pronounced. The twin fears of "abandonment" by Japan's alliance partner and of "entrapment" in U.S. military adventures were most evident during the 1991 Persian Gulf War. Japan's belated decision to send money, not troops, provoked so much hostility from U.S. politicians that Japanese politicians and defense intellectuals began to speak openly of Japan's need to become a "normal nation" (*futsū no kuni*), shedding at least some of the distinctiveness of the country's relatively light hand in matters of global security.[11] In 1994, the Pentagon's "Nye initiative" committed U.S. support for Japanese security over the long term, partly to mitigate concern that trade frictions were eating away at the alliance.[12] In response, the Japanese government, by this time led by an LDP-JSP coalition, revised the National Defense Policy Outline (often called New Taikō, or "new general principles") and developed a new set of defense guidelines, albeit controversial ones.[13]

Of course, "normality" has had consequences beyond commitments to support U.S. activities, as both the 1995 New Taikō and 1997 "new guidelines" suggest. As noted in chapter 2, first the Hanshin earthquake and then the Aum Shinrikyo attack prompted criticism of the government's ability to respond to domestic crises. And so the New Taikō, passed in November 1995, provided for a wider role for the SDF in dealing with domestic crises. The new guidelines also called for the creation of new "emergency laws" that would enable the SDF to operate domestically without first getting authorization from local governments for their actions. The SDF's inability to perform independently had long rankled leaders who dreaded having to check with prefectural and local authorities before moving personnel and matériel along the nation's roads in the event of a military attack. One general had stirred controversy in 1978 by remarking to a press conference that the SDF might be forced to take "extralegal" (*chōhōkiteki*) action in a moment of crisis, a frightening prospect especially to those moderates and leftists already suspicious of the SDF's presumptive inclination to supersede civilian authority.[14]

With the post–cold war rise of new security challenges—symbolized for many Japanese by the 1995–96 Taiwan Strait crisis in which China test-fired missiles near Taiwan and North Korea's August 1998 test firing of a missile over Japan—Japan's political hawks and their allies in the Japan Defense Agency and Self-Defense Forces have made extraordinary gains since the late 1990s. In addition to growing concerns about the rise of China, the 1998 Taepodong missile test reinforced Japanese suspicion of Pyongyang. This mistrust was rooted in the then-rumored (and later confirmed) abduction of Japanese by North Korean agents in the 1970s and 1980s, North Korea's continuing protection of Japanese Red Army members, and the country's nuclear weapons program. Conciliatory moves toward Pyongyang by the Clinton administration, particularly the construction of the KEDO (Korean Peninsula Energy Development Organization), and South Korea's "sunshine policy" toward the north exacerbated Japanese fears regarding its growing isolation on security issues.[15]

The Persian Gulf War and the Taepodong tests form neat bookends for 1990s Japanese security policies, representing the twin concerns about entrapment and abandonment. While pro-defense conservatives have generally extolled the merits of further cooperation with the United States, leftists have swayed moderates with fears of entrapment in U.S. adventures such as the decision to enter Kuwait and now the Iraq War. On the other hand, the prospect of facing regional rivals without clear U.S. protection has been a potent image in debates over Japan's need to follow U.S. leadership. The context for that leadership is now changing, shaped by a fundamental reconstruction of terrorism as a partly military phenomenon. In a follow-up to his prescient study of the connections between Japan's internal and external security policy, Peter Katzenstein argues that, in the wake of the September 11 attacks, the United States now views security in more comprehensive terms, as Japan and to some degree Germany already did.[16] The murkiness of the North Korean threat made it a complicated image in debates over specific security policies. Did North Korea present chiefly a military challenge, armed with nuclear missiles that could be stopped only with the development of "theater missile defense" (TMD)?[17] Or was it primarily a terrorist threat in its support for Japanese leftists or Korean residents of Japan to whom it might provide weapons of mass destruction?[18] Was it primarily an espionage or subversive threat, with North Korean agents aboard tiny vessels, coming to Japan to abduct citizens, commit sabotage, distribute narcotics, and spy on Japanese facilities? This ambiguity, particularly with the U.S.-led redefinition of counterterrorism norms, proved to be exploitable.

September 11 and Terrorism as External Security

In the immediate aftermath of the September 11 attacks, foreign policymakers in the Bush administration rapidly made the decision to build international support for planned military strikes against the Taliban in Afghanistan. Assistant Secretary of State and East Asia specialist Richard Armitage flew to meet officials in Tokyo, Seoul, and elsewhere. For Japan—whose significant but tardy financial contributions to the first Persian Gulf War had been derided as "checkbook diplomacy"—Armitage clearly had more in mind than eliciting kind words and offers of reconstruction assistance. Prime Minister Koizumi, no dove himself, had immediately called the attacks "unforgivable" and promised support to the United States in bringing to justice those responsible. Shortly after Armitage's visit, Koizumi guaranteed Japanese military support, particularly the dispatch of Maritime Self-Defense Forces vessels, including an Aegis-radar equipped cruiser, for the effort.[19]

In making this request (or demand, depending on how one judges U.S. diplomacy), the Bush administration embarked on its openly acknowledged road to militarizing counterterrorism norms. As noted in chapter 5, international counterterrorism had long focused specifically on applying police and intelligence tools to circumscribe and control nonstate security threats, particularly transnational movements. But in declaring a "war on terror," the Bush administration clearly aimed at moving beyond the limits of these norms, justifying the use of massive levels of military force (not just special "counterterrorism" units) against both terrorist organizations and state sponsors.[20] In doing so, the U.S. government chose one way to define security in "comprehensive" terms, linking the need to strike Kabul (and later, Baghdad) to tightened immigration procedures and protection of sensitive installations at home. In this sense, dispatching Japanese troops to support the maneuver was in part an effort to globalize this new approach to transnational terrorism.

The dispatch was almost purely symbolic, though Japanese ships refueled other nations' vessels. Afghanistan is a landlocked nation and, aside from the cleverly low-tech suicide attack on the USS *Cole* docked in Yemen in 1998, there was no reason to believe either in the existence of a threat to the U.S. Navy or that multinational naval cooperation near the theater of operations would provide much in the way of operational advantage to an already overpowering U.S. military effort. Symbols matter, of course, but their meaning depends on political and cultural contexts. For the United States, the appearance of Japanese forces meant both the promise of a longer-term financial commitment as well as enhanced international legitimacy for the U.S. attack. But in Tokyo, the dispatch of Japanese troops meant more chipping away at the shackles on the use of force to deal with international security: a hopeful moment for Japan's hawks, and a terribly worrisome sign for the doves.

In the same way that Diet debates on the Child Prostitution/Child Pornography Law focused partly on international norms and partly on distinctive Japanese problems, officials cleverly linked the U.S. demand for support to Japan's own troubling security issues. The government simultaneously proposed the Tero Taisaku Tokubetsu Sochihō (Anti-Terrorism Special Meaures Law), legally paving the way for SDF deployment to support the United States; a revision of the Self-Defense Forces Law allowing the SDF to guard their own and U.S. bases, replacing the police;[21] and a revision of the Coast Guard Law[22] to allow it to use weapons against unknown or suspicious foreign vessels in Japanese waters. Because of the apparent departure from established government norms regarding engagement in international disputes, the deployment to assist the United States in the Indian Ocean engendered the greatest amount of internal debate. With the Socialists a barely functioning political force in 2001, the primary stand against the deployment was taken by the DPJ, though the Democrats' mixed provenance (including a few former Socialists, former LDP members, and assorted others) made its position extraordinarily convoluted. After rejecting an initial proposal in October because it did not require subsequent Diet approval before individual deployment decisions,[23] the DPJ then supported a specific deployment proposal in November, in spite of clear dissent within its ranks.[24]

For the LDP, which had long pushed for an extension of Japan's overseas military role, the Afghanistan mission was very nearly a godsend. In fact, the LDP's plans greatly resembled its goals in the 1990–91 Persian Gulf War, when it had been stymied and embarrassed by domestic opposition to deployment, settling for financial contributions to the U.S. effort. This time, both the local and global contexts were different. Legally, the stage had been set with earlier peacekeeping missions and also with the 1999 Surrounding Areas Emergency Measures Law, which provided legal space for observation of the 1997 U.S.-Japan security guidelines. In theory, the troops could be deployed to support U.S. operations in "areas surrounding Japan," a term so elastic as to allow the Indian Ocean deployment. Koizumi's personal popularity, hovering in 2001 at about 80 percent, probably was not the deciding factor; only 50 percent of the Japanese public favored the dispatch and some sort of rear-guard support. Instead, the primary difference between the LDP's failure in the earlier Persian Gulf War and success in 2001 may have been in the willingness of South Korea and China to limit their criticism of Japan's dispatch. This reflected Tokyo's longstanding efforts to reassure both countries about its intentions,[25] and almost certainly also both nations' willingness to defer to U.S. interests in this most pressing of crises.

The development of a "war on terror" thereby provided the opportunity for the LDP to capitalize on altered regional and domestic political environments. By stipulating that Japan's obligations under the U.S.-Japan treaty should be interpreted to include support, however symbolic, of U.S. activities in Afghanistan, the Bush administration offered the Koizumi cabinet an extraordinary chance. The 2001 deployment debates permitted Koizumi to push for an SDF role that could be defined as humanitarian in terms of the planned reconstruction of Afghanistan and yet was distinctively military. Even more important, however, was the Bush administration's depiction of this particular military engagement as part of a global struggle against terrorism. Terrorism's nebulous meaning—a security threat defined more by the fear it creates than by any concrete identity or goals of the antagonists involved—would provide an opportunity to recast a number of long-debated security plans as essential components of a strategy against this scourge.

From *Fushinsen* to *Kōsakusen*

In the long run, October 29, 2001—the date of the Diet vote on the counterterrorism law—may be relevant primarily for the simultaneous revision of the Coast Guard Law and the trajectory it began to mark. Since 1999, the Japanese Maritime Self-Defense Forces and Coast Guard had vociferously argued for tougher measures against *fushinsen* (suspicious boats) in Japanese waters. Though some of the dozens of such boats spotted annually were almost certainly illegal fishing boats piloted by Chinese and other foreigners, some clearly originated in North Korea and were involved in drug smuggling or worse in Japan. Particularly with the still-unverified rumors of North Korean abductions of Japanese civilians, the Maritime Self-Defense Forces and Coast Guard experienced little criticism when, in 1999, they opened fire on a fushinsen, which then accelerated to a suspiciously high speed and escaped.[26] Lower house member Ishiba Shigeru, who later became head of the Japan Defense Agency, argued at a 2000 committee meeting that the fushinsen problem was not just one for the Coast Guard but the entire government, including the police, the military, and the political leadership. He argued for a revision of the Self-Defense Forces Law or the Coast Guard Law to allow for engagement.[27] At the time, however, it was unclear which of these legal routes would be more politically viable.

But the September 11 attacks offered the Japanese government the remarkable option of legitimizing increasingly muscular steps against North Korea by tying it to a global struggle against terrorism. Unlike al Qaeda, which had played virtually no role in the Japanese popular imagination, North Korea was a pressing and local threat already suspected to have engaged in sneaky transborder operations regarded by many Japanese as similar to those of the September 11 hijackers. This was a comparison used far more for domestic than for international consumption. Notably, the English-language website of the Ministry of Foreign Affairs does not list the revision of the Coast Guard Law as part of Japan's counterterrorism stance,[28] while the Japanese-language site of the Prime Minister's Office cites it as a feature of the government's efforts against terrorism.[29] With the revision of the Coast Guard Law, the Japanese government entered the thorny world of fights over the transnational nature of terrorism.

Prime Minister Koizumi opened up the discussion in the lower house on October 2, 2001, when he announced that the police, Coast Guard, and SDF were training and working together to prevent terrorist attacks in Japan, repeating the message next day in the upper house.[30] On October 10, 2001, the Diet's Steering Committee chairman, Fujii Takao, announced that a short revision (*ichibu no kaisei*) of the Coast Guard Law would be on the agenda of the Diet's extraordinary session.[31] One connection drawn between the proposed revision and September 11 was that the Coast Guard would need freer rules of engagement to deal with possible threats to U.S. ships and bases in Japan. Ōgi Chikage, who was the minister of Land, Infrastructure, and Transport, addressed the upper house Land, Infrastructure, and Transport Committee on October 18, explaining that in order to cooperate with the United States on terrorism, Japan would have to tighten up control of local waters. She specified that the Coast Guard Law would have to be revised to allow the preemptive use of force in order to protect U.S. bases from attack.[32] More commonly, however, conservative lawmakers directly pointed to the fushinsen as emblematic of the type of terrorist threat that the world now faced. In a main lower house session, LDP member Kamei Yoshiyuki explained that he represented the LDP and its coalition partners, New Kōmeito and the Conservative Party, in expressing how Japan would deal with the September 11 attacks. He pushed first for the Anti-Terrorism Support Law, but then added that there were foreign vessels, such as the fushinsen, that could be used for massive crimes or attacks (*jūdai kyōaku hanzai*) in Japan itself, implicitly drawing connections between what happened in New York and Washington and what North Korea might do in Japan. He then encouraged the revision of the Coast Guard Law.[33]

In the special Diet session to debate Japan's response to the September 11 attacks, virtually all of the opposition questions addressed the Anti-Terrorism Special Measures Law and the revision of the SDF law, not the Coast Guard Law. One of the few exchanges specifically about the proposed Coast Guard revision came late in the deliberations, in an October 25 meeting of the National Land and Infrastructure Committee of the upper house. Ōgi repeated her rationale—the possibility of attacks against U.S. bases—for the revision. This prompted a skeptical "And that's the most important reason for this proposal?" (*sono koto ga hōan teishutsu o okuraseta saidai no riyū desu ka*) from SDP member Fuchigami Sadao. Fuchigami questioned whether this was really about terrorism, or whether it was just a response to the embarrassment of earlier incidents in which Coast Guard patrol boats had been unable to capture fushinsen. Conceding that the suspicious boats were a concern that had helped to prompt the law, Ōgi turned for technical explanations of the rules of engagement to Nawano Katsuhiko, head of the Coast Guard, and Kitahara Iwao, a JDA specialist on military transport. Fuchigami then ran out of time and yielded the floor without pressing the issue further;[34] there ended the debate. The Coast Guard revision sailed through the Diet with less attention and opposition than the other two bills.

It turned out to be a bellwether, however. By forcing public acknowledgment of the fushinsen as threats to Japan and the right to use lethal force against them, the LDP created necessary political space for the Coast Guard to take action. Only two months later, it did so—though not directly using the revised law, thereby calling into question the necessity of the legal change. In the early morning hours of December 22, 2001, four Coast Guard vessels began to pursue a fushinsen in a chase that ended twenty hours later, with a brief firefight and an explosion, presumably from a self-destruct device, that sank the suspicious boat. These final events took place in China's, not Japan's, Exclusive Economic Zone. Two Coast Guard members were injured in the firefight, though both survived. The entire crew of the suspicious vessel—fifteen North Korean men—perished.

Depending on one's perspective, the story is either one of heroism and grit or of cynicism and opportunism. The Kyushu bureau of the right-leaning *Yomiuri Shimbun,* Japan's most popular newspaper, represented the former in a four-part series entitled "20 Jikan no Kōbō" (The 20-Hour Tug-of-War). Like any good battle story, this one focused on the tactics, worries, and thoughts of the heroes. We learn about the captains of all four Coast Guard boats, including seasoned veterans and a go-getter in his thirties. The lengthy series depicted the twenty-hour chase almost in real time (at least for someone who reads Japanese as slowly as I do), with the captains of Coast Guard patrol boats detecting and then beginning to follow the "suspicious boat."

The first boat to engage the fushinsen boat is the *Inasa,* helmed by Capt. Ishimaru Akira, who has gotten the call that a Coast Guard plane has spotted the boat. As Ishimaru turns his patrol boat to engage the chase, this veteran of the 1999 skirmish and other fushinsen encounters "has a hunch that this time is it" (*chokkanteki ni honmono to kanjita*). The *Kirishima*'s captain, Tsutsumi Masami, gets close enough to watch the crew of the fushinsen start to dump overboard equipment and suspicious-looking bags (which he guesses are filled with methamphetamines); "They're definitely destroying evidence" (*shōko inmetsu kōsaku ni chigainai*), he thinks. When the *Amami*'s captain, Kurusu Masao, watches the fushinsen use jet propulsion to race away at an alarming speed he realizes, "We're going to need to shoot to get this thing to stop" (*teishi saseru tame ni utsu koto ga aru ka mo shirenai*).

The head of the Coast Guard, Nawano Katsuhiko, is at headquarters, reviewing his options. Although there are Coast Guard teams with special weapons training suitable for counterterrorism (known as SSTs), they would not be able to mobilize quickly enough to join the chase. He also realizes that the boat is heading toward Chinese waters. Nawano himself reasons that as long as any firing begins while the fushinsen is in Japan's Exclusive Economic Zone, it is legitimate to pursue them under international laws on fish poaching—crucially, not relying on the revised law, which suggests its passage may have been more symbolic than practically relevant to Japan's handling of the suspicious boats. The Coast Guard's crisis management center radios the patrol boats at 2:11 p.m. saying that Nawano has authorized the use of weapons.

At about 5 p.m., Capt. Horii Kazuya of the *Mizuki*—the youngest of the captains—orders his men to fire on the ship with the ship's 20-mm automatic weapons. The fushinsen catches fire, though Horii is impressed with the speed with which the crew extinguishes it and resumes flight: "These guys are good. They must be trained professionals" (*tegiwa ga ii. Kunren sareta puro da*). The Coast Guard ships ultimately surround the fushinsen and try to subdue it peacefully, but at 10:09 p.m., the fushinsen—with no possibility of escape and at risk of being boarded—begins to fire at the *Amami, Kirishima,* and *Inasa,* wounding two Japanese. As Ishimaru of the *Inasa* watches missiles from the fushinsen flying over the boats, he realizes that he needs to open up full fire in self-defense. He gives the order to shoot but worries that his crew will hesitate out of bewilderment and concern for the safety of everyone, so he yells "Fire!" repeatedly. Ishimaru later says, "We needed to shoot straight at them, so it would have been weirder if we hadn't been hesitating. We're not soldiers, so haven't been trained to kill people" (*soko ni mukete utsu no dakara, tamerawanai hō ga okashii. Wareware wa guntai no yō ni hito o korosu kunren o uketeiru wake de wa nai*).[35]

The use of narrative style is important. The *Yomiuri*'s series tells us about the behavior of the Japanese crew, their frustration with the various constraints that have in the past prevented them from doing their job, and their determination not to allow the fushinsen to escape. And, of course, we also read about the frailties and vulnerabilities of the Japanese—they do not even know if they will have the stomach for killing—while the Koreans are mostly blank slates. The *Yomiuri* piece describes the Koreans as neither vindictive criminals nor hapless victims, either of which might have been a reasonable interpretation; they are instead trained professionals—like soldiers—competently going about their unknown but surely menacing business. The piece engages in no direct chest-thumping over Japanese naval superiority or moral virtue; instead, the Japanese are brave and gritty men, dealing personally with the ethical issues involved, and doing their dangerous jobs to protect Japan from suspiciously unspecified threats.

One might contrast this with Wada Haruki's careful and highly critical reconstruction of the incident. For Wada, one of Japan's foremost left-wing historians and perhaps its preeminent expert on North Korea, the proper narration of the incident is one of missed opportunities and questionable legal decisions that led to something very nearly an act of war. He argues that the decision to open fire on the ship and to continue the attack even as it had crossed into China's Exclusive Economic Zone raised a number of crucial issues involving the right to self-defense, the law of the sea, and the constitutionality of the Coast Guard's behavior. Using Nawano's own testimony to the Diet in October 2001 against him, Wada argues that the case was legally untenable.[36] He goes further and argues that the fushinsen incident was really an opportunity for the government to push its agenda of establishing broader Japanese rights for military engagement in "areas surrounding Japan." For Wada, the fushinsen incident was troubling not only on its own legal terms but also for what it meant about the disconcerting and extralegal trajectory of Japanese power.[37]

After getting Chinese permission to raise the ship and to collect the debris, the Coast Guard was able to shape public memory of the event for the huge crowds that went to see a special display of it in Tokyo in 2003. That September, I accompanied some colleagues to see the raised ship at the Museum of Maritime Science. Originally built in 1970, the museum sits in O-Daiba, a reclaimed land area in Tokyo Bay. By all accounts, the museum has been one of the less popular attractions in the area, falling far behind the O-Daiba Decks shopping complex or the "women's theme park," Venus Fort, a flamboyantly designed shopping mall. Although well-designed and informative, the museum had mostly served as a destination for school field-trips rather than tourists.

That changed in March 2003, when the Nippon Foundation (established by the conservative philanthropist Sasakawa Ryūichi) sponsored, in conjunction with the Kaijō Hoan Kyōkai (Maritime Safety Association) and the Coast Guard, a display of the raised vessel. No longer a fushinsen ("suspicious boat"), the rusted hull was now a kōsakusen, or "operations boat"; it was now confirmed as something very nearly an enemy ship, ordered by another government to undermine or harm Japan. When the exhibit first opened, the lines at the entrance would extend around the block, and around 3 p.m. employees would prevent people from joining the line so that they could close on time. By the time the exhibit closed in February 2004 (after several extensions of the display) it had attracted over 1.6 million visitors.[38] We rode out on the Yurikamome line, an ultramodern, driverless elevated train from Shimbashi Station. At the time of my visit, although most Yurikamome passengers were shoppers heading to O-Daiba, a substantial number got off at the exit for the museum to see the boat.

The exhibit began outdoors, where visitors could slowly walk in a line around the boat, as a guide explained the structure of the boat. There was space, we learned, for people to sleep and eat, and possibly for a smaller submersible craft for special operations. We could look in from the stern of the rusty, bullet-ridden husk, where the Nippon Foundation had placed a sign—in English, Japanese, and Korean—with a message from the group's president, Sono Ayako, dedicating the exhibit to the fifteen North Korean men who died in the incident. This sign was apparently added in reaction to some public criticism after the opening of the exhibit;[39] I overheard a person in another tour group chuckle, "Ah, tatemae da" ("They're just being politically correct"). Visitors could then enter the one-room indoor exhibit that contained remnants of the unlucky boat's debris.

My parents were opposed to the Vietnam War and raised me as a liberal, but even they could not resist taking my sisters and me to visit military museums when we were kids. I remember touring New England's Revolutionary War sites, including Bunker Hill and Lexington, as well as Gettysburg, and I am no stranger to the feeling of solemn pride one is supposed to have toward the men who did their grim duty in the higher cause of protecting me, or my ancestors, or the values my country ostensibly represents. And when I walked into the second part of the *kōsakusen* exhibit, I instinctively recognized that I was in a military museum, which I mention because almost every word written on each display card explained that this was *not* in fact a military museum. It was only one room, as I suppose was fitting for a skirmish that sank such a small boat; after all, even in an excruciatingly slow-moving crowd, I had just walked around the craft in less time that in would have taken me to slurp down a bowl of noodles at the ramen shop nearby.

All four walls had glass cases with material related to specific aspects of the incident, but the core of the exhibit was a display in the middle of the room. Here were the assorted and fearsome-looking weapons found on board: a rocket launcher, a deck-mounted machine gun, and a small collection of automatic weapons. I suspect that many Caribbean drug runners have similarly impressive arsenals, though I would not have relished the chance to be on board one of the Japanese patrol boats charged with stopping this boat.

This was one of the few times, however, in which I have really felt at ease in a military museum, largely because the exhibit so strenuously denied its military nature. Taking my time, I studied the small case that held a lighter with the face of the former North Korean dictator, Kim Il Sung, thus confirming the national origin of the ship. Another case displayed debris, such as Japanese cell phones and scuba diving equipment, hinting at the clandestine and probably illegal nature of the North Koreans' activities and the threat they posed to Japan.[40] And so, unlike in the United States, where we nearly fetishize weaponry on display, the *kōsakusen* exhibit asked us to be astounded by the destructive potential of the operations boat, as it assiduously reminded us that the Japanese government's actions had been legal, justified, and rational.

Here, I could really enjoy the weapons while assuaging my guilt at my own uncomfortably gleeful reaction to memorialized violence, because this was, after all, simply a story of crime and punishment, not of nationalism and war. A large plaque at the end of the exhibit explained (this time only in Japanese) that the Nippon Foundation and the Kaijō Hoan Kyōkai hoped that visitors would "tell as many of their compatriots as possible about the real situation in the waters surrounding Japan, and about the efforts and courage of those people who guard the ocean" (*dekiru dake ōku no kokumin ni nihon o kakomu umi no genjō o tsutae, nihon no umi o mamoru hitobito no doryoku to yūki ga shirareru koto o negatteiru*).[41] Like the exhibit, the statement was, in many ways, a masterpiece of ambiguity. One could experience the vicarious thrill of the chase and the firefight while still being committed to the peaceful settlement of international disputes. One could rest assured that these were no ordinary criminals—their escape would have imperiled Japan. Partly because of my natural restlessness and partly because I resent emotional manipulation, I have a low tolerance for museums, but even I felt cheerful after viewing this particular exhibit.

From Suspicion to Incident, from Terrorism to Emergency

Earlier fushinsen incidents had already indicated to some observers that Japan needed to rethink its approach to security. One American specialist, Ralph Cossa, argued in 1999 that the problems experienced by the Coast Guard and Navy in stopping the ship were emblematic of larger

problems for the Japanese government. Specifically, Japan needed to implement "emergency laws" that would give the military a freer hand in
the event of contingencies during crises. The new defense guidelines had
already called for these emergency laws, and their absence left a crucial
part of Japanese obligations unfulfilled. By engaging the issue of the
emergency laws and the defense guidelines, Japanese would have "a
golden opportunity to discuss the larger question of Japan's role not only
in assisting U.S. forces in maintaining or restoring peace in areas surrounding Japan but also in defending itself under normal circumstances
against a variety of potential military threats."[42]

In drawing connections between the fushinsen, the emergency laws,
and Japan's larger military role in regional security, Cossa tapped into
the sensitive debates highlighting the Japanese response to contingencies. "Emergency laws" provide special powers to the military in times of
crisis, ostensibly enabling them to respond quickly to unforeseen events
in ways that might, during peacetime, be considered to violate normal
rules and rights. For example, the Japanese Right tends to describe the
emergency laws as necessary so that Japanese military vehicles can ignore
red lights when responding to crises. For the Left, the operative example would be the use of emergency laws allowing the military to com-
mandeer vehicles, homes, and the like, potentially arresting or harming
those Japanese who refuse to cooperate even as a matter of pacifist conscience. Both sides have a point: Japan's exceptionally tight restrictions
on the military undoubtedly constitute a major impediment to domestic
military action,[43] though emergency laws have been used in other countries (e.g., South Korea) to justify appalling rights abuses. Crucially, the
revision of the Coast Guard Law would serve as a canary in the coal mine,
a proto-emergency law wedge for future expansion of military authority
in the event of a crisis.

As early as 1963, SDF officials were planning for contingency laws that
would free their hands in times of crisis. In cooperation with their U.S.
military counterparts, they undertook a study program known as the Mitsuya Kenkyū (Three Arrows Research) project, which envisioned a pin-
cer assault on South Korea by combined Communist forces. When a JSP
member, Okada Haruo, found out about the program and revealed it on
the floor of the lower house in 1965, he shocked leftists and moderates
in the Diet, and badly embarrassed Prime Minister Satō Eisaku. Satō evidently knew nothing of the Three Arrows project and faced heavy criticism for his apparent ineptitude as well as for the frightening secrecy
with which the supposedly reformed and pacifist Japanese military had

planned for the enhancement of its own authority. Satō had little choice but to kill the plan, at least as a specific research project.[44]

Through the 1970s and 1980s, however, planning for emergency laws continued, though under different names. In particular, two midterm reports actually spelled out the progress of ideas for the legislation. Even within the JDA, however, the plans were controversial, partly because they were premised on a contingency (a war between the United States and the Soviet Union) for which Japanese planning was largely beside the point. Nishihiro Seiki, at the time vice-minister of the Japan Defense Agency and known colloquially as "Mister Defense Agency," reportedly said, "If deterrence fails and there's a war with the Soviets, Japan's going to be scorched earth. You think Japanese are going to support that war? Fine, continue to study the issue, but let's keep the plans locked up in a safe." The plans gathered dust through the 1990s, as the end of the cold war fundamentally restructured the premises on which the research rested. Even so, after the 1997 U.S.-Japan security guidelines, and particularly after the September 11 attacks, JDA staff and LDP members turned back to the plans.[45]

With the fushinsen incident and heightened concerns regarding North Korea's intentions, Koizumi moved ahead in early 2002 with a proposal for three emergency laws, based almost entirely on the JDA's various midterm reports. When Koizumi traveled to Pyongyang that year for a historic summit with Kim Jong Il, the North Korean premier admitted that some in his government—described in essence as rogue figures—had in fact kidnapped over a dozen Japanese in the 1970s and 1980s, five of whom were still alive. Thus began one of the more grueling dramas in Japan's postwar Asian relations. When the North Korean government agreed to allow the five surviving Japanese to visit Japan, their families demanded that the government reject the condition that they return to North Korea, and ultimately all of the abductees themselves refused to return. Working with their families, a charismatic LDP hawk, Abe Shinzō, demanded that the government continue to take a tough line against North Korea until it received a full and verifiable account of those who were reportedly deceased, and until the abductees' (Korean) families were allowed to "return" to Japan as well. The most extreme and disturbing case involved Yokota Megumi, kidnapped at the age of thirteen and then apparently married to a North Korean man, with whom she had a daughter. With Yokota reportedly (and suspiciously) dead from suicide, Yokota's parents demanded the "return" of their grandchild, who had been born and raised in North Korea.[46]

The emotionally wrenching stories, clear evidence of North Korean wrongdoing, and the indisputable blamelessness of the victims made the event a lightning rod in Japanese politics. Perhaps more than anything else, the abductions issue cemented North Korea's place as a terrorist nation in the Japanese public imagination. If we work from the assumption that a minimal definition of terrorism would involve the use of political violence in order to intimidate an opponent into making concessions, it is hard to see how the term fits. Even in the most sinister of interpretations, North Korea undertook its actions in secret, hoping to teach its spies Japanese so that they might carry out operations in South Korea or Japan.[47] But the creepy, underhanded nature of the North Korean government's behavior—especially when disconnected from larger regional or historical issues, such as the much larger number of Koreans forced (some would say "abducted") to Japan during wartime—firmly established Kim Jong Il as the Japanese counterpart to America's Osama bin Laden. Economist and political commentator Hasegawa Keitarō argues that by having its agents move into Japan secretly, taking "innocent" (*tsumi mo nai*) people back to their own nation, North Korea had done the most "shocking" (*shōgeki*) thing to Japan that any country had done in the postwar era. The North Korean government was ostensibly doing something that the Japanese government would never consider: flaunting international law and rules, strictly to pursue its own selfish interest. This made it, in the eyes of many citizens, the "quintessential terrorist nation" (*moji-dōri tero kokka*).[48] For Koizumi, who had aimed to end a decades-long political struggle by passing the emergency laws, the North Korean government could hardly have made a more crucial contribution.

By this time, no Japanese politician or official would have dared to be seen as soft on North Korea. Anti-Pyongyang emotions ran so high that in September 2003 a rightist group placed a "bomb-like device" in the garage of Deputy Foreign Minister Tanaka Hitoshi, MOFA's top North Korea negotiator, who was seen by critics as overly soft on Pyongyang; Tokyo's right-wing governor, Ishihara Shintarō, quickly announced that Tanaka deserved it.[49] After the fall of the Taliban in early December 2001, the fushinsen incident (particularly with the boat's reclassification to "operations boat") helped to clarify the North Korean threat, which was confirmed by the abduction admission. In the view of one writer, this closed the circle, connecting "terrorism" to "North Korea," and led correspondingly from "counterterrorism" to "emergency laws."[50]

Leftists immediately charged that Koizumi's push for the laws was one more in a string of actions meant to throw off Japan's constitutional shackles. One of the most prominent, Hitotsubashi University's Watanabe Osamu, argued that Koizumi's vaunted "structural reforms," usually seen in strictly financial and economic terms, really demonstrated his intent to make Japan a "normal" nation, that is, one with a full military capable of extending Japanese power overseas. Koizumi had initially used his popularity to remove the antinationalism taboo associated with visits to the Yasukuni Shrine, where Japan's war dead (including war criminals) are venerated. In Watanabe's view, the handling of the fushinsen had been critical to Koizumi's long-term goal, by providing the government the opportunity to use deadly force against putative threats, thus justifying the further extension of power. If the establishment of the emergency laws went well, Koizumi would move to revise the constitution to allow for collective self-defense.[51]

Of course, conservatives concede all of these points, though they argue that the goal is nothing more sinister than making Japan "normal." In one typical exposition, military historian and former Defense University professor Nakayama Takashi laid out the case in virtually the same order. Nakayama's book, published as a *shinsho,* starts with a chapter on the fushinsen problem, covering the history of contacts and the fatal incident in 2001. More formal than the *Yomiuri* report, the chapter provides a brief chronology of the event and then draws lessons, which are primarily tactical in nature—though Nakayama argues that Japan and South Korea have to work together to deal with the threat. From there he moves to a brief chapter on the abductions and then more on the missile threat, including several intimidating charts regarding the missiles and their reach into Japan. He then moves to a long section dealing with the range of activities available to the SDF in the event of an emergency and to laying out the need for new emergency laws. The second half of the book calls for a complete reformation of Japan's defense system, including a fundamental rethinking of the constitution.[52]

Crucially, the emergency legislation that made its way to the Diet reflected its cold war origins, when the threat was of an invasion rather than a terrorist attack or other type of crisis. This legislation, however, has long been a goal of the increasingly powerful hawks in the Liberal Democratic Party, and for them its ratification represented a necessary step in the emergence of a normal Japan. When the emergency laws passed in June 2003, the Koizumi cabinet made relatively few concessions to the opposition. After promising to cooperate with the DPJ on a subsequent law to clarify citizens' rights vis-à-vis the military in the event of an emergency, the LDP-led coalition achieved passage of the emergency laws in June 2003. The three bills—including stipulations for new emergency powers for the Defense Agency, special responsibilities for other agencies and ministries, and specific limits on individual rights (e.g., restrictions on civil aviation)—passed with 90 percent support in the Diet. Abe and Ishiba, two leaders of the Bōei-zoku ("defense policy tribe") group in the lower house, took active roles in pushing for the citizens' rights stipulation in order to achieve DPJ backing. The Defense Agency's director general, Kyūma Fumio, and the DPJ's Maehara Seiji had hammered out an agreement in which the emergency laws would not be rewritten to guarantee the protection of civil liberties but the government would promise to respect freedom of association, expression, and conscience.[53] In an obvious nod to uncomfortable memories of the government's exploitation of emergency legislation to dominate civilian life during World War II,[54] the compromise required the Diet to pass subsequent legislation stipulating the need to protect human rights in the event of an emergency.[55]

Catch-Up Counterterrorism

For the Left, the emergency laws represented a cynical exploitation of fear to justify the extension of a state role beyond that constitutionally permitted. For conservatives, however, this was the natural thing for the government to do. The LDP's hawks did not need the September 11 attacks to convince them that their country faced threats that required the establishment of a larger military mission. Instead, it simply confirmed the type of consequence Japan would likely face if it were not to take a more responsible and assertive military stance. As noted in chapter 5, the Japanese government had long bracketed terrorism as crisis management, separating it from national security and viewing Japanese vulnerability as limited because of the country's relatively limited international profile. But September 11 provided a ghastly example of what can happen when a nation's guard is down; there are always enemies, including suspicious boats from countries occasionally test-firing missiles over your country's airspace.

In fact, the initial domestic counterterrorism steps taken after the September 11 attacks also reflect fears of potential attacks by North Korean special forces or guerrillas. Shortly after the attacks, the NPA authorized the deployment of special firearms units (jūki taisaku hen) to nuclear power plants (especially near the northwestern coast, seen as especially vulnerable to North Korean infiltration) and to Narita airport. These officers with automatic weapons were components of the existing riot police (*kidōtai*) in each prefectural police department. The decision seems partly in response to Asō Iku's widely read 1997 novel *Sensen Fukoku* (Declaration of War), in which North Korean agents plot to attack a nuclear power plant. In this two-volume work, which sold over a half million copies, Asō was so detailed about government plans against North Korea that, like Tom Clancy in the United States, he provoked concern because the book must have been based on leaks. The novel (later made into a film) even became a topic in the Diet, with legislators and journalists commenting on the author's access to classified information and on the frighteningly realistic scenario he presented.[56] The 2002 World Cup, jointly held with South Korea, also encouraged increased police-military cooperation in counterterrorism. By late 2002, the SDF and prefectural police forces were holding joint counterterrorism training exercises, first in Hokkaido and then in other prefectures.[57]

MOFA also upgraded its counterterrorism stance in subtle but possibly consequential ways. In late 2001, it established a special office within the powerful Foreign Policy Bureau to deal with counterterrorism; the unit engages in large-scale counterterrorism policy rather than simply tracking individual incidents involving Japanese overseas.[58] MOFA also overcame domestic resistance (specifically from the Ministry of Finance, which had not wanted to add new restrictions on banks) to Japan's signing the international convention on the financing of terrorism, as described in chapter 5. It additionally stepped up a schedule of counterterrorism programs run by the Japan International Cooperation Agency, with the cooperation of the NPA and MOFA, making them more frequent. These seminars bring bureaucrats from Asia's developing nations to Tokyo to study six issues related to counterterrorism: suppression of financing, CBRN cooperation, border control, customs, investigation, and community policing.[59]

MOFA has also cooperated with the NPA in a special police development program in Indonesia, where NPA officials have been training the Indonesian police in crime control techniques. The program actually began as a component of a multinational aid effort on governance reform[60] before the September 11 attacks, but afterward it was rechristened a counterterrorism program aimed at limiting varied threats of political violence. In contrast to, for example, the Antiterrorism Assistance program run by the U.S. State Department, which uses discrete courses on counterterrorism tactics, this ambitious program has essentially established "community policing" models based on the kōban (police box) system that served Japan so well in its struggle with the JRA. Because Japanese aid is distributed on a "request" basis, government agencies have to work with foreign governments to encourage them to request the kind of assistance that the Japanese government wants to give. In this case, the NPA representatives in Indonesia have worked to get beyond the merely fiscal requests and to try to engender an interest in specialized training designed to establish a trusted police force that can rely, as have the Japanese police at home, on dense social networks for information.[61] An English-language report outlines wide-ranging proposals by the Japanese government to improve the security situation in Indonesia, though these are tied much more closely to professionalization and training of the police than to specific concern with combating terrorism.[62] Now described as part of Japan's overall counterterrorism strategy, the program is at too early a stage for even the government to evaluate.[63]

Iraq, Internal Security, and Self-Responsibility

After the September 11 attacks, the Japanese government initiated a diverse array of external and internal security measures designed to meet assorted goals, many of them reflecting long-standing transnational norms of counterterrorism as policing. The most dramatic shift in policy came in the enhanced role and flexibility for the SDF, primarily through deployment to Afghanistan and the emergency laws. The U.S. decision to go to war with Iraq provided a dramatic test of Koizumi's determination to normalize Japan's military stance. With only limited popular support, Koizumi pushed through a law to authorize the dispatch of Air Self-Defense Forces to Kuwait and then SDF troops to Samawah, in southern Iraq, where they were to be entrusted with certain humanitarian projects, including repairing the water system.

This was not the first time the SDF had gone overseas; earlier peacekeeping operations in Cambodia, East Timor, Madagascar, and elsewhere had famously involved SDF troops. In those cases, however, the Japanese went under clear UN auspices to areas that were supposedly pacified; the Japanese troops were merely maintaining order. In Iraq, the troops were part of a military engagement that had been extraordinarily unpopular at the United Nations, had aroused strong suspicions in Japan of U.S. imperial intentions, and which seemed dangerously impulsive to boot. Japanese troops would be only lightly armed—mostly with sidearms and with a few recoilless rifles to destroy potential suicide car bombs—and they would be governed by strict rules of engagement. According to the law authorizing their dispatch, the troops would not be allowed to serve in "combat zones" (*sentō–chiiki*). Extraordinarily risky for his political fate, Koizumi's gambit relied on his popularity with voters and with the often vaguely stated but widely held view that cooperation with the United States on Iraq was essential for ensuring U.S. protection from North Korea.[64] This position received a boost when the U.S. State Department listed, for the first time, the abductions issue as one of the factors in its keeping North Korea on the "state sponsors of terrorism" list in April 2004.[65]

The public decision to support the United States provoked one early and unsettling response. An e-mail to an Arabic-language newspaper published in London announced that al Qaeda would be targeting Japan as well as other nations that supported the United States in the war. Immediately thereafter, the garish advertisements on the Tokyo subways for Japan's salacious weekly news magazines began to feature the face of Osama bin Laden, with headlines announcing that al Qaeda operatives were already in Tokyo. Each had a different scoop about the Uzbeks or Afghans or other Muslims who were ready and waiting to launch strikes in Tokyo. The fears only grew after the Madrid bombing, as well as the attacks on London's subways in July 2005. For the National Police Agency, which was in the process of reorganizing to add the new Foreign Intelligence Division (*gaiji jōhōbu*) inside the Security Bureau (*keibi kyoku*) and requesting budgetary outlays for ten thousand new police officers, the heightened fears came at an opportune moment. The NPA had primarily defended its proposal by overstating the threat of crime by immigrants,[66] and new fears of al Qaeda attacks in Tokyo made the request all the more urgent. The new division would combine analysis of international intelligence on terrorism with increased surveillance of foreign criminal threats in Japan, though foreign crime organizations are under the jurisdiction of the Organized Crime Division in the Detectives Bureau.[67]

Similarly, the additional officers at prefectural police departments would seemingly allow fuller staffing of Japan's police boxes and guarding of key installations. The largely unstated premise was that this terrorist threat was now partly an Islamist one, which could be countered through tightened immigration restrictions and surveillance of suspect foreign communities. Employing the kind of "straight talk" that has made him a populist hero for many at home and something of a villain abroad, Tokyo governor Ishihara (who had earlier said that MOFA's negotiator with North Korea deserved the bomb in his garage) went a step further. In trying to establish special crisis management units, Ishihara found that some of his intelligence-gathering plans against possible al Qaeda strikes in Tokyo were not feasible because he could not find Arabic-speaking staff. He then took a more direct approach, imploring the Metropolitan Police Department to have quick trigger fingers in the event of any suspicion of terrorism. "Don't hesitate—just shoot," he reportedly told them, "and I'll take responsibility."[68] There is little question as to who will take the bullet in the event of rapid police action. In early 2004, Sassa Atsuyuki, the crisis management specialist and former high-ranking NPA official, argued that effective counterterrorism would require racial profiling (which he simply calls "racial discrimination," or *jinshu sabetsu*) primarily of Arabs and Muslims, a move that he defended as "unavoidable" (*sezaru o enai*).[69]

The interest in tightening Japan's stance on international terrorism would later culminate in an action plan released in December 2004 by a taskforce headed by Fukuda's successor as chief cabinet secretary, Hosoda Hiroyuki. Announcing, for example, tighter coordination with the international Financial Action Task Force (FATF) for monitoring the flow of financial resources of terrorists, the plan also advocated taking tighter control over foreigners, including fingerprinting upon entry and exit of those foreigners other than permanent residents.[70] The plan aroused criticism among advocates of foreigners' rights,[71] becoming even more unnervingly Orwellian when Liberal Democratic Party members announced that foreigner registration cards would carry "integrated circuit chips" providing data that would be stored at an unnamed "intelligence" facility.[72] The *Yomiuri Shimbun*, however, had a point in suggesting that the real goal of the action plan was simply to bring Japan's counterterrorism laws into line with those of other advanced industrial nations.[73] But if international standards for counterterrorism were more important for Japan in 2004–2005 than in the 1980s, they reflected the potential costs of the nation's strategy in supporting the U.S.-led War on Terror, or of becoming a "normal" country with an operative military. After all, if Madrid (and, by July 2005, London as well) could become targets, why not Tokyo?

For Koizumi, increased public concern about al Qaeda was therefore a mixed blessing. Although it certainly provided additional impetus to NPA and LDP requests for increased police funding, worries about terrorism implicitly called into question his military strategy. Until the September 11 attacks, Japanese counterterrorism policy had been premised on the belief that the country's limited political profile meant that it was not a terrorist target. Even after September 11, the government had not changed its judgment about the likelihood of attacks by transnational terrorist groups, but had rather redefined its troubled relationship with North Korea as a counterterrorism issue. As such, it provided new justification for long-planned but politically costly security steps meant to deal with regional military concerns and only tangentially with the types of "homeland security" issues increasingly prevalent in other advanced industrial nations. As the Bush administration—representing Japan's closest ally—tried to rewrite international counterterrorism norms by justifying preemptive military action against Iraq to prevent future terrorism, the Japanese government seized on the opportunity to develop a larger international profile. This had now attracted unwelcome attention from a highly visible transnational terrorist organization that otherwise would likely have ignored Japan.

The decision to send troops to Iraq thus demonstrated not simply the mobilization of changing norms to take controversial steps but a wholesale revision of the political principle on which Japan's international counterterrorism stance had rested. Although the Tokyo Metropolitan Police Department and prefectural police forces went on higher alert at the time of the Iraq deployment, and MOFA instituted new travel warnings for Japanese overseas, the Koizumi cabinet's primary concerns lay with the safety of the lightly armed, legally constrained SDF units in the terribly unstable Iraqi environment. First relying on local bodyguards and then on Dutch forces for protection, the SDF became so immobilized that Koizumi's claim of offering humanitarian assistance seemed remarkably dubious; Ōnishi Kensuke, the head of one Japan's largest not-for-profit organizations, Peace Winds–Japan, explained that Japanese NPOs could do more for Iraqi reconstruction at less than 1 percent the cost of the SDF mission.[74] His claim received further validation when MOFA announced on April 20, 2004, that it would pay a Paris-based aid organization to supply water to Iraqis, the same type of mission charged to the SDF. With the grant of ¥39 million (about $350,000), France's Agency for Technical Cooperation and Development would supply 550 tons of water per day to help sixty-four thousand Iraqis. The SDF, at a cost of ¥40.3 billion (about $36 million), supplied eighty tons of water for sixteen thousand people—at least on those days when the security situation permitted them to leave their base camp.[75]

For leftists Iraq represented a crucial case, both as an opportunity to demonstrate the superiority of the nonmilitary route for humanitarian assistance and to uncover the violent conditions that the Koizumi cabinet implicitly endorsed by supporting the U.S. invasion. And the hostage crisis involving Imai, Takato, and Kōriyama played directly into this political battle. This was hardly the first time that Japanese had been victimized in the post-9/11 deployments; a Japanese journalist had briefly been held hostage by a Taliban-affiliated faction in Afghanistan in 2001, and two Japanese diplomats were killed by unknown gunmen in Iraq in early 2003. But in this instance the Saraya al-Mujahideen demanded that the government withdraw its troops from Iraq and threatened to burn the hostages alive, releasing a video in which hooded militants held knives to the hostages' throats. Although often discussed, these portions of the video did not appear widely on Japanese television until after the hostages returned home safely. Given earlier hostage crises—for example, the Dhaka incident, described in chapter 5, in which Prime Minister Fukuda had declared that "a human life is heavier than the earth"— Koizumi and his chief cabinet secretary, Fukuda Yasuo (the son of the earlier prime minister), clearly saw the risk. The brutal deaths of the hostages, if ascribed to a failed policy and the prime minister's unwillingness to make concessions, might be shocking enough to knock out the cabinet.

But something unexpected happened, largely because the ground for debating Japan's global responsibilities had shifted. Koizumi himself was likely surprised when the hostage crisis gave him and his deputy a political fissure to exploit. When the hostages' families began to appear on television, with Takato's brother Shūichi being the most voluble and critical of the government, Japanese opinion split. Nationalists on "Channel 2," Japan's massive chat room website, immediately identified the hostages as naive, unpatriotic "idiots" (*baka*), whose effort to embarrass the government had landed them in hot water.[76] Now their Communist families (Imai's parents quickly were exposed as members of the Japanese Communist Party) were demanding that Japan take the disgraceful step of complying with terrorist demands by withdrawing the Self-Defense Forces.

Dispatching a MOFA/NPA team to Jordan to attempt to secure the release of the hostages, the Koizumi cabinet quickly moved to ensure that critics focused on the hostages rather than on the government. In a press briefing on April 8, as news was breaking about the incident, Chief Cabinet Secretary Fukuda, asked whether he could have predicted that Japanese would become hostages, said, "We don't know what's happening. But we've told Japanese not to enter Iraq."[77] In the following days, Fukuda, Koizumi, and Foreign Minister Kawaguchi Yoriko consistently emphasized that although the government was taking extraordinary steps to secure the safe return of the hostages, responsibility ultimately lay with the five people (two more hostages were subsequently taken) who had ignored repeated MOFA warnings not to travel to Iraq. On April 10, a second note, purportedly from the Saraya al-Mujahideen, promised to release the hostages unharmed; it seemed so calibrated to Japanese left-wing rhetoric—including a reference to the illegality of the Self-Defense Forces[78]—that a number of Japanese conservatives, including some in the government, began to suspect and hint darkly that the hostages had actually been in on the scheme.

Within days, conservative media voices consistently began to deploy the term "*jiko sekinin*" (self-responsibility), which had been at the core of government public relations efforts on counterterrorism in the 1990s. In this instance, however, it became less a tactical reminder of the limits of government counterterrorism capabilities and more a moral statement about fault and accountability. For left-wing critics of the Iraq policy, the Koizumi cabinet was at fault; after all, seven Chinese taken hostage had been released immediately, suggesting that only those nations dispatching troops would be targets. For conservatives, however, the ir-responsible young people—in their version, a highly unprofessional photographer, a marijuana-smoking single woman, and an eighteen-year-old with delusions of government conspiracies—clearly had placed themselves and the nation's reputation at risk.[79] The families, who had started to receive threats by telephone and e-mail, moderated their rhetoric and dropped their demands, moving instead to request politely that the government do everything possible to prevent their loved ones' immolation. For conservatives, the hostages had been far worse than naive and unprepared—they had been disloyal and perhaps seditious, undermining the government's ability to play a proper and respectable role in international affairs.

Japan's "unique" culture once again became a favorite explanation for the handling of the hostage situation, though in a way that differed dramatically from similar arguments in earlier terrorist incidents. In the hijacking cases described in chapter 5, intense public and private pressure to return hostages had convinced policymakers that failure to do so would ultimately require their resignations. Many described this to me in cultural terms—for example, Japanese are exceptionally interested in human connections rather than in adherence to abstract principles of counterterrorism—that displayed at least a fundamental misunderstanding of similar pressures facing counterparts in other governments. In 2004, however, the vindictive treatment of the hostages in the Japanese press and by the government (which ultimately demanded that each reimburse the government for medical examination and airfare home) drew cultural explanations from abroad, including the *New York Times,* which referred to Japan's "hierarchical ties that have governed this island nation for centuries and that, at moments of crises, invariably reassert themselves."[80] Naturally, in the course of the five years from the 1999 Kyrgyzstan case to the 2004 Iraq hostage crisis, Japanese culture had not undergone a sea change from generosity to mendacity.

But the political context had been dramatically altered. As Japanese observers rushed to analyze *jikosekininron* (discourses of self-responsibility), they underscored the tensions facing Koizumi's cabinet. Liberals pointed to Koizumi's rejection of the term "combat zone" to describe Iraq, as doing so would legally require the withdrawal of troops, and his simultaneous claim that the situation was so self-evidently dangerous that Japanese unaffiliated with the government were there at their own risk. Japan's most famous investigative journalist, Tachibana Takashi, argued that in the rush to send troops, the Koizumi cabinet had forgotten to create a real policy (*musaku no saku*); in his view, the U.S.-led occupation and the Japanese government's shameful capitulation to U.S. policy were responsible for the hostage crisis and other terrorist incidents.[81]

On the other hand, conservatives continued to take the opportunity to bash antimilitarists intent on undermining Japanese foreign policy. For Morimoto Satoshi, a well-known former Defense Agency official and self-described "Japanese neocon," the hostage crisis had been an unwelcome sideshow, the sort of thing that might make the Koizumi administration change its stance on keeping troops in Iraq.[82] Others focused on the selfishness of these young people who had gone off to Iraq to "find themselves" (*jibun sagashi*) without considering the consequences for anyone else. In the most widely read monthly opinion magazine, *Bungei Shunju,* journalist Aonuma Yōichirō ridiculed their slapdash efforts by distinguishing between formal (and, in Japan, state-licensed) NPOs and the chaotic NGOs that allowed selfish young people to travel the world carelessly, pretending to help. Specifically with reference to Imai and Takato (who belonged to NGOs but had not been specifically sent by them to Iraq), Aonuma wrote, "One or two people, reinforcing one another's extreme comments at some bar can declare 'we're an NGO' [and become one] even if they don't actually do any real overseas activity" (*kyokutan na hanashi, izakaya de iki tōgō shita futari ga sono bāi de 'ore wa NGO da' to sengen shite shimaeba, kaigai ni mukete katsudō o okonawakutemo*).[83] In a less malicious but similar critique, social psychologist Okamoto Kōichi argued in *Chūō Kōron* that NGOs and NPOs have a naive view of human nature, and that in a dangerous world, it would be better to leave these functions to governments.[84]

The release of the hostages prompted speculation about how much money the government had spent in its rescue effort, especially by conservatives who demanded that the hostages be forced to foot the bill. In contrast to previous incidents, however, the general consensus held that there was no ransom payment. The Japanese government may have somehow "compensated" the Sunni clerics who served as intermediaries between the Saraya al-Mujahideen and MOFA representatives in Amman, and if such payment was made, a portion might have gone to the kidnappers. More likely, the decision to release the hostages came out of the unclear political alliances in war-torn Iraq, in which groups seen as killing sympathetic foreigners could have faced censure or worse from their embattled compatriots. Whether one believes, as do conservatives, that the release represented Sunni clerics' recognition of the Japanese government's good intentions, or, as do liberals, that it reflected Iraqi sympathy for the antigovernment Japanese, most observers evidently concluded that the government paid no direct ransom. The safe release of Imai, Takato, and Kōriyama, after eight days of captivity, was a momentary reprieve for the hostages, before an aggressive debriefing by MOFA and NPA officials in Amman[85] and public excoriation on their return to Tokyo.

Safety and Responsibility

With my obsessive-compulsive tendencies, I usually check two or three times to make sure I have turned off all the electrical devices in my apartment before leaving for a day. Before a trip, I double-check my preparations for all manner of emergencies, including travel or evacuation insurance when I go anywhere more dangerous than, say, central Wisconsin. By my high though emotionally unhealthy standards, Kōriyama, Imai, and Takato were a remarkably irresponsible, careless bunch. Who travels to a country in the midst of a violent occupation without being formally connected to some kind of functioning organization? Or without securing protection from their government? Or without having hired local bodyguards in advance, and then engaging in background checks on the bodyguards?

Japanese, apparently—or at least one might have determined after having seen the "overseas safety" animated videos described in chapter 5. But when Nicholas Berg, a U.S. contractor in Iraq, was kidnapped and beheaded in early 2004, no one suggested that he had been personally reckless in a manner reflecting American naiveté about the outside world. And even if the Japanese hostages had had remarkably innocent views of human nature and personal safety, one might judge it as a sign not of their personal failure but rather of the state's success: in having established a nearly impeccable public safety record at home and reasonably friendly relations abroad. Japan's international counterterrorism policies before September 11 were in fact predicated on this assumption. Because Japanese were accustomed to internationally unrealistic standards of public order and human decency, they were allegedly unprepared for the chaos and criminality awaiting them overseas. Before September 11, "self-responsibility" had been the buzzword for a government effort to get Japanese to take better care of themselves in places where the state might not be able to protect them. Afterward, it became an opportunity to remove a terrorist crisis from the thorny world of international politics, in which the Japanese government might be newly accountable, and to place it squarely in a familiar divide between loyal conservatives and disloyal leftists.

At another time, the hostage crisis might have been seen as bad luck, the fate of typically innocent Japanese in a world they did not create and could not understand. In 2004, however, it fundamentally challenged a strategy that had ironically been explained as Japan's new adherence to global efforts against terrorism. When Japan's most important partner, the United States, rewrote international counterterrorism norms to legitimate military action against sources of fear and uncertainty, the Japanese government seized the moment. Long prevented from going beyond minimal steps toward the development of a more expansive military capacity, conservatives in the Diet and the defense bureaucracy were able to reposition their distinctive national insecurities—of North Korean villainy and even of general foreign crime—as part of a global struggle. These were fears against which military tools, the kinds available to "normal" nations, would now be useful.

And so the capture of the hostages and the angry demands from their families were not a reminder of Japan's "wet" human connections and its social mindedness but rather a threat to the conservative effort to rebuild Japan. In Iraq, Japanese could be targeted as occupiers; at home, they might face the promised al Qaeda attacks for their cooperation with the United States. One might agree that the hostages had been irresponsible, but in Japanese debates their capture represented something other than simple youthful foolishness. Combined with the politically contested effort to expand the nation's regional military role, their trip to Iraq and treatment back home together tell us something about the goals and consequences of the government's adherence to changing counterterrorism norms. In their effort to operate outside of the state's authority and to critique military engagement, implicitly or explicitly, the hostages had undermined Japan's trajectory toward becoming the normal nation to which many conservatives aspire. Their violent deaths, like the increasingly assertive counterterrorism preparations at home, might have served as an unwelcome sign of what normality now meant.

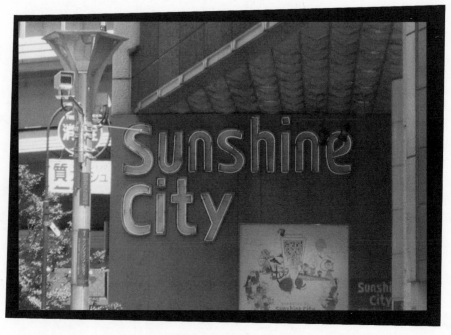

A police crime prevention camera (upper left) on Ikebukuro's Sunshine-Dōri, in front of the Sunshine City shopping complex, June 2004.

CHAPTER SEVEN

LOCAL SCAPEGOATS AND OTHER UNINTENDED CONSEQUENCES

As it had done twice before, in 1994 and 2000, the *Yomiuri Shimbun*—Japan's most widely read newspaper—released a proposal in 2004 for the revision of Japan's constitution. And, as it was twice before, the major target was Article IX, which renounces the right to war and explicitly forbids the maintenance of "war potential," including formal armed forces. This long-standing source of resentment among conservatives, however, was not the only item on the *Yomiuri*'s agenda. In terms somewhat reminiscent of the nineteenth-century proclamations such as the Imperial Rescript on Education,[1] the *Yomiuri* also recommended the insertion of a new clause into the document's preamble, stipulating that the family is the foundation of Japanese society (*shakai no kisō*).[2] The proposal's varied purposes included encouraging the reliance on families rather than on the state for social welfare. The *Yomiuri* saw Japan as threatened by both internal and external forces, not only poorly prepared to deal with persistent regional military threats but facing growing social disorder that they saw as a consequence of the breakdown of families. To be sure, gangs of bleached-blonde teenagers drinking, smoking, and loitering around nightclubs after midnight pose a different problem than the existential threat of a rickety North Korean government armed with nuclear missiles. In expanding the suggestions for revision, the *Yomiuri*'s editors gambled that readers feared both the military menace from abroad and the seemingly chaotic social transformations within.

Even if they become law, the *Yomiuri*'s proposed constitutional revisions would almost be legal exclamation points on ongoing debates: dramatic, to be sure, but not necessarily revolutionary. After all, frequent constitutional "reinterpretations" have already provided Japan's Self-Defense Forces overseas military opportunities that would have been nearly unimaginable in the 1960s. And government social programs and the handling of juvenile delinquency reflect relatively conservative notions regarding the proper structure and behavior of the family. But the proposals to revise the constitution aim at making its primary emphases—on individual rights, on pacifism—negotiable rather than foundational. For many on the right, Japan's oft-debated but completely unrevised constitution has been a shameful and imposed burden, preventing the government from taking the kinds of steps it really needs to protect the nation from a menacing world and a crumbling social order. And yet the very distinctiveness of the Japanese constitution's constraints on state power provides conservatives with a crucial tool for legitimizing their efforts to alter it: they can claim that they are simply trying to make Japan normal.

In the preceding chapters, I focused on two cases—child prostitution and terrorism—in which international norms became crucial tools for those trying to enhance the Japanese state's authority. Particularly in their struggles with left-leaning forces that have used the constitution as a bulwark against remilitarization and the recrudescence of an older family ideal, conservative leaders have been able to point to global standards and argue that Japan needs to comply. Normal governments, for example, have military forces capable of fighting real wars; in normal nations, middle-class high school girls do not sell their used panties to businessmen. According to the liberal and conservative forces facing off against one another, each of these issue areas cuts to the core not only of what Japan is but also what it is supposed to become. And so when political figures in Japan fight over sex and violence, they believe themselves to be in competition over Japan's future, and they are constantly on the lookout for tools that might be used to ensure their victory. By finding evidence that their preferred policies adhere to some kind of global standard, legislators, activists, bureaucrats, and intellectuals can argue that they want Japan to contribute to international society or to recognize its international responsibility. In this view, quashing deviant sexual behavior and rewriting the rules on the state's use of force should not be seen as controversial bids for authority; they instead represent necessary steps for normality.

Busy Undertakers

I originally planned to open this book with an epigraph from one of my favorite hip-hop artists; I simply could not decide which one. I might have gone with Mos Def's line "Gunmen and stockholders try to merit my fear."[3] After the 2004 release of *The Tipping Point* by the Roots, I had been leaning toward the post-9/11 line "When the undertaker's busy and the prisons is crowded / People livin' in fear because they vision is clouded."[4] At first, the lyrics seemed to me to have nearly universal meaning, to be as useful in setting the tone for my book about Japan as they had been in anchoring songs about the United States by especially shrewd and nuanced rappers. Mos Def urges defiance against those with awesome claims about their own power; the Roots point to the difficulty of seeing clearly in times of apparent peril. But I am already too inclined to see other countries' problems through American lenses, and I realized that this story—while not, I think, an exclusively Japanese story—has a different moral than the common recognition that leaders use fear in ways that we should challenge rather than simply accept.

Instead, in these cases, fear is shaped in part by global norms, even by those designed to craft a better world, one free from cruelty, random violence, and exploitation; norms serve both as information about proper behavior and as tools that political agents can employ. By using two radically different cases of international norms of criminal justice in this book, I have addressed local actors from across Japan's political spectrum, from the radical feminists in the Tokyo ECPAT office to the conservative counterterrorism experts in the Council for Public Policy. In both cases, however, I have ended up focusing especially on the successes of conservatives in implementing the norms. In doing so, I know I may sound vaguely paranoid, as if the Japanese Right has something approximating a hegemonic ability to frame issues in Japanese politics. It is fair to say, I think, that my own political biases make me far more likely to react critically to conservative constructions than to liberal ones, though I have tried to maintain an open mind.

Even so, at this time, in this place, and on these issues, I believe the emphasis to be fair. Japan's political climate has undergone a sea change since 1993, particularly with the collapse of the traditional Left and the rise of a primarily moderate opposition to the conservative ruling party. Japan's conservatives are, of course, a diverse lot, and trying to shoehorn all of their opinions into one large box is both unfair and inaccurate. But it seems reasonable to suggest that on matters of law enforcement, Japan's conservatives generally support a more active state role in challenging the kind of disorder many describe as threatening Japan from both within and without. For them, the anxiety produced by Japan's troubles in the 1990s has made it even more imperative to dismantle at least some of the constitutional and legal constraints on the government's surveillance of and responses to those problems that jeopardize Japan's physical safety and social order.

Who am I to disagree? I acknowledged in chapter 1 that the September 11 attacks, coming only a year after my departure from my role as token left-winger in the State Department's counterterrorism office, left me a particularly tremulous critic of conservative demands for more authority. From the perspective of Japanese conservatives, both sets of issues jeopardizing Japanese security—the collapse of its traditional moral order, as evidenced by the shocking behavior of the kogals, and the threats of physical violence posed by North Korea and by outsiders in Japan's midst—obviously call for action. After all, to use language common to American social reformers, would it not be worth it to give police more authority over teens if doing so can save the life of even one child? And on terrorism, how much more villainous would Kim Jong Il have to become before liberals like me would be willing to acknowledge that Japan needs greater leeway in its application of military force?

But of course, the solutions are older than the problems at hand, and the solutions themselves rest in part on assumptions regarding what other (normal) states can do that the Japanese government cannot. Japan's parliamentary hawks have pushed for decades against the plastic wall created by Article IX, and the police have found themselves blocked for decades by the courts and civil libertarians from gaining a freer hand vis-à-vis Japanese teens. In fact, it is only because conservatives have *not* been hegemonic that they have turned to the legitimacy afforded to them by international norms. By framing greater coercive authority over teens and an expanded role for the Japanese military as the contributions of a normal nation to international society, conservatives have sought to justify steps they had long wanted to take. In his study of Japanese and Italian leadership, Richard J. Samuels uses the term *bricoleur* to refer to actors who struggle to use and to reconstruct history, rather than to rebel against it, in order to justify change.[5] I have something similar in mind. The social role of norms suggests that they constitute actors' identities in vital ways, while actors also use them for their own purposes. Images of defense policy in "normal" countries like the United States,

Great Britain, China, and Australia have clearly shaped and informed the judgments of Japan's security hawks. And yet, in stressing Japan's abnormality, conservatives make selective and strategic use of these norms to justify their distinctive and sometimes idiosyncratic positions. Norms therefore constrain ideas even as they become instruments in prevailing domestic debates. But local application requires local threats; the globalization of security rests on the "glocalization" of fear.

Whose Intentions?

If international norms on security and crime are turned against locally available scapegoats who are not themselves at the core of the globally recognized problem, we might view the outcomes to be the "unintended consequences" of norms. Doing so would give us a way to collapse the problem into more conventional discussions in political science; after all, unintended consequences are now considered crucial issues in comparative politics.[6] But it raises the question: Whose intentions? Surely, the Japanese political actors pushing for penalties on schoolgirls for compensated dating, or for a more expansive security strategy, have very much intended to use norms in the ways in which they did. Because norms are not self-enacting, they rely for their adoption on the actions of real people, who bring with them the baggage of prior debates, positions, and goals. This is the kind of language that makes norms theorists despair, because if norms differ across national contexts according to the interpretive schema and political machinations of different individuals, what is the point of talking about them? Surely, this admission risks the larger enterprise; perhaps norms do not matter at all.

My sense, however, is very much the opposite: norms do matter. Neither of the cases I examine in this book would have played out as it did without the influence of transnational movements or changing global standards of problem solving. But their deviations from straightforward projections of what norms do suggest that the local context matters as well, and in specific and perhaps predictable ways. In this case, the nature of the local fears—the available scapegoats—shaped the ways in which policymakers tweaked and shifted the meaning of norms to fit them to more immediate problems. Because these policy arenas involved law enforcement and security norms, which essentially stipulated a larger coercive role for the state in people's lives, political actors have needed to justify the wider range of state action by identifying those people who need to be controlled, punished, or eliminated. As a general proposition, this probably speaks more to the nature of security norms than it does to the nature of Japan, and we would do well to investigate similar types of norms across nations to consider the way in which scapegoating might become the predictable—if unintended—consequence.

The logic would likely differ for other norms that stipulate specific enlargement of or limits on the sphere of state activity, though I do not wish to suggest that norms are bad or undesirable. In fact, my daily experience of politics relies on my own normative claims about the types of rights all people should have, regardless of their national or cultural context. But norms that generate a larger role for certain state actors will empower them to tackle or move into certain issue areas that they had previously been unable to touch. Even if unintentional from a global politics perspective, certain consequences might be anticipated. Environmental norms might become pretexts for agricultural protectionism, to the disadvantage of farmers in developing nations; property rights norms might be used to legitimize continuing global inequality, both within and across national borders. These consequences too might be viewed as the unintentional results of global standards and agreements, but they are generally acknowledged and should affect the ways in which we theorize about politics.

Counterterrorism norms offer among the more obvious examples. Even as states converge on specific law enforcement practices, the effects are far from uniform; they will likely be exercised especially on ethnic or religious minorities judged to be supporters of or synonymous with the terrorist threat. And so in the United States, even before the September 11 attacks, counterterrorism efforts focused especially on Arab-American and Muslim communities rather than Christian fundamentalists, Cuban expatriates, or other groups whose members have occasionally carried out terrorist violence.[7] The experiences of other countries, where common law enforcement techniques differentially target Irish Catholics, Moros, or Basques, reinforce the notion that there are common problems in the spread of counterterrorism policies. Sexual exploitation norms would seem to be less likely to produce unintended consequences, as they ostensibly target only pedophiles. Even so, with the political connections between children and innocence on the one hand, and sex and shame on the other, we should not be surprised to find the mixture combustible. And the demand for a larger police role will likely be premised in part on notions of proper morality as much as it will on a universal understanding of children's rights. In both cases, transnational norms, through which other international actors demand that Japan contribute to the solution of a global criminal problem, are refracted through local prisms of fear, threat, and danger, and become political instruments for those actors looking to legitimize their larger goals. On balance, both sets of policies might be good; Japanese might be safer with tougher security rules and better policing of sexually active (and, in many ways, vulnerable) schoolgirls. But we should neither forget nor relegate to the category of unintended consequences ways in which tighter state authority over morality and an increasingly active military stance partly define the country that Japan is becoming.

Asking the Question

And so my goal in this book has been to examine how law enforcement and security norms lend themselves well to a specific type of manipulation, and how their "glocalization" will likely follow a reasonably predictable path. By choosing Japan, I have stacked the deck in my favor; this is a country in which international norms have often played a crucial legitimating role for policy change, and also a country in which widespread anxiety is the crucial context for the extension of state authority. Even so, I have come up with a decidedly mixed and complex picture, in which international norms partly work in the way in which theorists generally suppose, but then veer off in directions that depend largely on the country's existing political fissures. My expectation, then, is hardly that this book will have made a clear causal link or that it will have uncovered the multi-issue orientations of key actors, like the Liberal Democratic Party, the Japan Defense Agency, or the National Police Agency. My objective is more modest: by paying more attention to domestic debates and the presumptive policy effect of norms, we might be able to anticipate some of the unintended consequences by considering how they will likely animate and reflect longstanding political divisions.

At the very least, I hope that this book will encourage people to inquire differently about norms. In addition to our research, for example, on how various countries respond to specific norms, I would like to see us group norms in alternative ways, and ask about how different prescriptions for the state's role lend themselves to assorted methods of political exploitation. Doing so may enable us to envision different connections between norms and rationality. We can recognize the crucial role played by political interests but embed those interests in long-term

political cleavages. We might even gain new insight into politics, globalization, and the interpretive frames that local actors use to understand
the world and its omnipresent, though shifting, cultural expectations.

In mid-March 2004, I traveled to Ikebukuro—the shopping and
nightlife district in northeastern Tokyo that, as noted in chapter 1, had
been my transportation hub and my introduction to the enjo kōsai topic
eight years earlier—to pick up a DVD as a present for a friend. While
walking down Sunshine-Dōri,[8] I overheard two young women talking behind me. One of them said to the other, "Kowai, gaijin wa kowai" ("Foreigners are really scary"). The other replied, "Ee, kowai, kowai" ("Yeah,
definitely").

Admittedly, I was not looking my best that day. My efforts to cut my
own hair—because I am afraid of Japan's relatively high levels of He-
patitis B and had grown tired of barbers drawing blood every time they
go after me with one of their electric clippers—had resulted in yet another mishap. Part of the back of my head was nearly bald, a fact I was
trying to disguise with a baseball cap. Add to that my unshaven face and
my gray hooded sweatshirt, and I barely looked presentable for attend-
ing a Star Trek convention let alone qualified to be a visiting researcher
at Japan's most prestigious university.

I could tell from the tone of the conversation behind me, though, that
I had missed an important bit of context. I sensed they were not talking
about me but rather about some foreigners they came across in some
other part of their lives. Given the extraordinarily international nature
of Ikebukuro, where one would not be more than a few meters from an
Asian, African, Latino, or white foreigner, I found the conversation
vaguely hilarious. I quickly turned around, smiling, just to see who they
were and what they were chatting about, and I realized that they were
uniformed schoolgirls, no older than the ones I had seen stripping on the
subway in 1996. One of them saw me looking, and I turned away both embarrassed and a bit unnerved. The girls started laughing, and one called
after me, "Chigau, chigau, omae ja nai" ("No, no, not you,"—though "you"
hardly captures the casual, even dismissive quality of "omae"). I kept
walking.

The most common reaction of my colleagues to this story is that I am
an idiot; the girls were practically inviting me into a conversation, using
informal language that implied a gruff friendliness rather than hostility,
remote deference, or aloofness. How could I not have taken the chance
to chat with them, to ask them about what they meant or the way they—
as schoolgirls—think about their place in contemporary Japan? Or

about their views of foreigners, who serve as alternate bogeymen for many in the media when they tire of schoolgirls? Researchers are supposed to thrive in moments like this, seizing the opportunity to expand and contextualize their knowledge; I had manifestly failed, especially embarrassing given that I was writing a book exploring the political uses of fear.

In imagining how they might have explained their comments to me, I have considered the possibility that they might find foreigners scary in general, though I think it unlikely. They seemed intimidated neither by me nor by the African men trying to hawk hip-hop clothing a few meters in front of us. I wonder if perhaps, as Governor Ishihara has encouraged them to do, they consider foreigners (particularly Muslims or Arabs) to be terrorist threats. I suppose that is somewhat more likely, though I doubt this too. Maybe they were simply talking about merchants at the various flea markets around Tokyo, and find the foreigners to be more menacing traders; *kowai* means scary, but it can be used in a variety of ways, most of them less rather than more terrifying. Most often, however, my imagination turns puerile. I envision the girls involved in some kind of media-hyped drama, either in enjo kōsai dalliances or in drug deals where foreign johns or foreign pushers are especially frightening counterparts.

And so when I ask myself why I did not take this surely harmless opportunity to ask which foreigners the girls found scary, I realize that I was far more frightened of them than they were of me. Part of this was male insecurity, of being laughed at or ridiculed, especially by teenage girls. But more to the point, my reaction to them reflected in part my own unconscious acceptance of widespread claims about dangerous Japanese high school girls. Does this make me especially credulous? Or does it drop uncomfortable hints about my motives, as a white man, for studying sex in Asia? Because it happened so fast—a comment, a turn, another comment, and finally escape, no more than ten seconds in all—I believe that my brain articulated nothing more substantial than discomfort followed by a desire to flee. But it is clear that the discourses surrounding schoolgirls in Japan—discourses of which I am suspicious, just as I am of those invoking terrorists and criminals—have affected me as well. At the very least, Japanese fears have merged with my own continual misgivings about my place as a researcher and about Asia's place in my imagination, and so I instinctively made a bad decision, as people often do when they are anxious or afraid.

Which is too bad. I have no doubt that I would have found the conversation with them enlightening, possibly surprising, and almost certainly enjoyable. Maybe I would have understood better how they think of the police and the role of the state in their lives. And perhaps their interaction with me would have encouraged them to think about the diversity of foreigners, about the ways in which we live our lives in Japan, and about the people whose unseen and unknown activities now animate media discussions of the security threats facing the country. I do not mean to overstate what this conversation might have accomplished. I seriously doubt that it would have revealed anything useful to me about how political figures use fear to accomplish specific policy changes, or about how international norms facilitate the process. Even our enriched pictures of one another (this is, of course, based on the insane premise that they were as interested in my life as I was in theirs) would have been incomplete, filled in by our larger beliefs and uncertainties.

But I wish I had had the courage to ask.

NOTES

1. Fear, Norms, and Politics in Contemporary Japan

1. Threat and reassurance were crucial issues in the work of Murray Edelman. See especially *The Symbolic Uses of Politics* (1964; repr., Urbana: University of Illinois Press, 1985), 188–89; and *Constructing the Political Spectacle* (Chicago: University of Chicago Press, 1988), 12–36.

2. Joseph R. Gusfield, *The Culture of Public Problems: Drinking-Driving and the Symbolic Order* (Chicago: University of Chicago Press, 1981). For a "pre-scientific" version of a similar process, see Paul Boyer and Stephen Nissenbaum, *Salem Possessed: The Social Origins of Witchcraft* (Cambridge: Harvard University Press, 1974).

3. See, for example, Arthur J. Clark, "Scapegoating: Dynamics and Interventions in Group Counseling," *Journal of Counseling and Development* 80 (Summer 2002): 271–76.

4. René Girard, "The Plague in Literature and Myth," *Texas Studies in Literature and Language* 15, special classics issue (1974): 883–50, reprinted in Girard's collection *"To Double Business Bound": Essays in Literature, Mimesis, and Anthropology* (Baltimore: Johns Hopkins University Press, 1978), 136–54; René Girard, *Violence and the Sacred*, trans. Patrick Gregory (Baltimore: Johns Hopkins University Press, 1972), especially 1–67.

5. Barry Glassner, *The Culture of Fear: Why Americans Are Afraid of the Wrong Things* (New York: Basic Books, 2000).

6. See, for example, Corey Robin, *Fear: The History of a Political Idea* (Oxford: Oxford University Press, 2004); and contributions by Robin, Cass Sunstein, Jessica Stern, and others to the special issue "Fear: Its Political Uses and Abuses," *Social Research* 71, no. 4 (Winter 2004).

7. Kenneth Waltz, *Theory of International Politics* (Reading, Mass.: Addison-Wesley, 1979); Waltz, "Reflections on *Theory of International Politics*: A Response to my Critics," in *Neorealism and Its Critics*, ed. Robert O. Keohane (New York: Columbia University Press, 1986), 322–45; Stephen M. Walt, *The Origins of Alliances* (Ithaca: Cornell University Press, 1987); John J. Mearsheimer, *The Tragedy of Great Power Politics* (New York: W. W. Norton, 2003).

8. See, for example, Robert Axelrod and Robert O. Keohane, "Achieving Cooper-

ation under Anarchy: Strategies and Institutions," in *Neorealism and Neoliberalism: The Contemporary Debate*, ed. David A. Baldwin (New York: Columbia University Press, 1993), 85–115; Joseph S. Nye, "Maintaining a Nonproliferation Regime," *International Organization* 35, no. 1 (Winter 1981): 15–38.

9. Mark C. Suchman and Dana P. Eyre, "Military Procurement as Rational Myth: Notes on the Social Construction of Weapons Proliferation," *Sociological Forum* 7, no. 1 (March 1992): 137–61.

10. Alexander E. Wendt, "Anarchy Is What States Make of It: The Social Construction of Power Politics," *International Organization* 46, no. 2 (Spring 1992): 391–425; Alexander E. Wendt, "The Agent-Structure Problem in International Relations Theory," *International Organization* 41, no. 3 (Summer 1987): 335–70.

11. Audie Klotz, *Norms in International Relations: The Struggle against Apartheid* (Ithaca: Cornell University Press, 1995). For similar cases, including prostitution and slavery, see Ethan A. Nadelmann, "Global Prohibition Regimes: The Evolution of Norms in International Society," *International Organization* 44, no. 4 (Autumn 1990): 479–526, especially 491–98.

12. Ronald J. Jepperson, "Institutions, Institutional Effects, and Institutionalism," in *The New Institutionalism in Organizational Analysis*, ed. Paul J. DiMaggio and Walter W. Powell (Chicago: University of Chicago Press, 1991), 143–63.

13. See, for example, Thomas J. Bierstaker and Cynthia Weber, eds., *State Sovereignty as Social Construct* (Cambridge: Cambridge University Press, 1996); Bruce Cronin, *Institutions for the Common Good: International Protection Regimes and International Society* (Cambridge: Cambridge University Press, 2003).

14. Martha Finnemore, *National Interests in International Society* (Ithaca: Cornell University Press, 1996); John Boli and George M. Thomas, eds., *Constructing World Culture: International Nongovernmental Organizations since 1875* (Stanford: Stanford University Press, 1999).

15. Audie Klotz, "Norms Reconstituting Interests: Global Racial Equality and U.S. Sanctions against South Africa," *International Organization* 49, no. 3 (Summer 1995): 451–78; Richard Price, "Reversing the Gun Sights: Transnational Civil Society Targets Land Mines," *International Organization* 52, no. 3 (Summer 1998): 613–44.

16. Peter M. Haas, "Introduction: Epistemic Communities and International Policy Coordination," *International Organization* 46, no. 1 (Winter 1992): 1–35.

17. See, for example, Michael C. Desch, "Culture Clash: Assessing the Importance of Ideas in International Security," *International Security* 23, no. 1 (Summer 1998): 141–70. For an overview of the debate, see Miles Kahler, "Rationality in International Relations," *International Organization* 52, no. 4 (Autumn 1998): 919–41.

18. Jeffrey Checkel, "The Constructivist Turn in International Relations Theory," *World Politics* 50, no. 2 (January 1998): 324–48; Martha Finnemore and Kathryn Sikkink, "Taking Stock: The Constructivist Research Program in International Relations and Comparative Politics," *Annual Review of Political Science 2001*, 391–416.

19. Thomas Risse, for example, builds from Jürgen Habermas's theory of communicative action to emphasize the role that argument and debate can have in shaping norm adoption. See Risse, "International Norms and Domestic Change: Arguing and Communicative Behavior in the Human Rights Area," *Politics & Society* 27, no. 4 (December 1999): 529–59; "'Let's Argue': Communicative Action in World Politics," *International Organization* 54, no. 1 (Winter 2000): 1–39.

20. During the 2000 campaign, Condoleezza Rice wrote a *Foreign Affairs* article in which "norms" became synonymous with the ostensibly wishy-washy, idealistic foreign policy of Bill Clinton. See Rice, "Campaign 2000: Promoting the National Interest," *Foreign Affairs* 79, no. 1 (January–February 2000): 45–62.

21. R. Charli Carpenter, "'Women and Children First': Gender, Norms, and Humanitarian Evacuation in the Balkans 1991–1995," *International Organization* 57, no. 3 (Fall 2003): 661–94.

22. Kay B. Warren, *Indigenous Movements and Their Critics: Pan-Maya Activism in Guatemala* (Princeton: Princeton University Press, 1998), 52–85.

23. Rodney Bruce Hall, "The Discursive Demolition of the Asian Development Model in the Asian Financial Crisis," *International Studies Quarterly* 47, no. 1 (March 2003): 71–99.

24. Decoupling of practices from institutions has been a central theme in the institutionalist and world polity literature. See, for example, John W. Meyer and John Boli, "World Authority and the Nation-State," *American Journal of Sociology* 103, no. 1 (July 1997): 144–81, at 154–55. For an application to international norms, see Antje Wiener, "Towards a Transnational Nomos: The Role of Institutions in the Process of Constitutionalization," in *European Integration: The New German Scholarship,* Jean Monnet Working Paper 9/03 (Heidelberg: Max Planck Institute for Comparative Public Law and International Law, 2003).

25. The key postmodern study of the constitutive function of the prison is Michel Foucault, *Discipline and Punish: The Birth of the Modern Prison,* trans. Alan Sheridan (New York: Vintage, 1995 [1977]).

26. See the comments by Grand Mufti Sheik Abdulaziz bin Abdullah al-Sheik in the Reuters wire report "Saudi Arabia's Top Cleric Condemns Calls for Women's Rights," *New York Times,* January 22, 2004, A13.

27. Antonio Sérgio Alfredo Guimarães, "Racial Insult in Brazil," *Discourse & Society* 14, no. 2 (March 2003): 133–51. On the continuing idealization of violent criminals as poor, unemployed, black Brazilians, see Marcelo Gomes Justo and Helena Singer, "Sociology of Law in Brazil: A Critical Approach," *American Sociologist* 32, no. 2 (Summer 2001): 10–25, at 15–18.

28. See, for example, Karl-Dieter Opp, "When Do Norms Emerge by Human Design and When by the Unintended Consequences of Human Action?" *Rationality and Society* 14, no. 2 (May 2002): 131–58; Dennis Chong, *Rational Lives: Norms and Values in Politics and Society* (Chicago: University of Chicago Press, 2000); Michael Hechter and Satoshi Kanazawa, "Sociological Rational Choice Theory," *Annual Review of Sociology* 23 (1997): 191–214; and, specifically with regard to constructions of identity, David D. Laitin, *Identity in Formation: The Russian-Speaking Populations in the Near Abroad* (Ithaca: Cornell University Press, 1998); and James D. Fearon and David D. Laitin, "Violence and the Social Construction of Ethnic Identity," *International Organization* 54, no. 4 (Autumn 2000): 845–77.

29. For examples, see Norma Field, *In the Realm of a Dying Emperor* (1991; repr., New York: Vintage, 1993); Clayton Naff, *About Face: How I Stumbled onto Japan's Social Revolution* (New York: Kodansha America, 1996); John Nathan, *Japan Unbound: A Volatile Nation's Search for Pride and Purpose* (New York: Houghton Mifflin, 2004).

30. Peter J. Katzenstein, *Cultural Norms and National Security* (Ithaca: Cornell University Press, 1996); Thomas U. Berger, *Cultures of Antimilitarism: National Security in Germany and Japan* (Baltimore: Johns Hopkins University Press, 1998); Elizabeth Kier, *Imagining War: French and British Military Doctrine between the Wars* (Princeton: Princeton University Press, 1999); David Leheny, *The Rules of Play: National Identity and the Shaping of Japanese Leisure* (Ithaca: Cornell University Press, 2003); Jennifer Chan-Tiberghien, *Gender and Human Rights Politics in Japan: Global Norms and Domestic Networks* (Stanford: Stanford University Press, 2004); Petrice R. Flowers, "International Norms and Domestic Policies in Japan: Identity, Legitimacy and Civilization," PhD diss., University of Minnesota, 2003; Isao Miyaoka, *Legitimacy in International Society: Japan's Reaction to Global Wildlife Preservation* (New York: Palgrave Macmillan, 2004).

31. See Peter Carey's *Wrong about Japan: A Father's Journey with His Son* (New York: Knopf, 2005) for an account of how the Booker Prize–winning novelist tries to come to grips with the complexity of contemporary Japan. Sofia Coppola's film *Lost in Translation* similarly uses images of an oddball modern Japan but also relies on brief glimpses of the "traditional" Japan of geisha and shrines in Kyoto.

32. Kent E. Calder, "Japanese Foreign Economic Policy Formation: Explaining the Reactive State," *World Politics* 40, no. 4 (July 1998): 517–41.

33. See Peter Dauvergne, *Shadows in the Forest: Japan and the Politics of Timber in Southeast Asia* (Cambridge: MIT Press, 1997).

34. Although the country has been the world's leading or second-largest aid donor, its per capita generosity is limited, and critics have accused the government of using aid to promote national industrial objectives. See, for example, David Arase, *Buying Power: The Political Economy of Japan's Foreign Aid* (Boulder: Lynne Rienner, 1995).

35. Katherine Tegtmeyer-Pak, "Outsiders Moving In: Identity and Institutions in Japanese Responses to International Migration," PhD diss., Department of Political Science, University of Chicago, 1998; Amy Gurowitz, "Mobilizing International Norms: Domestic Actors, Immigrants, and the Japanese State," *World Politics* 51, no. 3 (April 1999): 413–45.

36. Chan-Tiberghien, *Gender and Human Rights Politics in Japan*.

37. Sheldon Garon, *Molding Japanese Minds: The State in Everyday Life* (Princeton: Princeton University Press, 1997).

38. Christine Ingebritsen refers to Norway's leadership in international environmental movements in spite of its pariah status over whaling: "The Politics of Whaling in Norway and Iceland," *Scandinavian Review* 85, no. 3 (Winter 1997–1998): 9–15.

39. William J. Long, "Nonproliferation as a Goal of Japanese Foreign Assistance," *Asian Survey* 39, no. 2 (March–April 1999): 328–47.

40. For an exploration of the tensions between democratization and Japan's economic interests in Asia, see Mikio Oishi and Fumitaka Furuoka, "Can Japanese Aid Be an Effective Tool of Influence?" *Asian Survey* 43, no. 6 (November–December 2003): 890–907.

41. Christina Davis, *Food Fights over Free Trade* (Princeton: Princeton University Press, 2003), 62, 163–65.

42. James Risen, "Broader Spy Powers Gaining Support," *New York Times,* September 16, 2001, A1.

43. Michael J. Bulzomi, "Foreign Intelligence Surveillance Act: Before and After the USA PATRIOT Act," *FBI Law Enforcement Bulletin* 72, no. 6 (June 2003): 25–32.

44. Quoted on *All Things Considered,* National Public Radio, March 18, 2004.

45. By most accounts, *Chūō Kōron* has been more conservative since its 1999 purchase by the *Yomiuri Shimbun.*

46. See, for example, Michael Schatzberg's example regarding the unmentionable possibility of "nationalizing" Microsoft during its recent legal battle with the U.S. government. In Michael G. Schatzberg, *Political Legitimacy in Middle Africa: Father, Family, Food* (Bloomington: Indiana University Press, 2001).

2. A "Vague Anxiety" in 1990s Japan

1. When acknowledged, the women often became the subject of moralistic accounts of their sex habits and other activities that would, in the end, lead to ruin. Marginalization was as much active as it was passive. I thank Laura Miller for making this point in correspondence.

2. William W. Kelly and Merry I. White, "Students, Slackers, Seniors, Singles, and Strangers: Transforming a Family-Nation," in *Beyond Japan: The Dynamics of East Asian Regionalism,* ed. Peter J. Katzenstein and Takashi Shiraishi (Ithaca: Cornell University Press, 2006).

3. Ueno Chizuko, "Modern Patriarch and the Formation of the Japanese Nation State," in *Multicultural Japan: Paleolithic to Postmodern,* ed. Donald Denoon, Mark Hudson, Gavan McCormack, and Tessa Morris-Suzuki (Cambridge: Cambridge University Press, 1996), 213–23; Nishikawa Yūko, "The Modern Japanese Family System: Unique or Universal?" in *Multicultural Japan,* ed. Denoon et al., 224–32.

4. Hiroshi Ishida, "Does Class Matter in Japan? Demographics of Class Structure and Class Mobility in Comparative Perspective," paper presented to the "Researching Social Class in Japan" workshop at the Institute of Social Science, University of Tokyo, January 2005.

5. John Price, *Japan Works: Power and Paradox in Postwar Industrial Relations* (Ithaca: Cornell University Press, 1996).

6. Oguma Eiji, *Tan'itsu minzoku shinwa no kigen: 'Nihonjin' no jigazō no keifu* [The Myth of the Homogeneous Nation: A Genealogy of Self-Images of Japaneseness] (Tokyo: Shin'yōsha, 1995).

7. John Lie, *Multiethnic Japan* (Cambridge: Harvard University Press, 2001).

8. Yumiko Iida, "Between the Technique of Living an Endless Routine and the Madness of Absolute Degree Zero: Japanese Identity and the Crisis of Modernity in the 1990s," *Positions* 8, no. 2 (Fall 2000): 423–64, at 425.

9. See, for example, Jon Woronoff, *The Japanese Social Crisis* (London: Macmillan, 1997), 5–10.

10. Ulrike Schaede, "The 'Old-Boy' Network and Government-Business Relationships in Japan," *Journal of Japanese Studies* 21, no. 2 (1995): 293–317; Chalmers Johnson, "The Reemployment of Retired Government Bureaucrats in Japanese Big Business," *Asian Survey* 14 (November 1974): 953–65.

11. Ulrike Schaede, "The 1995 Financial Crisis in Japan," Berkeley Roundtable on the International Economy, Working Paper 85, February 1996. Accessed from Columbia International Affairs Online (CIAO).

12. William W. Grimes, *Unmaking the Japanese Miracle: Macroeconomic Politics, 1985–2000* (Ithaca: Cornell University Press, 2001), 145–47.

13. Koichi Hamada, "The Incentive Structure of the 'Managed Market Economy': Can It Survive the Millennium?" *American Economic Review* 88, no. 2 (May 1998): 417–21.

14. Haruhiro Fukui and Shigeko N. Fukai, "Japan in 1996: Between Hope and Uncertainty," *Asian Survey* 37, no. 1 (January 1997): 20–28, at 22–23.

15. Nakatani Iwao, "A Design for Transforming the Japanese Economy," *Journal of Japanese Studies* 23, no. 2 (Summer 1997): 399–417, at 413.

16. Chalmers Johnson, *MITI and the Japanese Miracle: The Growth of Industrial Policy, 1925–1975* (Stanford: Stanford University Press, 1982).

17. See, for example, the essays in Meredith Woo-Cumings, ed., *The Developmental State* (Ithaca: Cornell University Press, 1999).

18. For a brief overview, see Hashimoto Jurō, "The Heyday of Industrial Policy Activity," *Social Science Japan* 12 (March 1998).

19. See, for example, Richard N. Rosecrance, *The Rise of the Trading State: Commerce and Conquest in the Modern World* (New York: Basic Books, 1996); James Fallows, *Looking at the Sun: The Rise of the New East Asian Economic and Political System* (New York: Pantheon, 1994).

20. Richard Katz, *Japan: The System That Soured* (Armonk, N.Y.: M. E. Sharpe, 1998); Robert M. Uriu, *Troubled Industries: Confronting Economic Change in Japan* (Ithaca: Cornell University Press, 1996); Scott Callon, *Divided Sun: MITI and the Breakdown of Japanese High-Tech Industrial Policy, 1975–1993* (Stanford: Stanford University Press, 1995).

21. T. J. Pempel, *Regime Shift: Comparative Dynamics of the Japanese Political Economy* (Ithaca: Cornell University Press, 1998).

22. Edward J. Lincoln, *Arthritic Japan: The Slow Pace of Economic Reform* (Washington, D.C.: Brookings Institution, 2001), 94–120.

23. Jennifer Amyx, "The Ministry of Finance and the Bank of Japan at the Crossroads," in *Japanese Governance: Beyond Japan Inc.*, by Jennifer Amyx and Peter Drysdale (London: Routledge/Curzon, 2003), 55–76; Akiyoshi Horiuchi, "The Big Bang Financial System Reforms: Implications for Corporate Governance," in Amyx and Drysdale, *Japanese Governance*, 77–95.

24. Ethan Scheiner, *Democracy without Competition: Opposition Failure in One-Party Dominant Japan* (London: Cambridge University Press, 2005), chap. 2.

25. I leave women out of the equation because of their systematic exclusion from a number of the institutions seen as central to Japan's economy. Japanese women have long faced employment discrimination, with many younger women expected to leave their positions upon marriage and then becoming reabsorbed as part-time workers, depending on firm needs. This is commonly described as the "M-shaped curve." See, for example, Omori Maki, "Gender and the Labor Market," *Journal of Japanese Studies* 19, no. 1 (Winter 1993): 79–102, at 95.

26. Kelly and White, "Students, Slackers, Seniors, Singles, and Strangers," 13–16.

27. Ichiko Fuyuno, "A Silent Epidemic," *Far Eastern Economic Review* (September 28, 2000), 78–80.

28. Ulrike Schaede, "Private Debt and Social Welfare in Japan: Consumer Finance, the 'Middle-Risk Gap', and Japan's Social Contract," Graduate School of International Relations and Pacific Studies, University of California-San Diego, January 2005, 12.

29. The most complete study of this period of reform comes in Sasaki Takeshi, *Seiji kaikaku 1800 nichi no shinjitsu* [The Truth behind 1,800 Days of Political Reform] (Tokyo: Kodansha, 1999). For excellent English-language overviews, see Gerald L. Curtis, *The Logic of Japanese Politics* (New York: Columbia University Press, 1999), and Jacob Schlesinger, *Shadow Shoguns: The Rise and Fall of Japan's Postwar Political Machine* (Stanford: Stanford University Press, 1997).

30. Curtis, *Logic of Japanese Politics*, 180.

31. See, for example, Okano Kaoru and Fujimoto Kazumi, eds., *Murayama seiken to demokurashii no kiki: Rinshō seijigakuteki bunkseki* [The Murayama Administration and Democracy in Crisis: Sickbed Political Analysis] (Tokyo: Toshindo, 2000). For an angry, left-leaning critique, see political scientist Yamaguchi Jirō's *Kiki no Nihon seiji* [Japanese Politics in Crisis] (Tokyo: Iwanami, 1999).

32. Sassa had criticized Murayama's "crisis management" capabilities even before the earthquake, as in "Kore de ii no ka: Kyokutō no kiki kanri" [Is This All We Have? Crisis Management for the Far East], *Chūō Kōron* (March 1995), 51–69. Immediately after the quake, he published the blistering "'Gominkan' ga inakatta Sōri Kantei" [Protection of the People: There's Nobody Home in the Prime Minister's Office], *Chūō Kōron*, April 1995, 62–73. Two months later, he wrote the remarkably angry "Mō damatte wa irarenai" [We Can Be Silent No Longer], *Bungei Shunju* (June 1995), 94–103.

33. See, for example, the conversation between hawks Shīna Motō and Okazaki Hisahiko, in "Shin no hoshu seiken o kibō suru" [Hoping for a Real Conservative Administration], *Chūō Kōron* (April 1995), 90–98, esp. Hisahiko's comments on 91–92.

34. Mizushima Asaho, "Dono yō na bōsai kyūjo soshiki o kangaeru ka" [Considering the Right Organization for Disaster Relief and Rescue] " *Sekai* (March 1995), 46–51; Maeda Tetsuo, "Jieitai bōsai betsu soshikiron" [Considering the Separation of Disaster Relief Functions from the SDF], *Sekai* (May 1995), 89–99.

35. Ishibashi Katsuhiko, "Shizen no setsuri ni sakarawanu bunka o" [Creating a Culture That Doesn't Disobey Mother Nature], *Sekai* (March 1995), 62–66. Uchihashi Katsuto adds that some of the worst-hit places in Kobe were "reclaimed land" areas whose existence reflected the increasingly irresponsible demands by business for more land no matter what the human costs. See Uchihashi, "Pōto Airando de nani ga okita ka" (What Happened on Port Island?), *Sekai* (May 1995), 76–82.

36. Susan J. Pharr, Robert D. Putnam, and Russell J. Dalton, "Trouble in the Advanced Democracies? A Quarter-Century of Declining Confidence," *Journal of Democracy* 11, no. 2 (April 2000): 5–25.

37. Robert Pekkanen, "Japan's New Politics: The Case of the NPO Law," *Journal of Japanese Studies* 26, no. 1 (Winter 2000): 111–43.

38. Helen Hardacre, "After Aum: Religion and Civil Society in Japan," in *The State*

of Civil Society in Japan, ed. Frank J. Schwartz and Susan J. Pharr (Cambridge: Cambridge University Press, 2003), 135–53, at 138–41.

39. Nakamura also points out Asahara's skill in gaining believers in post-Soviet Russia, shifting the discussion away from an overly Japan-centric focus. See Nakamura Yūjirō, *Nihon bunka ni okeru aku to tsumi* [Evil and Sin in Japanese Culture] (Tokyo: Shinchōsha, 1998), 45–47.

40. Kariya Takehiko, *Chiteki fukugō shiko hō* [Laws for Thinking with an Intellectual Compound Eye] (Tokyo: Kodansha, 1996), 38, 250.

41. Yoshimi Shun'ya, "Wareware no naka no Oumu" [The Aum in Ourselves], *Sekai* (July 1995).

42. Hosoi Shin'ichi, in Haruki Murakami, *Underground: The Tokyo Gas Attack and the Japanese Psyche*, trans. Alfred Birnbaum and Philip Gabriel (New York: Vintage, 2000), 320.

43. Ruth Benedict, *The Chrysanthemum and the Sword: Patterns of Japanese Culture* (1946; repr., Tokyo: Tuttle, 1988); Nakane Chie, *Japanese Society* (Berkeley: University of California Press, 1986); Doi Takeo, *The Anatomy of Dependence*, trans. John Bester (Tokyo: Kodansha, 1994 reissue).

44. See, for example, Peter Dale, *The Myth of Japanese Uniqueness* (London: Routledge, 1986); Yoshio Sugimoto and Ross Mouer, *Images of Japanese Society: A Study in the Social Construction of Reality* (London: KPI Press, 1986).

45. David Leheny, *The Rules of Play: National Identity and the Shaping of Japanese Leisure* (Ithaca: Cornell University Press, 2003).

46. Like Asahara, Manson's charisma was lost on those not in the cult, and he was found hiding in a tiny crawl space in the cult's compound at the time of the arrest. Both were indisputably in charge of their cults, yet both denied involvement in their crimes. See Vincent Bugliosi with Curt Gentry, *Helter-Skelter: The True Story of the Manson Murders* (New York: W. W. Norton, 2001).

47. Although he focuses predominantly on the presumptive spiritual crises facing Japanese young people, Daniel Metraux includes a comparative chapter on Aum's presence (which he describes as having "weak roots") in Russia and other nations. Daniel A. Metraux, *Aum Shinrikyo and Japanese Youth* (Lanham, Md.: University Press of America, 1998), 87–97.

48. Sharon Kinsella, "Japanese Subculture in the 1990s: Otaku and the Amateur Manga Movement," *Journal of Japanese Studies* 24, no. 2 (Summer 1998): 289–316, at 292–94 (see esp. 293 n. 15).

49. Kenji Otani, "Time Distributions in the Process to Marriage and Pregnancy in Japan, *Population Studies* 45, no. 3 (November 1991): 473–87.

50. For a thoughtful critique of the "parasite single" school of thought, see James M. Raymo, "Premarital Living Arrangements and the Transition to First Marriage in Japan," *Journal of Marriage and Family* 65 (May 2003): 302–15, at 314–15.

51. Kelly and White, "Students, Slackers, Seniors, Singles, and Strangers," 15–21.

52. Because Fukasaku died early in the filming of the sequel, *Battle Royale II: Requiem*, it was completed by his son, Kenta. It moves into even stranger territory, though apparently a direction that Fukasaku himself authorized. The survivors of the first *Battle Royale* have moved to Afghanistan and have become an al Qaeda–like terrorist group, dedicated to destroying an unnamed hegemon (clearly the United States) and its sycophantic allies, like Japan.

53. Aoki Tamotsu, "Kaihatsu to shūmatsuron—posuto baburu nihon no futatsu no kyoku" [Development and Decline: The Two Poles of Post-Bubble Japan], *Chūō Kōron* (May 1995): 30–35.

54. Conversations between public intellectuals are a staple, and an easily ridiculed one, of Japan's leading monthly opinion magazines. In one of his brilliant one-man skits, comic actor Ogata Issei plays a deferential magazine editor who arranges a con-

versation between two famous authors, only to find through his increasingly frantic prodding that they have not read one another's books.

55. Yōrō Takeshi and Aoki Tamotsu, "Nani ga Oumu o unda no ka" [What Produced Aum?], *Chūō Kōron* (June 1995), 56–67, at 62–63.

56. Perhaps most famous among these was his claim that the Self-Defense Forces should prepare to deal harshly with foreigners who riot after a major earthquake. In addition to his use of the racial slur *sangokujin* (literally, "third-country people"), referring primarily to non-Japanese Asians, his comments were especially pernicious given the brutal treatment of Koreans after the 1923 Tokyo earthquake, when many were accused of looting and were lynched. See Tessa Morris-Suzuki, "Packaging Prejudice for the Global Marketplace: Chauvinism Incited by Tokyo Governor Ishihara" (2001), Iwanami's *Japan in the World* website http://www.iwanami.co.jp/jpworld/text/packaging01. html. Accessed March 20, 2004.

57. See, for example, the excellent profile by John Nathan in *Japan Unbound: A Volatile Nation's Quest for Pride and Purpose* (New York: Houghton Mifflin, 2004), 169–202.

58. Ishihara Shintarō, "Nani o mamori, nani o naosu ka" [What to Preserve, and What to Fix], *Bungei Shunjū* (July 1995), 94–106, quote from 96.

59. Ishihara Shintarō, "Kanryō no fuhai, seijika no mukiryoku" [Lifeless Politicians and the Rot in the Bureaucracy], *Bungei Shunju* (November 1995), 110–17.

60. See, for example, Oguma Eiji, *Minshū to aikoku: Sengo nihon no nashonarizumu to kōkyōsei* [Democracy and Patriotism: Nationalism and Community in Postwar Japan] (Tokyo: Shin'yōsha, 2002), 811–22.

61. The debates about Japan's new nationalism are now extensive, working along well-established fault lines. The right-wing side is well represented by Kobayashi Yoshinori's *Shingomanizumu no sengen* [Declaration of Arrogance] series of political manga, while on the left, Korean-Japanese University of Tokyo professor Kang Sang Jung has now written or contributed to well over a dozen books critiquing the country's nationalistic turn.

62. This is not an effort to excuse either Ishihara's or Koizumi's behavior, which has sometimes been appalling, particularly with regard to sensitivities in other Asian nations. But their popularity owes at least as much to their reputations for independence as to any clear desire to deny Japan's past or to express Japanese superiority.

63. Yamada Taiichi and Kawamoto Sanjurō, "Aimai na fūan no jidai," *Sekai* (March 1995), 24–35, at 33.

64. Kina Shoukichi and Shin Sugok, "Nihon Bunka tte Nan Da?" [What the Hell Is Japanese Culture?] *Sekai* (April 1998), 115–29.

65. Douglas McGray, "Japan's Gross National Cool," *Foreign Policy* (May–June 2002): 44–54; Jim Frederick, "What's Right with Japan?" *Time* (Asia edition), August 11, 2003.

3. "Whatever It Is, It's Bad, So Stop It"

1. The "mo-gal" (modern girl) moniker in early twentieth century Japan described those young women rejecting traditional manners in favor of modern (generally Western) alternatives. For illustrative biographies, see Phyllis Birnbaum, *Modern Girls, Shining Stars, and the Skies of Tokyo: Five Japanese Women* (New York: Columbia University Press, 1999).

2. For a discussion of the etymology, see Laura Miller, "Those Naughty Teenage Girls: Japanese Kogals, Slang, and Media Assessments," *Journal of Linguistic Anthropology* 14, no. 2 (2004): 225–47, at 227–28.

3. See, for example, Cecilia Segawa Seigle, *Yoshiwara: The Glittering World of the Japanese Courtesan* (Honolulu: University of Hawaii Press, 1993).

4. For example, Nicholas Bornoff's *Pink Samurai: The Pursuit and Politics of Sex in Japan* (London: Grafton, 1991).

5. *Shūkan Posuto,* April 16, 2004.

6. T. R. Reid of the *Washington Post* is almost certainly correct, however, in arguing that American journalists, particularly those who are new to Japan, overstate the role of the sex industry in everyday life here. One does not need many linguistic skills to find porn, whereas the rest of the social environment can be bewildering if one doesn't read and speak the language. Adult-oriented industries are, of course, important in Japan, but they are not as popularly accepted as some of the literature would have it. For example, the phrase "hen na ojīsan" roughly corresponds to "dirty old man," and in Japanese video stores, adult video titles are generally sequestered in a relatively private area. See the interview with Reid in *Warawareru Nihonjin* [also in English: *Japan Made in U.S.A.*], ed. Zipangu (New York: Zipangu, 1998), 52–57 (English), reverse 59–64 (Japanese).

7. See, for example, Sabine Frühstück, *Colonizing Sex: Sexology and Social Control in Modern Japan* (Berkeley: University of California Press, 2003); Sabine Frühstück, "Then Science Took Over: Sex, Leisure, and Medicine at the Beginning of the Twentieth Century," in *The Culture of Japan as Seen through Its Leisure,* ed. Sepp Linhart and Sabine Frühstück (Albany: State University of New York Press, 1998), 59–79.

8. For excellent studies, see Sharon Kinsella, "Cuties in Japan," in *Women, Media, and Consumption in Japan,* ed. Lise Skov and Brian Moeran (Honolulu: University of Hawaii Press, 1996), 220–54; and Brian J. McVeigh, *Wearing Ideology: State, Schooling, and Self-Presentation in Japan* (Oxford: Berg, 2001), 135–82.

9. The predictably grotesque and hilarious lyrics of Frank Zappa's 1979 song "Catholic Girls" nicely capture this in the American context.

10. Carol Gluck, *Japan's Modern Myths* (Princeton: Princeton University Press, 1985). Kawaji quote on 187, imperial rescript information on 132–33.

11. Kashiwame Reihō, *Gendai jidō fukushiron* [Contemporary Child Welfare], 3rd ed. (Tokyo: Seishin, 1999), 7–8. Kashiwame here builds on work by Nakagawa Nobutoshi and Nagai Yoshikazu, whose edited volume *Kodomo to iu retorikku: muku no yūwaku* [The Rhetoric of the Child: Temptation of the Innocent] (Tokyo: Seikyūsha, 1993) addresses the issue in more depth.

12. George W. Bush, 2004 State of the Union address, text available at http://www. whitehouse.gov/news/releases/2004/01/20040120-7.html.

13. Neil Postman, *The Disappearance of Childhood* (New York: Vintage, 1994).

14. Kashiwame, *Gendai jidō fukushiron,* 5–7.

15. Kawahara Kazue, *Kodomokan no kindai: 'Akai tori' to 'dōshin' no risō* (Modernity and Views of Childhood: "Red Bird" and the Ideal of a Second Childhood) [Tokyo: Chūō Shinshō, 1998), esp. 3–13.

16. Jidō Fukushi Hōki Kenkyūkai [Child Welfare Laws and Regulations Research Association], ed., *Saishin jidō fukushihō, boshi oyobi kafu hō, boshi hōken hō no kaisetsu* [Interpretation of the Child Welfare Law, the Law for Widows and Mothers and Children, and the Mothers and Children Insurance Law: Newest Edition] (Tokyo: Jijitsūshinsha, 1999), 7.

17. Kawahara, *Kodomokan no kindai,* 118–23.

18. Sheldon Garon, *Molding Japanese Minds: The State in Everyday Life* (Princeton: Princeton University Press, 1997), 159.

19. The law has undergone only one major revision, largely dealing with daycare, a crucial issue amid concerns about Japan's rapidly declining birth rate. See Roger Goodman, *Children of the Japanese State: The Changing Role of Child Protection Institutions in Contemporary Japan* (Oxford: Oxford University Press, 2000), 59–60

20. Chūō shakai jigyō iinkai, "Jidō hogohō yōkōan o chūshin to suru jidō hogo ni kan suru ikensho" [Opinion Paper on Child Protection, Focusing on the Proposed Outline for a Child Protection Law]. Cited in Jidō Fukushi Hōki Kenkyūkai, *Saishin jidō fukushihō,* 9–10.

21. Ayukawa Jun, "Shōnen shihō no poritikkusu" [The Politics of Juvenile Justice], in Nakagawa and Nagai, *Kodomo to iu retorikku,* 201–37, at 205–7.

22. Masami Izumida Tyson, "Revising Shonenho: A Call to Reform a System That Makes the Already Effective Japanese Juvenile System Even More Effective," *Vanderbilt Journal of Transnational Law* 33, no. 3 (May 2000): 739–77, at 764–66.

23. Ibid., 754–55.

24. Okabe Takeshi argues that unless one takes an artificially short-term perspective on juvenile delinquency, tracking from the unusually low rates of the mid-1980s, it is impossible to argue that there has been a major increase in youth crimes, even the serious ones at the center of the debate. See Okabe Takeshi, "Hikō to kazoku no kankei o toinaosu" [Reexamining the Relationship between Families and Delinquency], in *'Risō no kazoku' wa doko ni aru no ka* [Where is the "Ideal Family"?], ed. Hirota Teruyuki (Tokyo: Kyoiku Kaihatsu Kenkyūjo, 2002), 146–54, at 150–51.

25. Ayukawa, "Shōnen shihō no poritikkusu," 210–16.

26. For a discussion, see Niikura Osamu and Sasaki Mitsuaki, "Kaikaku wa sōsa no arikata no minaoshi kara—yamagata matto shijiken kara manabu" [Considering Reform by Rethinking Investigative Techniques: Learning from the Yamagata Mat Case], in *Chotto matte shōnenhō 'kaisei'* [Wait a Minute! Reforming the Juvenile Law], by Dandō Shigemitsu, Murai Toshikuni, Saitō Toyoji, et al. (Tokyo: Nihon Hyōronsha, 1999), 172–82. See also Tyson, "Revising Shonenho," 761–62.

27. Tyson, "Revising Shonenho," 756–57.

28. Oda Susumu, "Thoughts on the Child Murder Suspect," *Japan Echo* (October 1997): 15–17. This is an abridged and translated version, provided by the conservative *Sankei Shimbun*, of Oda's piece "14-sai no hanzai, Jun-kun jiken o kangaeru," published in the newspaper on July 8–9.

29. Tyson, "Revising Shonenho," 760.

30. Dandō Shigemitsu, "Shōnenhō kaisei hihan" [Criticism of the Juvenile Law Reform], in *Chotto matte shōnenhō 'kakusei'*, by Dandō et al., 14–27, at 19–20.

31. Yamaguchi Naoya, "Kokusai jinken kijun ni han suru 'kaisei' hōan" [The Revision Bill That Opposes UN Human Rights Standards], in Dandō et al., *Chotto matte shōnenhō 'kakusei'*, 163–70, at 165–66.

32. Victoria James, "Out of Control Youth," *New Statesman* (September 10, 2001), 23–25.

33. Iwao Sumiko, "Problems among Japan's Young," *Japan Echo* (June 1998), 6–8, at 8.

34. This figure is from an October 2000 poll by the Japanese polling association Yōron Chōsakai; it also found that only 40% supported "severe punishment" (*genbatsu*) for youth. Gotō Hiroko, "Keiji shobun no han'i no kakudai to sono kadai" [Issues in the Expansion of the Scope of Investigative Procedures], *Jurist* 1195 (March 1, 2001): 10–16.

35. Although the Meiji government encouraged girls' education (particularly after 1880), the political construction of the nation as an extended family, with the state as a generous patriarch, rested in part on the continued subservience of women as well as girls. Sasaki Shizuko, *Josei ga kaeru seikatsu to hō* [How Women Changed Laws and Lifestyles] [Tokyo: Minerva, 2000], 246–55.

36. Saeki Junko, *Ren'ai no kigen: Meiji no ai o yomikaku* [The Origins of Romance: Reading and Unraveling Meiji Era Love] (Tokyo: Nihon Keizai Shimbunsha, 2000), 223–29.

37. Andrew D. Morrison, "Teen Prostitution in Japan: Regulation of Telephone Clubs," *Vanderbilt Journal of Transnational Law* 31, no. 2 (March 1998): 457–97, at 463–65.

38. Garon, *Molding Japanese Minds*, 104–5.

39. Yamazaki Tomoko, *Sandakan Brothel No. 8: An Episode in the History of Lower-Class Japanese Women*, translated by Karen Colligan-Taylor (Armonk, N.Y.: M. E. Sharpe, 1999). See also the review essay by James F. Warren, "New Lands, Old Ties, and Prostitution: A Voiceless Voice," *Journal of Southeast Asian Studies* 31, no. 2 (2000): 396–404.

40. J. Mark Ramseyer, chap. 6: "Promissory Credibility: Sex," in *Odd Markets in Japanese History: Law and Economic Growth* (Oxford: Oxford University Press, 1996).

41. See Takashi Shiraishi's essay on prostitutes in Saya S. Shiraishi and Takashi Shiraishi, eds., *The Japanese in Colonial Southeast Asia* (Ithaca: Cornell University Southeast Asia Program, 1993).

42. There is little doubt that the ugliness of this story has contributed heavily to anti-Japanese rhetoric and sentiment in and around Asia, particularly with regard to issues of sexual exploitation. The literature on the comfort women is abundant in both Japanese and English. See in English, Maria Rosa Henson, *Comfort Woman: A Filipina's Story of Prostitution and Slavery under the Japanese Military* (Lanham, Md.: Rowan and Littlefield, 1999); George L. Hicks, *The Comfort Women: Japan's Brutal Regime of Enforced Prostitution in the Second World War* (New York: W. W. Norton, 1997). In Japanese, see the 1997 issue of *Sekai* for the articles under the heading "Koshoron ni hanron suru—nihongun 'ianfu' mondai no honshitsu to wa" [Against the Licensed Prostitute Arguments: The Truth about the Japanese Army's "Comfort Women"]. Yoshimi Yoshiaki's "Rekishi shiryō o do yomu ka" [How to Read Historical Documents] takes on the historical revisionists who argue that the comfort women were simply licensed prostitutes; Suzuki Yuko's "Sekando reipu ni hoka naranai" [Nothing More Than a Second Rape] also criticizes the handling of the issue. It should be noted that Yoshimi in particular is one of the most famous activists working on this issue from the Japanese Left.

43. On the relationship between the U.S. armed forces and sex markets in Asia, see Saundra Pollack Sturdevant and Brenda Stoltzfus, *Let the Good Times Roll: Prostitution and the U.S. Military in Asia* (New York: New Press, 1993); Katherine H. Moon, *Sex among Allies: Military Prostitution in U.S.-Korea Relations* (New York: Columbia University Press, 1997). On a more theoretical level, see Cynthia Enloe, *Bananas, Beaches, and Bases: Making Feminist Sense of International Politics* (Berkeley: University of California Press, 1990).

44. Children are defined in the law as those under the age of eighteen, though girls can marry at sixteen and can be at that point defined as adults. See Hirose Kenji, "Jidō ni inkō o saseru kōi" [Activities Exposing Children to Obscenity], in *Keiji saiban jitsumu taikei, dai san kan: Fūzoku eigyō, baishun bōshi* [Overview of Criminal Cases in Practice, Vol. 3: Sex Oriented Businesses Law and Anti-Prostitution Law], ed. Satō Fumiya (Tokyo: Aoki, 1994), 424–38.

45. Jidō Fukushi Hōki Kenkyūkai, *Saishin jidō fukushihō*, 260–61.

46. Kashiwame Reihō, *Jidō fukushihō kaikaku to jisshi taisei* [Enforcement and Reform of the Child Welfare Law] (Tokyo: Minerva, 1997), 31–32.

47. There are, of course, national judicial rulings on what constitutes obscenity (*waisetsu*), which necessarily involve debates over freedom of expression. But the issue of "lewd behavior," which is central to the Child Welfare Law, appears to be a more complex matter engaging both national rulings and local regulations. On obscenity, see Uematsu Tadashi, "Waisetsu no gainen" [The Concept of Obscenity], in *Sōgō hanrei kenkyū sōsho: Keihō 19* [Comprehensive Judicial Precedent Research Series: Criminal Law, no. 19] (Tokyo: Yūhikaku, 1963), 1–56. See also Uchida Fumiaki and Nagai Madoka, "Seihyōgen to keihō" [Sexual Expression and Criminal Law], in *Gendai keibatsuhō taikei, dai 4 kan: Shakai seikatsu to keibatsu* [Overview of Contemporary Criminal Penalties, Vol. 4: Social Lifestyle Issues and Penalties], ed. Ishihara Kazuhiko, Nishihara Haruo, and Sasaki Shirō (Tokyo: Nihon hyōronsha, 1982), 257–92.

48. Itō, *"Sei" no nihonshi*, 40.

49. Garon, *Molding Japanese Minds*.

50. Fumiko Kanazumi, "Sei no jikō ketteiken o kakuritsu suru hōseido to wa" [What's the Legal Framework Guaranteeing Sexual Self-Determination?], in *Sei no jiko kettei genron—enjo kōsai, kaibaishun, kodomo no sei* [The Right of Sexual Self-Determination: Enjo Kōsai, Prostitution, and Child Sexuality], by Miyadai Shinji, Hayami Yukiko, et al. (Tokyo: Kinokuniya, 1998), 181–217, at 200.

51. Garon, *Molding Japanese Minds*, 202.

52. The text of the law appears as an appendix in Itō, *"Sei" no nihonshi*, 238–41.

53. I have made this argument before, in David Leheny, "A Political Economy of Asian Sex Tourism," *Annals of Tourism Research* 22, no. 2 (1995): 367–84. On the yakuza, see Peter B. E. Hill, *The Japanese Mafia: Yakuza, Law, and the State* (Oxford: Oxford University Press, 2003).

54. A breezy history appears in "Nippon no enjo kōsai hisutorii" [The History of Enjo Kōsai in Japan], in *Enjo Kōsai Dokuhon: Otoko to Onna no Seikimatsu* [Readings on *Enjo Kōsai*: The End of the Century for Men and Women], ed. Yoshioka Tekkyo (Tokyo: Futabasha, 1997), 157–62.

55. Morrison, "Teen Prostitution in Japan," 494.

56. Itō Hosaku, *"Sei" no nihonshi* [The History of "Sex" in Japan] (Tokyo: Sōbasha, 1997), 37–40. *Kimin* appears to be Itō's neologism, combining one of the characters meaning "dispose" or "cast-off" (*suteru*, or *ki*) with that of "people" (*min*). I am presuming the use here of *kimin* as the proper reading.

57. Nagasawa Mitsuo, *AV Joyū* [Adult Video Actress] (Tokyo: Village Center, 1996). I thank Yamanouchi Mihoko for her reflection on the publishing world's reaction to the book.

58. I thank Sharon Kinsella and Laura Miller for having made this point to me.

59. For a fascinating overview, see especially journalist Nagasawa Mitsuo's *Fūzoku no hitotachi* [People in the Sex Industry] (Tokyo: Chikuma, 1997), a collection of his pieces in *Kurasshu* magazine between 1990 and 1996.

60. Hideko Takayama, "Sex: A Booming Business in Japan," UPI, December 17, 1984. Takayama, however, repeats fairly tiresome assertions about why the sex industry is so large: "Like other Asians, Japanese are troubled less by guilt than by shame." "It is typically Japanese to maintain appearances while overlooking realities."

61. For an official overview, see the Keisatsuchō Hōzaika Fūzoku Mondai Kenkyūkai (National Police Agency Crime Prevention Division, Fūzoku Problem Research Council), ed., *Shinpan—fūzoku tekiseikahō handōbukku* [Handbook on the Fūzoku Correction Law—New Edition] (Tokyo: Tachibana, 1984).

62. "NPA Plans Tighter Controls on Sex Businesses," Kyodo News Service, March 5, 1984.

63. Asahi Shimbunsha, *Asahi Nenkan 1985* [Asahi Yearbook 1985] (Tokyo: Asahi shimbunsha, 1985), 123–24.

64. Keisatsuchō Hōzaika Fūzoku Mondai Kenkyūkai, *Shinpan—Fūzoku Tekiseikahō Handōbukku*, 1–9.

65. Itō, *"Sei" no nihonshi*, 138.

66. Morrison, "Teen Prostitution in Japan," is particularly good in his overview of the telephone club industry.

67. "Japan's Typical Prostitute, Aged 29, Meets Clients by Arrangement," Kyodo News Service, March 8, 1986.

68. Futabasha Henshūbu (Futabasha Editorial Group), "Nippon no Enjo Kōsai Hisutorii" [The History of *Enjo Kōsai* in Japan], in *Enjo kōsai dokuhon*, at 161.

69. "Meeting Mortgages—And Husbands," *Economist* (July 6, 1991), 36.

70. Yoshida Sawako, "Otto igai no hito to sekkusu wa yappari shinsen na yorokobi ga atta" [The Fresh Thrill of Sex with Someone Other Than Your Husband], in *Enjo kōsai dokuhon*, 94–97.

71. Cameron W. Barr, "Why Japan Plays Host to the World's Largest Child Pornography Industry," *Christian Science Monitor*, April 2, 1997, 1.

72. Most reports of payments made to high school girls for enjo kōsai indicate that they are two to three times as high as those for housewives, likely reflecting greater demand. One estimate given was ¥30,000 for a single date and ¥200,000 per month to act as a "girlfriend." Jonathan Watts, "Schoolgirls Trade Sex for Designer Goods," *Guardian*, June 9, 1997.

73. Ueno Chizuko, "Sekushuariti no chikaku hendo ga okiteiru" [The Seismic Shift

in Sexuality], excerpted in *Enjo kōsai "shakai" no yukue* [The Enjo Kōsai Society], by Murao Kenkichi (Tokyo: Rokusaisha, 1999), 140.

74. Saeki, *Ren'ai no kigen*, 232-33.

75. Terumitsu Otsu, "Prostitution without Sexual Intercourse," *Daily Yomiuri*, November 25, 1996.

76. Perry Kishita interview with Fujii Yoshiki, "Kanojotachi ni genzai no moraru wa nan no chikara ni mo naranai" [For the Girls, Contemporary Morals Have No Power], in *Enjo Kōsai Dokuhon* [Readings on *Enjo Kōsai*], 16-21.

77. Noriko Sato, "Schoolgirls and 'Enjo Kōsai'—A Good Deal of Hype," Kyodo News Service, May 30, 1997.

78. "Survey Disputes 'Enjo-kosai' Hype," Asahi News Service, April 24, 1998.

79. But some schoolgirls were active even at this time. Nagasawa Mitsuo's first chapter in his book on the sex industry, *Fūzoku no hitotachi*, written in April 1990, begins with a conversation between a twenty-something salaryman and someone who describes herself as a seventeen-year-old high school student: even in the early days of the terekura, schoolgirls were using them. *Fūzoku no hitotachi* [People in the Sex Industry] (Tokyo: Chikuma, 1997), 10-17.

80. Miyadai Shinji, *Seifuku shojotachi no sentaku* [The Options for Girls in Uniform] (Tokyo: Kōdansha, 1994), 1. Even if most of these girls had actually gone on dates with men met through these exchanges (and few people believe that this is true), many encounters would have been coffee dates rather than sex. In other words, one should not interpret these figures to mean—as some panicky observers immediately did—that one in four high school girls had traded sex for cash.

81. "Live Television Till Morning," a monthly six-hour roundtable discussion program that takes on a different issue each month. Its tone falls somewhere between a typical news analysis program and a free-for-all at a bar. This information can be found in Japanese at its website, http://www1.tv-asahi.co.jp/broadcast/asanama/.

82. In the *Mainichi Shimbun*, February 2, 1998. Excerpted in Murao, *Enjo kōsai "shakai,"* 148-49.

83. Kawai Hayao, "Kaisetsu," in *Enjo Kōsai*, by Kuronuma Katsushi (Tokyo: Bunshun, 1998).

84. Sawada Kantoku, *Rakuen no Datenshi* [Paradise's Fallen Angels] (Tokyo: Gendai Shorin, 1997), 25.

85. Ibid., 12.

86. Quoted by Terumitsu Otsu, "Schoolgirls Involved in Dating Clubs—A Wake-up Call to Society," *Daily Yomiuri*, December 9, 1996.

87. Miyadai, *Seifuku shojotachi no sentaku*, 45-50.

88. Ibid., esp. chap. 6.

89. Sagisawa Megumu, "Enjo kōsai ni kansuru kōsatsu" [Considering *Enjo kōsai*] *Gunzō*, May 1997, excerpted in Murao, *Enjo kōsai "shakai,"* 123-24.

90. Murakami Ryū, *Rabu & Poppu* [Love and Pop] (Tokyo: Gentosha, 1997).

91. Kuronuma, *Enjo Kōsai*, 156-65. See also Richard James Havis, "Teens on the Make," *Asiaweek* (July 10, 1998), 48.

92. "Hit-and-Run Suspect in Girl's Death Hangs Self," Kyodo News Service, October 2, 2001. Accessed through Lexis-Nexis.

93. "Court Upholds 6-Year Sentence on Ex-Teacher for Girl's Death," Kyodo News Service, November 26, 2002. Accessed through Lexis-Nexis.

94. Murakami Ryū, "Tokubetsu Intabyū: Enjo kōsai to bungaku no kiki" [The Crisis of Literature and Enjo Kōsai], *Bungakkai* (January 1997), excerpted in Murao, *Enjo kōsai "shakai,"* 90-92.

95. Ueno Chizuko, "Sekushuariti no chikaku hendo ga okiteiru," excerpted in Murao, *Enjo kōsai "shakai,"* 138-40.

96. Hayami Yukiko, "Enjo kōsai o sentaku suru shōjotachi" [The Girls Who Choose Enjo Kōsai], in Miyadai, Hayami, et al., *Sei no jiko kettei genron*, 15-38.

206 NOTES TO PAGES 79-88

NOTES TO PAGES 79-88

206 NOTES TO PAGES 79-88

97. Kanazumi, "Sei no jikō ketteiken," 203–4.

98. "Ministry to Update Sex Education Rules," *Mainichi Daily News,* June 8, 1997.

99. Murase Yukihiro, "Intabyū: 'Enjo kōsai' o umu haikei to otona ga nasubeki koto" [Interview: The Environment That Creates "Enjo kōsai," and What Adults Must Do], in *Enjo kōsai no shōjotachi: Dō sureba otona? Dō sureba gakkō?* [The Little Girls of Enjo Kōsai: What Should Adults Do? What Should Parents Do?], by Shōji Akiko, Shimamura Arika, et al. (Tokyo: Tōken, 1997), 41–63.

100. Yuriko Yamaki, "Middle-aged Men Are Played Like a Fiddle," in *Warawareru Nihonjin* [In English: *Japan Made in U.S.A.*], ed. Zipangu, trans. Yuriko Yamaki and Steve Cohen (New York: Zipangu, 1998), 20–21.

101. "Teachers Publish Booklets to Fight Teen Prostitution," *Daily Yomiuri,* May 15, 1997.

102. See, for example, Shōji Akiko, Shimamura Arika, et al., *Enjo kōsai no shōjotachi.*

103. Maeda leaves no doubt about this. Chap. 2 of his book is entitled "The End of 'Safe Japan'" ['Chian no yoi kuni nihon' no shūen]. Chapter 9, on the rise in crime by teenage girls, is "Zōdai suru josei no hanzai" [Increasing Female Crime]. Maeda Masahide, *Shōnen hanzai: Tōkei kara mita sono jishō* [Juvenile Crime: The Real Image in Statistics] (Tokyo: University of Tokyo Press, 2000), 137–50, cited photo on 145.

4. Guidance, Protection, and Punishment in Japan's Child Sex Laws

1. Ethan A. Nadelmann, "Global Prohibition Regimes: The Evolution of Norms in International Society," *International Organization* 44, no. 4 (Autumn 1990): 479–526, esp. 513–16; see also Kathleen Barry, *The Prostitution of Sexuality* (New York: New York University Press, 1995), 220–49.

2. Alison Jaggar, "Contemporary Western Feminist Perspectives on Prostitution," *Asian Journal of Women's Studies* 3 (1997); Ronald J. Berger, Patricia Searles, and Charles E. Cottle, *Feminism and Pornography* (New York: Praeger, 1991), 31–49.

3. S. Ryan Johansson, "Complexity, Morality, and Policy at the Population Summit," *Population and Development Review* 21 (1995): 361–86, at 378.

4. Thanh-Dam Truong, *Sex, Money, and Morality: Prostitution and Tourism in Southeast Asia* (London: Zed, 1990); Jeremy Seabrook, *Travels in the Skin Trade: Tourism and the Sex Industry* (London: Pluto, 1997); Ryan Bishop and Lillian S. Robinson, *Night Market: Sexual Cultures and the Thai Economic Miracle* (London: Routledge, 1998); Cleo Odzer, *Patpong Sisters: An American Woman's View of the Bangkok Sex World* (New York: Blue Moon, 1995).

5. ECPAT, "Tourism and Children in Prostitution," report prepared for the 1996 Stockholm World Congress against Commercial Sexual Exploitation of Children. Available through the CSEC website (in English) at http://www.csecworldcongress.org/en/index.htm. Accessed August 10, 2003.

6. Louise Waugh, "AIDS Time Bomb Feared in Mongolia as Child Sex Booms," *Guardian* (November 17, 1997), 14. This piece, like most of the other English-language news articles cited, is available in Lexis-Nexis.

7. David Leheny, "A Political Economy of Asian Sex Tourism," *Annals of Tourism Research* 22 (1995): 367–84.

8. Carol Smolenski, "Sex Tourism and the Sexual Exploitation of Children," *Christian Century* 112, no. 33 (November 15, 1995).

9. Ron O'Grady, *The Child and the Tourist* (Bangkok: ECPAT, 1991); Ellen Lukas, "Children for Sale: The Stockholm Congress against the Commercial Exploitation of Children," *Insight on the News,* December 1996.

10. International Conference on Population and Development, "Program of Action at the 1994 International Conference on Population and Development (Chapter I–VIII)," *Population and Development Review* 21 (1995): 187ff., at 191.

11. Lukas, "Children for Sale."

12. Karen Mahler, "Global Concern for Children's Rights: The World Congress against Sexual Exploitation," *International Family Planning Perspectives* 13 (1997): 79–84.

13. Ibid., 82.

14. Yuri Kageyama, "Japan Criticized for Slack Policing of Internet Child Pornography," Associated Press, November 24, 1998. Accessed through Lexis-Nexis.

15. Cameron W. Barr, "Japan Hit for Allowing Child Porn on the Web," *Christian Science Monitor,* December 16, 1998.

16. Sachiko Nakagome, "Sexual Exploitation: The Gravest Infringement against Children's Rights," Asahi News Service, December 10, 1998.

17. Kanazumi Fumiko, "Sei no jiko ketteiken o kakuritsu suru hōseido to wa" [What Legal Framework Will Guarantee Sexual Self-determination?], in *Sei no jiko kettei genron* [Principles of Sexual Self-determination], ed. Miyadai Shinji (Tokyo: Kinokuniya, 1998), 181–217.

18. Cameron W. Barr, "Why Japan Plays Host to World's Largest Child Pornography Industry," *Christian Science Monitor,* April 2, 1997.

19. Ibid.

20. Sheldon Garon, *Molding Japanese Minds: The State in Everyday Life* (Princeton: Princeton University Press, 1998), 114–45 and 178–205.

21. In her study of gender norms in Japan, Jennifer Chan-Tiberghien notes that the number of child advocacy organizations increased dramatically from the 1970s onward, with particularly high jumps in the 1980s. *Gender and Human Rights Politics in Japan: Global Norms and Domestic Networks* (Stanford: Stanford University Press, 2004), 65–66.

22. ECPAT-Kansai, "Kodomo seigyakutai kinshi hōan" [Counterproposal: The Bill to Abolish the Sexual Abuse of Children], July 1998. On the ECPAT-Kansai website (in Japanese) at http://homepage3.nifty.com/ecpat/ECPAT/law/horitsu_an.htm. Accessed June 20, 2004.

23. Perry Kishita, "Okane o wataseba taiho de wa, purezento nara" [If I Can Get Arrested for Paying Money, How About Presents?], in *Enjo kōsai dokuhon,* 152–56. Oddly enough, one of the best and clearest overviews of the laws governing enjo kōsai comes in this article, which essentially is an explanation of where and under what conditions it is legal, presumably to help would-be offenders from running afoul of the letter of law, even if flagrantly violating its spirit.

24. Exchanges with Sharon Kinsella were particularly important in turning my attention to these processes, and I thank her for her generous advice and help.

25. Interviews, April 5 and 7, 2004.

26. Andrew D. Morrison. "Teen Prostitution in Japan: Regulation of Telephone Clubs," *Vanderbilt Journal of Transnational Law* 31, no. 2 (March 1998): 457–97.

27. "Posters Discouraging Paid Dates Approved by Osaka School Board," *Daily Yomiuri,* April 10, 1997. Accessed through Lexis-Nexis.

28. Mitsuaki Nishikawa, "Police Adopt More Aggressive Approach toward Teen Prostitutes," *Mainichi Shimbun,* reprinted (in English) in the *Mainichi Daily News,* April 16, 1997, 12. Accessed through Lexis-Nexis.

29. Sonoda Hisashi, *Kaisetsu: Jidō kaishun/jidō poruno shobatsuhō* [Interpreting Laws for Punishing Child Pornography and Child Prostitution] (Tokyo: Nihon Hyōronsha, 1999), 2–3, 78–87.

30. Suvendrini Kakuchi, "Law Banning Teen Prostitution May Have Little Impact," Interpress Service, October 17, 1997.

31. "Tokyo Revises Rules to Ban Teen Prostitution," *Daily Yomiuri,* October 11, 1997.

32. Although I visited with guidance professionals and watched them on duty, I did not participate in their activities or interact with the children themselves.

33. The box was in this form at the time of my visit; I know nothing else about the girl and would not use the anecdote if I had met her personally. I am not sure if she had done the design the previous day or weeks earlier.

34. I thank Manuel Metzler (Heidelberg University) for informing me about his fieldwork in other prefectures.

35. In accordance with confidentiality rules, neither the girl's nor her contacts' identities were revealed to me, and although I suspect the transcript is a real one, I have no way of verifying its authenticity.

36. This view is in line with David Johnson's judgment of the Japanese criminal justice system as a whole; its flaws notwithstanding, Japanese justice seeks to rehabilitate wrongdoers, making it "uncommonly just." See David T. Johnson, *The Japanese Way of Justice: Prosecuting Crime in Japan* (New York: Oxford University Press, 2001), 280.

37. *Sangiin Honkaigi Gijiroku* [Records of the Upper House Meeting], January 24, 1997, 4.

38. *Shū Yosan Iinkai Gijiroku* [Records of the Lower House Budget Committee] No. 3, January 28, 1997, 26.

39. *Sangi Chihō Gyōsei Iinkai Bōryokudan kōinkai* [Upper House Regional Affairs Committee, Subcommittee on Organized Crime], June 17, 1997.

40. Japan's legislative body, the Diet, is a bicameral parliament. The upper house, or House of Councillors, is the weaker of the two houses. At the time, the governing coalition of the Liberal Democratic Party, the Japan Socialist Party, and the New Harbinger Party–Sakigake was an uneasy group, fending off attacks from the center-left Democratic Party and the more conservative New Frontier Party.

41. Kaoruko Sunazawa, "Crimes," *Asahi Shimbun*, June 24, 1997.

42. Keisuke Iida notes that the LDP's weakened position in the Diet, which forced it to work in coalition with other parties, enhanced the ability of Socialists to push a pro-human rights agenda in key cases, including this one. See Keisuke Iida, "Human Rights and Sexual Abuse: The Impact of International Human Rights Law on Japan," *Human Rights Quarterly* 26, no. 2 (May 2004): 428–53, at 430.

43. The text of the original proposal is available in Japanese on ECPAT's Japanese web page, at http://homepage3.nifty.com/ecpat/ECPAT/law/yoko.htm. Accessed June 21, 2004. Its title was *Jidō kaishun, jidō poruno ni kakawaru kōi no shochi oyobi jidō no hogo ni kan suru hōritsuan* [Bill for the Protection of Children as well as for Measures to Deal with Acts Involving Child Prostitution and Child Pornography].

44. It is an open question, of course. Where Chalmers Johnson sees bureaucrats as the crucial figures who feed laws to sometimes poorly informed legislators, Mark Ramseyer and Frances Rosenbluth see harried officials trying to draft legislation that will please their constitutional bosses in the Diet. See Chalmers Johnson, *Japan: Who Governs? The Rise of the Developmental State* (New York: W. W. Norton, 1996); J. Mark Ramseyer and Frances McCall Rosenbluth, *Japan's Political Marketplace* (Cambridge: Harvard University Press, 1993).

45. For a discussion of the path of the law through the Diet, see Moriyama Mayumi, *Yoku wakaru jidō kaishun/jidō poruno kinshihō* [Understanding the Law to Prohibit Child Prostitution and Child Pornography] (Tokyo: Gyōsei, 1999).

46. The Women's Christian Temperance Union, which is related to the Tokyo EC-PAT office, also cooperates with the HELP shelters for Asian women working in Japan's sex industry.

47. Kageyama, "Japan Criticized for Slack Policing."

48. See (in Japanese) www.jimin.or.jp/jimin/giindata/moriyama-ma.html. Moriyama was also praised by the conservative Japanese National PTA for her activities in promoting Japanese *kenzen ikusei*. Accessed March 31, 2000. See (in Japanese) www.nippon-pta.or.jp/oshirase/s07–baishun-kinshi.htm. It is important here to note that ECPAT-Kansai, angry about the linking of enjo kōsai to child prostitution and pornography in sex tourism, stressed that *kenzen ikusei* was part of an effort to maintain a normative order rather than to defend the rights of children. See ECPAT-Kansai, "Kodomo seigyakutai kinshi hōan," 1998.

49. The text of the Japanese National PTA's statement was available at www.nippon-pta.or.jp/oshirase/s07–baishun-kinshi.htm. Accessed October 1999.

50. See her remarks in "Bill Takes Aim at Under-18 Set Trade," Asahi News Service, March 18, 1998.

51. Also at ECPAT-Kansai's web page (in Japanese): http://homepage3.nifty.com/ecpat/ECPAT/law/nichibenren.htm. Accessed June 20, 2004.

52. This text is also available at ECPAT's home page, at http://homepage3.nifty.com/ecpat/ECPAT/law/minsyutoan.htm. Accessed June 20, 2004.

53. Miyadai Shinji, statement to the Shūgi Seishōnen Mondai ni kansuru Tokubetsu Iinkai [Lower House Special Committee on Juvenile Problems], April 27, 1999, 5–8.

54. Sonozaki Toshiko, "Jidō kaishun/jidō poruno kinji sangiin tsūka" [The Child Prostitution/Child Pornography Bill's Process through the Lower House]. *ECPAT-Kansai Newsletter,* April 1999. On ECPAT-Kansai's web page, at http://homepage3.nifty.com/ecpat/ECPAT/wings/wings99/newsletter99.4.htm. Accessed June 20, 2004.

55. Iida, "Human Rights and Sexual Abuse," 435.

56. Scantily clad teen models still appear in the pages of major magazines, but former fetish magazines like *Beppin School, Cream,* and *Waffle* now seem less inclined to have underage models stripping off their school uniforms, relying instead on teenagers in bikinis and on models over eighteen to handle the school uniform pictorials.

57. Keisatsuchō Seikatsu Anzen Kyoku Shōnenka (National Police Agency, Lifestyle Safety Bureau, Juvenile Division), *Shōnen hikō nado no gaiyō* [Overview of Juvenile Delinquency and Related Matters, 2003] (Tokyo: NPA, 2004), 15.

58. Miyamoto Junko, "The Second World Congress against the Commercial Sexual Exploitation of Children: The Third Panel," December 19, 2001.

59. In 2002, there were 1.1 million cases of "guidance" to juveniles, almost double the number of a decade earlier. Of these, approximately 485,000 were scoldings for smoking, and 475,000 for staying out late at night. Sexual offenses thus represented less than 1% of the total. Keisatsuchō (National Police Agency), *Keisatsu Hakushō Heisei 15-nen* [National Police White Paper 2003] (Tokyo: Ministry of Finance, 2003), 157.

60. Keisatsuchō Seikatsu Anzen Kyoku Shōnenka, *Shōnen hikō nado no gaiyō,* 2.

61. Inō Kamie, "Deaikei saito kisei hō to kodomo no jinken" [The Law to Restrict Dating Sites and the Human Rights of Children], *Koseki Jihō* 559 (August 2003): 38–46, at 38.

62. "Jidō kaishun mokuteki no kakikomi ni bakkin" [Fines for Leaving Messages for Child Prostitution], *Hōgaku seminā* 583 (July 2003): 126.

63. "Diet Outlaws Online Solicitation of Sex with Minors," *Japan Times,* June 7, 2003.

64. Gotō Hiroko, "Deaikei saito kisei hō ni tsuite—intanetto jō no kodomo no komyunikēshon kisei" [About the Law to Restrict Dating Rights: Regulating the Communication of Children on the Internet], *Gendai keijihō* 6, no. 1 (2004): 65–71.

65. "New Law to Ban Kids from Online Dating Sites," *Mainichi Daily News,* December 26, 2002. Accessed through Lexis-Nexis.

66. "'Jidō kaishun' no hōkisei wa tōzen'" [Legal Restrictions on 'Child Prostitution' Are Natural]. *Kahoku Shimpō,* March 22, 1999. Available in Japanese at www.kahoku.co.jp/shasetsu/1999/03/19990322s.htm. Accessed July 30, 1999.

67. UNICEF's Japanese web page contains the text (in Japanese) of the law, at www.unicef.or.jp/sif/kaisyun.html. The new law reflects some of the changes proposed by the Democrats and some of the clarifying questions of the Japan Federation of Bar Associations. It does not ban possession of child pornography, nor does it prohibit non-photographic images of child sexuality, focusing instead on photographs and videotapes. It maintains, however, the initial definition of children as those under eighteen and the right to prosecute even in the absence of a complaint or accusation from the victims.

"Jidō kaishun kinshihō no shuchi taitei" [Making the Law to Abolish Child Prostitution Common Knowledge], *Ehime Shimbun,* May 17, 1999. Originally found online (in October 1999) in Japanese at www.ehime-np.co.jp/arc/1999/shasetu/np-shasetu-0517. html.

68. Roger Goodman, "Child Abuse in Japan: 'Discovery' and the Development of Policy," in *Family and Social Policy in Japan: Anthropological Approaches,* ed. Roger Goodman (Cambridge: Cambridge University Press, 2002), 130–55.

69. Shū Gaimu Iinkai Gijiroku, March 18, 2004, 1–3.

5. Trust in Japan, Not in Counterterrorism

1. *Sakusen kōdo Tokyo,* produced by Keisatsu Kyōkai (National Police Association), 1996.

2. For some famous examples from the United States, see Richard A. Clarke, *Against All Enemies: Inside America's War on Terror* (New York: Free Press, 2004); Michael Scheuer, *Imperial Hubris: Why the West Is Losing the War on Terror* (Dulles, Va.: Potomac Books, 2004).

3. Peter J. Katzenstein, *Cultural Norms and National Security: Japanese Security Policy in Comparative Perspective* (Ithaca: Cornell University Press, 1996).

4. John M. Maki, "Japan's Subversive Activities Prevention Law," *Western Political Quarterly* 6, no. 3 (September 1953): 489–511.

5. "Cloak, Dagger, and Muddle," *Economist,* February 8, 1997, 38.

6. Patricia G. Steinhoff, "Hijackers, Bombers, and Bank Robbers: Managerial Style in the Japanese Red Army," *Journal of Asian Studies* 48, no. 4 (November 1989): 724–40.

7. Patricia G. Steinhoff, "Kidnapped Japanese in North Korea: The New Left Connection," *Journal of Japanese Studies* 30, no. 1 (2004): 123–41, at 126–27.

8. Patricia G. Steinhoff, "Portrait of a Terrorist: An Interview with Kozo Okamoto," *Asian Survey* 16, no. 9 (September 1976): 830–45.

9. Sassa Atsuyuki, *Rengō Sekigun 'Asama Sarsō' Jiken* [The Japanese Red Army's Asama Sansō Incident] (Tokyo: Bungei Shunju, 1996). Critics pointed out that Sassa's self-serving account was riddled with inaccuracies. Director Harada Masato popularized the account in his 2002 film *Totsunyūseyo: Asama Sansō Jiken,* which has a radically different English title, *The Choice of Hercules.*

10. Patricia G. Steinhoff, "Death by Defeatism and Other Fables: The Social Dynamics of the Rengō Sekigun Purge," in *Japanese Social Organization,* ed. Takie Sugiyama Lebra (Honolulu: University of Hawai'i Press, 1992), 195–224.

11. David E. Apter and Nagayo Sawa, *Against the State: Politics and Social Protest in Japan* (Cambridge: Harvard University Press, 1984).

12. Karl Dixon, "The Growth of a 'Popular' Japanese Communist Party," *Pacific Affairs* 45, no. 3 (Autumn 1972): 387–402.

13. "Security Officials Accused of Secretly Filming JCP Office," Kyodo News Service, November 16, 1988.

14. The kōban system is discussed in virtually every major study of the Japanese police. See, for example, David H. Bayley, *Forces of Order: Policing Modern Japan,* rev. ed. (Berkeley: University of California Press, 1991).

15. Lisa Sansoucy, "Aum Shinrikyo and the Japanese State," unpublished paper, Cornell University Department of Government, 2003, 3–4, 11–16; H. Richard Friman, Peter J. Katzenstein, David Leheny, and Nobuo Okawara, "Immovable Object? Japan's Security Policy in East Asia," in *Beyond Japan: The Dynamics of East Asian Regionalism,* ed. Peter J. Katzenstein and Takashi Shiraishi (Ithaca: Cornell University Press, 2006).

16. Katzenstein notes, for example, the difficulty of getting reliable information from Koreans in Japan, who are suspicious of being discriminated against by the police. Katzenstein, *Cultural Norms and National Security,* 66.

17. There are a number of excellent studies of the Aum case. Because it is well covered by other authors and because I am primarily concerned with trajectories of state

activity, I touch on it here only impressionistically. For longer studies, see (among many others) Ian Reader, *Religious Violence in Contemporary Japan: The Case of Aum Shinrikyo* (Honolulu: University of Hawaii Press, 2000); Robert Jay Lifton, *Destroying the World in Order to Save It: Aum Shinrikyo, Apocalyptic Violence, and the New Global Terrorism* (New York: Metropolitan Books, 1999); Mark Juergensmeyer, *Terror in the Mind of God: The Global Rise of Religious Violence* (Berkeley: University of California Press, 2000), 102–16.

18. Indeed, the major innovations in the late 1990s in U.S. counterterrorism policy focused so narrowly on WMD that the September 11 attacks were more surprising to policymakers than were the subsequent anthrax attacks.

19. Brian Jenkins, "Will Terrorists Go Nuclear?" *Orbis* 29, no. 3 (Autumn 1985): 507–16.

20. National Commission on Terrorism, *Countering the Changing Threat of International Terrorism* (Washington, D.C.: Report of the Commission to Congress, 2000), 2.

21. For examples, see Jessica Stern, *The Ultimate Terrorists* (Cambridge: Harvard University Press, 1999); Walter Laqueur, *The New Terrorism: Fanaticism and the Arms of Mass Destruction* (New York: Oxford University Press, 1999); Ian O. Lesser, Bruce Hoffman, John Arquilla, David F. Ronfeldt, Michele Zanini, and Brian Michael Jenkins, *Countering the New Terrorism* (Santa Monica: RAND Corporation, 1999).

22. Sassa Atsuyuki, *Kiki kanri* [Crisis Management] (Tokyo: Gyōsei, 1997), 183–85. In 1999, he elaborated further on his idea that Japanese leaders are almost pathologically unable to handle emergencies. See Sassa Atsuyuki, *Heiji no shikikan, yūji no shikikan: Anata wa buka ni mirareteiru* [Leaders in Peacetime, Leaders in Emergency: Your Subordinates Are Watching You] (Tokyo: Bunshun Bunko), 1999.

23. Sassa, *Kiki kanri*, 233–34.

24. Robyn Pangi, "Consequence Management in the 1995 Sarin Attacks on the Japanese Subway System," BCSIA Discussion Paper 2002–4, ESDP Discussion Paper ESDP-2002–01, John F. Kennedy School of Government, Harvard University (February 2002), 20; Isao Itabashi, Masamichi Ogawara, with David Leheny, "Japan," in *Combating Terrorism: Strategies of Ten Countries*, by Yonah Alexander (Ann Arbor: University of Michigan Press, 2002), 337–73. Pangi in particular notes lingering problems related to the hierarchical structure of Japanese crisis management routines, which can hamstring "first responders" in emergency situations.

25. Toshikawa Takao, *Nihon no Kiki Kanri* [Japan's Crisis Management] (Tokyo: Kyōdō Tsūshinsha, 2002), 96.

26. Helen Hardacre, "After Aum: Religion and Civil Society in Japan," in *The State of Civil Society in Japan*, ed. Frank J. Schwartz and Susan J. Pharr (Cambridge: Cambridge University Press, 2003), 135–53, at 146–48.

27. Friman et al., "Immovable Object?"

28. Itabashi, Ogawara, and Leheny, "Japan," 363.

29. James Risen and David Johnston, "FBI Report Found Agency Not Ready to Counter Terror," *New York Times*, June 1, 2002. Accessed through Lexis-Nexis. This became one of the points of contention in Attorney General Ashcroft's April 14, 2004, testimony to the congressional commission investigating the September 11 attacks.

30. David Leheny, "Symbols, Strategies, and Choices for International Relations Scholarship after September 11," *Dialogue-IO* (Spring 2002): 57–70, at 60–61.

31. Richard A. Falkenrath, "Problems of Preparedness: U.S. Readiness for a Domestic Terrorist Attack," *International Security* 25, no. 4 (Spring 2001): 147–86.

32. Peter J. Katzenstein and Yutaka Tsujinaka, *Defending the Japanese State: Structures, Norms, and the Political Responses to Terrorism and Violent Social Protest in the 1970s and 1980s* (Ithaca: Cornell University East Asia Program, 1991).

33. Alessandro Politi, "European Security: The New Transnational Risks," *Chaillot Working Paper* No. 29 (Paris: European Union Institute for Security Studies, 1997).

34. Joanna Apap and Sergio Carrera, "Progress and Obstacles in the Area of Justice and Home Affairs in an Enlarging Europe," *CEPS Working Document* No. 194 (Brussels: Centre for European Policy Studies, 2003).

35. Therese Delpech, "International Terrorism and Europe," *Chaillot Working Paper* No. 56 (Paris: European Union Institute for Security Studies, 2002).

36. Padraig O'Malley, *Biting at the Grave: The Irish Hunger Strikers and the Politics of Despair* (Boston: Beacon, 1990).

37. For the text of all the conventions, including signatories and ratification status, see the United Nations counterterrorism convention web page at http://untreaty.un.org/English/Terrorism.asp.

38. Soviet support (and that of its satellite states) for terrorist groups has been well documented, if in heavily biased works of the 1980s (e.g., Claire Sterling, *The Terror Network: The Secret War of International Terrorism* [New York: Holt, Rinehart and Winston 1981]). For a scholarly discussion of East Germany's support of terrorist groups, see Peter J. Katzenstein, "September 11 in Comparative Perspective: The Anti-terrorism Campaigns of Germany and Japan," *Dialogue-IO* (Spring 2002): 45–56, at 47–48. For one example of a treaty with Soviet support, see the International Convention for the Suppression of the Unlawful Seizure of Aircraft, text and status available at http://untreaty.un.org/English/Terrorism.asp. Accessed May 5, 2003.

39. On the use of terrorism as a kind of "asymmetric strategy," see Ian O. Lesser's introduction to Lesser et al., *Countering the New Terrorism*, 1–5, at 3.

40. Bruce Hoffman, *Inside Terrorism* (New York: Columbia University Press, 1999), 15–17.

41. The 1999 Convention of the Organisation of the Islamic Conference on Combating International Terrorism allowed the Arab states and many other primarily Muslim countries to voice general disapproval of terrorism while allowing individual members to retain the right to define terrorist activity in different ways. See the OIC-UN's website at http://www.oic-un.org/26icfm/c.html. Even so, U.S. counterterrorism policy dictates that "state sponsors" of terrorism will be held responsible for violating even those rules to which they have not agreed.

42. The "no concessions" pledge is best expressed in agreements at the G8 level. See the report of the G8 Venice conference at the website of Japan's Ministry of Foreign Affairs, http://www.mofa.go.jp/policy/economy/summit/2000/past_summit/13/e13_d.html. Accessed May 5, 2003.

43. The text of these conventions can be found on the United Nations website, http://untreaty.un.org/English/Terrorism.asp.

44. "International Legal Developments," *Journal of Money Laundering Control* 6, no. 3 (Winter 2003): 201–16.

45. Robert Looney, "Hawala: The Terrorist's Informal Financial Mechanism," *Middle East Policy* 10, no. 1 (Spring 2003): 164–67; Council on Foreign Relations, *Terrorist Financing: Report of an Independent Task Force* (New York: Council on Foreign Relations, 2002).

46. Laura K. Donohue, "In the Name of National Security: U.S. Counterterrorist Measures, 1960–2000." BCSIA Discussion Paper 2001–6, ESDP Discussion Paper ESDP-2001–04, John F. Kennedy School of Government (August 2001), 12–13.

47. Statement of Louis J. Freeh, director of the FBI, before the Senate Committee on Appropriations, April 21, 1998. Online at http://www.fbi.gov/congress/congress98/intrcrime.htm.

48. "The Antiterrorism Assistance Program: Report to Congress for Fiscal Year 2002," *U.S. Department of State*, February 2003.

49. Al Baker, "Police Receive Antiterrorism Training in Israel," *New York Times*, May 20, 2002, B6. Accessed through Lexis-Nexis.

50. Alex Hannaford, "Missions Abroad to Keep the Peace," *Evening Standard* (London), November 11, 2002, 13. Accessed through Lexis-Nexis.

51. The rationale for Japan's increasingly heavy police training for Asian nations appears in Foreign Minister Kawaguchi Yoriko's January 31, 2003, comments to the Diet. Online at the Liberal Democratic Party's website, http://www.jimin.jp/jimin/kokkai/156/002.html. Accessed October 12, 2003.

52. Statement of Sam Brinkley, policy advisor, Office of the Coordinator for Counterterrorism at the U.S. Department of State, to the House Armed Services Committee, May 22, 2001. Online at http://www.house.gov/hasc/openingstatementsandpressreleases/ 107thcongress/01–05–22brinkley.html.

53. Larry Niksch, "Abu Sayyaf: Target of Philippine-U.S. Anti-Terrorism Cooperation," Congressional Research Service Report to Congress, January 25, 2002.

54. Juergensmeyer, *Terror in the Mind of God.*

55. Paul Wilkinson, *Terrorism and the Liberal State* (New York: Wiley, 1977). For more recent examples, see Paul Wilkinson, *Terrorism versus Democracy: The Liberal State Response* (London: Frank Cass, 2000); Philip B. Heymann, *Terrorism and America: A Commonsense Strategy for a Democratic Society* (Cambridge: MIT Press, 2000).

56. Walter Enders and Todd Sandler, "The Effectiveness of Antiterror Policies: A Vector-Autoregression-Intervention Analysis," *American Political Science Review* 87, no. 4 (December 1993): 829–44.

57. Bryan Brophy-Baermann and John A. C. Conybeare, "Retaliating against Terrorism: Rational Expectations and the Optimality of Rules vs. Discretion," *American Journal of Political Science* 38, no. 1 (February 1994): 196–210.

58. R. James Woolsey, foreword to Alexander, *Combating Terrorism,* v–vii. In the interest of full disclosure, I coauthored one of the chapters in this book.

59. Martha Crenshaw's 1989 conference on "Terrorism in Context" was an unusual effort to reintegrate studies of politics and violence, essentially problematizing terrorism as a concept rather than deploying it uncritically across contexts. Martha Crenshaw, ed., *Terrorism in Context* (University Park: Pennsylvania State University Press, 1995).

60. For a representative sample of the debate, see Richard Ned Lebow and Janice Gross Stein, "Deterrence: The Elusive Dependent Variable," *World Politics* 42 (April 1990): 336–69; Paul Huth and Bruce Russett, "Testing Deterrence Theory: Rigor Makes a Difference," *World Politics* 42 (July 1990): 466–501.

61. See, for example, Martha Crenshaw, "Terrorism, Security, and Power," paper presented at the Annual Meeting of the American Political Science Association, Boston, Massachusetts, 2002.

62. I thank Martha Crenshaw for making this point in correspondence.

63. I thank John Meyer for suggesting this formulation in correspondence.

64. See Bruce Hoffman, "Is Europe Soft on Terrorism?" *Foreign Policy* (Summer 1999): 62–76.

65. Hugo Dobson, *Japan and the G7/G8: 1975–2002* (London: Routledge/Curzon, 2004), 67–68.

66. Itabashi, Okawara, and Leheny, "Japan," 346–47.

67. The opinion poll of "The Japan Air Lines' Hijacking Case" (by the Office of Public Relations in the Prime Minister's Office). The survey had more than thirty-five hundred respondents, based on a stratified two-stage random sample, taken from forty-four hundred queries made from October 19 to 23, 1977.

68. Quoted in Itabashi Isao, "Kaigai no tero/yūkai, kigyō taishō bōryoku to anzen taisaku," [Overseas Terrorism and Kidnapping: Security Measures and Violence against Firms], in *Kigyō taishō bōryoku to kiki kanri* [Crisis Management and Violence against Firms], ed. Saiki Shōichi and Hayashi Norikiyo (Tokyo: Gyōsei, 1998), 159–92, at 190–91.

69. U.S. Department of State, *Patterns of Global Terrorism, 1999* (Washington, D.C.: Department of State, 2000), iii.

70. Shortly after the event, the Kyodo News Service published *Perū nihon taishi kōtei hitojichi jiken* [The Hostage Crisis at the Japanese Ambassador's Residence in Peru] (Tokyo: Kyōdō Tsūshin, 1997). This journalistic account gives a good overview of the chronology of the crisis as well as the personalities of the key actors.

71. For a brief discussion of the Hashimoto-Fujimori connection, see Fukuda Kazuya, "Hashimoto wa naze Fujimori ni maketa ka" [Why Did Hashimoto Lose to Fu-

214 NOTES TO PAGES 134-139

jimori?], *Bungei Shunju* (June 1997): 160–66. Fujimori evidently was concerned that by informing Hashimoto of the attack in advance (which he had promised to do), he risked the secrecy of the mission.

72. Ministry of Foreign Affairs, *Zai perū nihon taishi kōtei senkyo jiken chōsa iinkai hōkokusho* [Report of the Committee Investigating the Occupation of the Residence of the Japanese Ambassador to Peru] (Tokyo: MOFA, 1997).

73. Ibid., special section "Jiken o furikaette (teigen)" [Looking Back on the Crisis (Suggestions)], 6.

74. CPP, "Perū nihon taishi kōtei senkyo, hitojichi jiken o keiki to shita teigensho: Jiken no tōtoi kyōkun o fūka sasenai tame ni" [Suggestions following the Occupation and Hostage Crisis at the Japanese Ambassador's Residence in Peru: To Ensure That Its Valuable Lessons Are Remembered] (Tokyo: CPP, 199), 7.

75. Nihon zaigai kigyō kyōkai (JOEA). "Perū nihon taishi kōtei hitojichi jiken o keiki to suru teigen: Nichigaikyō Perū jiken chōsai iinkai hōkokusho" [Suggestions following the Hostage Crisis at the Residence of the Japanese Ambassador in Peru: Report of the JOEA's Peruvian Crisis Research Team] (Tokyo: JOEA, 1997). After all, Japanese firms, like their American and European counterparts, have been known to pay ransoms—as quietly as possible—to free employees held overseas.

76. *Yomiuri Shimbun,* October 16, 1999.

77. *Yomiuri Shimbun,* October 18, 1999.

78. *Yomiuri Shimbun,* October 28, 1999.

79. Interview, December 1999.

80. *Yomiuri Shimbun,* November 12, 1999.

81. Interview, January 2000.

82. Ibid.

83. For details, see the Enforcement Regulations of Police Law, Article 1, Clause 24.

84. Itabashi, Ogawara, Leheny, "Japan," 357.

85. Margaret G. Herrman and Charles F. Herrman, "Hostage Taking, the Presidency, and Stress," in *Origins of Terrorism: Psychologies, Ideologies, Theologies, States of Mind,* ed. Walter Reich (Washington, D.C.: Woodrow Wilson Center Press, 1999), 211–29.

86. "Tourists Are Seized in Malaysia: Tie to Philippine Clash Claimed," Associated Press, April 25, 2000. Accessed through Lexis-Nexis.

87. As noted, the payment reportedly came from the European governments via Libya. Other U.S. hostages were subsequently taken by the ASG. One, Guillermo Sobero, was beheaded by the group, and another, Martin Burnham, was killed during a firefight with Filipino troops; a Filipina hostage, Deborah Yap, also perished in the raid. See "Rescue Raid Ends in Hostage Deaths," CNN, June 8, 2002, online at *http://www.cnn.com/2002/WORLD/asiapcf/southeast/06/07/phil.hostages/.* Accessed May 1, 2004.

88. Interviews, January 2000.

89. According to one expert, the Diet has otherwise taken little interest in international terrorism, leaving it primarily to the NPA to handle. Interview, May 2000.

90. Interview, December 2000.

91. Interview, January 2000.

92. Like the distinctions noted above between "individualistic" Westerners and "collectivistic" Japanese, these claims draw from *nihonjinron,* or "theories of Japaneseness," that posit essential cultural differences between the Japanese and "others," usually idealized Westerners. I have argued elsewhere that these are crucial elements in Japanese political legitimacy. See David Leheny, *The Rules of Play: National Identity and the Shaping of Japanese Leisure* (Ithaca: Cornell University Press, 2003). For another critique, see Tessa Morris-Suzuki, *Re-Inventing Japan: Time, Space, Nation* (Armonk, N.Y.: M. E. Sharpe, 1998). These theories are enormously elastic, meaning that there are other and contradictory logical corollaries. One might be the possibility that the Japanese who are skilled at distinguishing between "inside and outside" (*uchi/soto*), another hallmark of

nihonjinron, would be deeply suspicious and cagey overseas, as foreigners are not part of the trusted Japanese environment.

93. Interviews, January 2000.

94. These firms provide a variety of services, including consultations on security preparations, threat assessments, and the like. One of the more ambiguous elements of U.S. and European security politics is that these firms can also send representatives to act as mediators in the event of a hostage crisis involving employees of the contracting firm. After all, a government can follow a no concessions policy if it so chooses, but firms face severe recruitment problems for overseas posts if they develop a reputation for allowing their employees to die at the hands of captors. Although the CPP espouses a no concessions line, as does the U.S. government, in this case it recognizes that firms will often do what they have to do to secure the safe release of their employees, and that they may be better able to do so quietly and securely if an experienced security firm handles the negotiations.

95. "Trust," written by Michael G. and Oshima Michiru. Performed by Donna Burke.

96. For example, see U.S. Department of State, Bureau of Diplomatic Security, *Hostage Taking: Preparation, Avoidance, and Survival* (Washington, D.C.: U.S. Department of State, 1988); U.S. Department of State, Overseas Security Advisory Council, *Security Awareness Overseas: An Overview* (Washington, D.C.: U.S. Department of State, 1991, 1994).

6. The Self-Fulfilling Afterthought

1. One of his essays on a left-leaning "citizen journalists and NPO-oriented" website, *Janjan*, had argued that Shōnen A, the fourteen-year-old identified as "Sakakibara Seito" in the brutal Kobe child murder, was innocent and had been framed by the police. Imai Noriaki, "Sakakibara Seitō wa shōnen A de wa nai?!" October 10, 2003. Online at http://www.janjan.jp/living/0310/0310067103/1.php. Accessed April 10, 2004.

2. On hearing of the government's commitment to maintain its troops in Iraq, U.S. Defense Secretary Donald Rumsfeld called it a "good, sound position."

3. "Perception Gap," Asahi News Service, April 21, 2004.

4. Norimitsu Onishi, "For Japanese Hostages, Release Only Adds to Stress," *New York Times*, April 22, 2004.

5. Jennifer M. Lind, "Pacifism or Passing the Buck? Testing Theories of Japanese Security Policy," *International Security* 29, no. 1 (Summer 2004): 92–121.

6. The term is now widely used, but it is originally associated with Thomas Berger. See Thomas U. Berger, "From Sword to Chrysanthemum: Japan's Culture of Antimilitarism," *International Security* 17, no. 4 (Spring 1993): 119–50; Thomas U. Berger, *Cultures of Antimilitarism: National Security in Germany and Japan* (Baltimore: Johns Hopkins University Press, 1998).

7. Peter J. Katzenstein, *Cultural Norms and National Security* (Ithaca: Cornell University Press, 1996).

8. Fujiwara Kiichi, *Demokurashii no teikoku: Amerika, sensō, gendai sekai* [Democracy's Empire: America, War, and the Modern World] (Tokyo: Iwanami shinsho, 2002).

9. Marc Gallichio, "Occupation, Dominion, and Alliance: Japan in American Security Policy, 1945–1969," in *Partnership: The United States and Japan, 1951–2001*, ed. Akira Iriye and Robert A. Wampler (Tokyo: Kodansha, 2001), 115–34, at 120–21. See also Richard J. Samuels, *Machiavelli's Children: Leaders and Their Legacies in Italy and Japan* (Ithaca: Cornell University Press, 2003), 204–11.

10. Yoshihide Soeya, "Japan: Normative Constraints versus Structural Imperatives," in *Asian Security Practice: Material and Ideational Influences*, ed. Muthiah Alagappa (Stanford: Stanford University Press, 1998), 198–233, at 211–13.

11. Most famous was Ozawa Ichirō's *Nihon kaizō keikaku*, which Louisa Rubinfien

translated into English as *Blueprint for New Japan: The Rethinking of a Nation* (Tokyo: Kodansha International, 1994). See also Kitaoka Shin'ichi, *"Futsū no kuni" e* [Becoming a "Normal Nation"] (Tokyo: Chūō Kōronsha, 2000).

12. Michael Jonathan Green, "The Search for an Active Security Partnership: Lessons from the 1980s," in *Partnership,* ed. Akira and Wampler, 135–60, at 144–49. Green also discusses the tension between "abandonment" and "entrapment" at some length in this chapter.

13. Yoshihide Soeya, "Japan's Dual Identity and the U.S.-Japan Alliance," Stanford University Asia-Pacific Research Center Working Paper, May 1998, 19–21.

14. Eiichi Katahara, "Japan: From Containment to Normalization," in *Coercion and Governance: The Declining Political Role of the Military in Asia,* ed. Muthiah Alagappa (Stanford: Stanford University Press, 2001), 69–91, at 75.

15. Michael J. Green, "Japan-ROK Security Relations: An American Perspective" *Asia-Pacific Center Occasional Paper,* May 1999, 15–18.

16. Peter J. Katzenstein, "Same War, Different Views: Germany, Japan, and Counterterrorism," *International Organization* 57, no. 4 (October 2003): 731–60; Peter J. Katzenstein, "September 11 in Comparative Perspective: The Antiterrorism Campaigns of Germany and Japan," *Dialogue-IO* (Spring 2002): 45–56.

17. This has been the preferred position of many in the Japan Defense Agency, who have argued assiduously for a joint U.S.-Japan theater missile defense program consistent with the Bush administration's Pacific basin strategy. See the report by former Maritime Self-Defense Forces admiral Kaneda Hideaki and the hawkish Okazaki Institute, *TMD nyūmon: Nihon kokumin ni totte dandō misairu bōei to wa nani ka* [Introduction to TMD: What Japanese Need to Know about Missile Defense] (Tokyo: Okazaki Institute, 1999). Online at http://www.okazaki-inst.jp/kanetmd/kaneda.tmdcover.html. Accessed November 8, 2005.

18. Sonia Ryang argues that the legal situation for Korean residents in Japan, including those strongly sympathetic to North Korea, has improved significantly, which has curtailed at least some of the anti-Korean stereotyping that might have accompanied increased concerns about North Korean intentions. Sonia Ryang, *North Koreans in Japan: Language, Ideology, and Identity* (Boulder: Westview, 1997), 120–28.

19. Gavan McCormack, "Japan's Afghan Expedition," first published in Japanese in *Sekai* (December 2001), with English translation available at Japan in the World, http://www.iwanami.co.jp/jpworld/text/Afghanexpedition01.html. Accessed May 9, 2004.

20. Stephen M. Walt, "Beyond Bin Laden: Reshaping U.S. Foreign Policy," *International Security* 26, no. 3 (Winter 2002–3): 56–78.

21. These responsibilities had traditionally belonged to the police, prompting some to worry about larger military goals and insufficient civilian control over military action. Fujii Haruo, "Jieitaihō no henshitsu to gunji himitsu hōsei" [Law on Military Secrets and the Changing SDF Law], in *Yūji hōsei o kentō suru: '9.11 igo' o heiwa kenpō no shiza kara toinaosu* [Considering the Emergency Laws: Using the Peace Constitution to Question the Aftermath of 9/11], ed. Yamauchi Toshihiro (Tokyo: Hōritsu bunkasha, 2002), 168–83.

22. For the sake of simplicity, I refer to the Kaijō Hoanchō as the Coast Guard, which is the official English-language translation as of April 2000. Prior to that, it was the Maritime Safety Agency, and critics have charged that the name change was meant to symbolize its shift toward a "paramilitary" stance. See Maeda Tetsuo, "Kaijō hoanchō hō kaitei to ryōiki keibi" [Territorial Protection and the Revision of the Coast Guard Law], in Yamauchi, ed., *Yūji hōsei o kentō suru,* 184–200, at 186. I use the later name for clarity rather than as a statement of political support for the change.

23. For the Democrats' reasoning, see Watanabe Shū, "Tero taisaku tokubetsu sochi hōan hoka 3 hōan e no tōron" [Comments on the Three Bills—Including Special Mea-

sures for Counterterrorism Law], October 18, 2001, Democratic Party of Japan website, http://www.dpj.or.jp/seisaku/gaiko/BOX_GK0055.html. Accessed May 18, 2003.

24. "Diet OK's Deployment of SDF," *Japan Times,* December 1, 2001.

25. Paul Midford, "Japan's Response to Terror: Dispatching the SDF to the Arabian Sea," *Asian Survey* 43, no. 2 (March–April 2003): 329–51.

26. One rumor has it that the Coast Guard and Navy deliberately allowed the ship to escape in order to force the issue onto the political agenda. I have no way of verifying the claim.

27. In a June 2001 meeting of the lower house's National Security Committee, future Defense Agency head Ishiba Shigeru said that the fushinsen problem was not one for the Defense Agency, the MSA, or the police, but rather for the entire government. *Shū Anzen Hoshō Iinkai Gijiroku* [Minutes of the Lower House National Security Committee] No. 8, June 14, 2001, 6.

28. "Counterterrorism," Ministry of Foreign Affairs website, http://www.mofa .go.jp/policy/terrorism/index.html. Accessed May 9, 2004.

29. To be fair, the prime minister's page specifies "domestic" responses, but many of these are clearly international in nature and are also featured on MOFA's page, including measures against money laundering and hijacking, as well as protection of Japanese citizens overseas. See "Kokunai tero taisaku nado jūten suishin jikō" [Key Issues and Points in Domestic Counterterrorism], at http://www.kantei.go.jp/jp/kakugiketei /2001/1219terojyutensuisin.html. Accessed May 9, 2004.

30. *Shū Honkaigi Gijiroku* 3 (October 2, 2001): 18; *San Honkaigi* 3 (October 3, 2001): 19.

31. *Shū giin un'ei iinkai gijiroku* 5 (October 10, 2001): 1.

32. *San Kokuchi Kōtsū Iinkai Gijiroku* 1 (October 18, 2001): 1.

33. *Shū Honkaigi Gijiroku* 7 [Minutes of the Main Session of the Lower House], October 18, 2001, 7.

34. *San Kokuchi Kōtsū Iinkai Gijiroku* 3 (October 25, 2001): 18–20.

35. The series was originally published in August 2002 in the *Yomiuri Shimbun,* according to the Nippon Foundation's archive, http://nippon.zaidan.info/seik abutsu/ 2001/00997/contents/00211.htm. "Rensai: 20 Jikan no Kōbō" [Serial: The Twenty-Hour Tug-of-War] online at http://kyushu.yomiuri.co.jp/special/fushinsen/fushinsen-main.htm. Accessed May 13, 2004.

36. This point is seconded by Mark J. Valencia and Ji Guoxing, who compare the handling of the fushinsen incident with the downing of a U.S. spy plane off the Chinese coast to suggest that conditions are rife for a crisis in the Pacific over the use of police and military force in exclusive economic zones. See "The 'North Korean' Ship and U.S. Spy Plane Incidents," *Asian Survey* 42, no. 5 (October 2002): 723–32.

37. Wada Haruki, *Chōsen yūji o nozomu no ka: fushinsen, rachi giwaku, yūji rippō o kangaeru* [Do We Want a Korean Crisis? Considering the Fushinsen, Abduction Suspicions, and Emergency Legislation] (Tokyo: Sairyūsha, 2002), 41–69. Because of its criticism of the then-unproved allegations of abductions of Japanese by North Korean agents, Wada's book is dismissed in many policy circles.

38. Statistics provided by the Fune no Kagakukan public website, http://www. funenokagakukan.or.jp/other/kousakusen/kousakusen.html. Accessed May 9, 2004.

39. I thank Rich Friman for informing me about this in correspondence.

40. A brochure available at the exhibit, "Kōsakusen no subete" [All about the Operations Boat], provides photos of the materials found on board and information on the boat's special design to carry out missions and to evade capture.

41. From the sign at the end of the kōsakusen exhibit, photographed by author, September 2003.

42. Ralph A. Cossa, "Beyond the Defense Guidelines: Responding to Intruders," Center for Strategic and International Studies, *PacNet Newsletter,* April 2, 1999.

43. After all, contingency laws are considered standard in most nations.

44. Koji Murata, "The Origins and Evolution of the Korean-American Alliance: A Japanese Perspective," Stanford University Asia-Pacific Center, America's Alliances with Japan and Korea in a Changing Northeast Asia Project Discussion Paper, August 1998, 9; Yuki Tatsumi, "Yuji Hosei: Japan Should Not Repeat the Mistake of the Past," Center for Strategic and International Studies, *PacNet Newsletter* 17, April 26, 2002, online at http://www.csis.org/pacfor/pac0217.htm. Accessed May 11, 2004.

45. Furukawa Atsushi, "Yūji hōsei no rekishiteki hatten: 'Mitsuya kenkyū' kara nichibei gaidorain kanrenhō made" [The Historical Development of Emergency Laws, from the "Three Arrows Research" to the U.S.-Japan Guidelines Legislation], in Yamauchi, ed., *Yūji hōsei o kentō suru*, 85–105, at 96.

46. Gavan McCormack, "North Korea in the Vice," *New Left Review* 18 (November–December 2003): 5–26, at 13–14. The reported deaths—in traffic accidents in a country with few cars; because of gas leaks; and by suicide—of the majority of abductees have left most Japanese deeply suspicious.

47. "How North Korea's Abductions Got Started," *Japan Echo* 30, no. 5 (October 2003): 44.

48. Hasegawa Keitarō, *Kitachōsen no saishū ketsumatsu—Higashi ajia no reisen wa kaku hōkai suru* [The Final Outcome for North Korea: The Collapse of the East Asian Cold War] (Tokyo: PHP, 2003), 42.

49. Kyodo News, September 10, 2003.

50. Kawabe Katsurō, *Rachi wa naze fuseganakatta no ka—nihon keisatsu no jōhō haisen* [Why Couldn't We Prevent the Abductions? How the Japanese Police Lost the Intelligence Battle] [Tokyo: Chikuma Shinshō, 2004], 110–11.

51. Watanabe Osamu, "9.11 jiken to nihon no taigai, kokunai seisaku" [9/11 and Japan's Diplomatic and Domestic Policies], in *Yūji hōsei o kentō suru*, ed. Yamauchi, 19–38, at 25–26.

52. Nakayama Takashi, *Nihonkai gunji kinchō* [Military Tensions in the Sea of Japan] (Tokyo: Chūō Shinsho La Clef, 2002); chronology and lessons, 17–18.

53. "Contingency Laws: Overcoming the Taboo; Diet Lays Groundwork for New Defense Policy," *Yomiuri Daily News*, June 8, 2003.

54. Reji Yoshida, "War Contingency Bills a Wobbly First Step," *Japan Times*, May 22, 2003.

55. Brad Glosserman, "U.S.-Japan Relations: Still on a Roll," *Comparative Connections* 5, no. 2 (July 2003): 21–30, at 25.

56. Kawabe, *Rachi wa naze fuseganakatta no ka—nihon keisatsu no jōhō haisen*, 107.

57. Gunji jānarisuto kaigi (Katō Kenjirō and Kuroi Buntarō), "Tero taisaku de minaosareru 'jieitai vs. keisatsu' bimyō na kankei" [A New Counterterrorism Look at the Delicate Relations between the Police and the SDF], in *Saishin! Jieitai 'senryaku' hakusho* [Breaking! The SDF 'Strategy' White Paper], ed. Katō and Kuroi (Tokyo: Takarajimasha, 2004), 74–76, at 76.

58. H. Richard Friman, Peter J. Katzenstein, David Leheny, and Nobuo Okawara, "Immovable Object? Japan's Security Policy in East Asia," in *Beyond Japan: The Dynamics of East Asian Regionalism*, ed. Peter J. Katzenstein and Takashi Shiraishi (Ithaca: Cornell University Press, 2006).

59. Interview, March 2004.

60. International Crisis Group, "Indonesia: National Police Reform," *ICG Asia Report* No. 13 (Jakarta–Brussels: International Crisis Group, 2001), 13.

61. Yamazaki Hiroto, the head of the NPA team dispatched to Jakarta, discusses these issues diplomatically in "Indoneshia kokka keisatsu kaikaku shien jigyō suishin no chūkiteki kōsō (Miteikō)" [Midterm Comments on Propelling Reforms of Indonesia's National Police], report to the National Police Agency, January 6, 2002. This section does not appear in Yamazaki's published version in the journal *Keisatsu gakuronshū,*

which provides an update on the NPA's successes in Indonesia. Yamazaki Hiroto, "Indoneshia kokka keisatsu shien" [Assistance for the Indonesian National Police], *Keisatsu gakuronshū* 56, no. 10 (October 2003): 42–72.

62. NPA Jakarta Team, "Police Reform," unpublished paper.

63. Interview, March 2004.

64. See, for example, Hara Osamu, "Jieitai iraku haiken wa tai kitachōsen seisaku de mo aru," *Seiron* (June 2004): 84–95.

65. Office of the Coordinator for Counterterrorism, United States Department of State, *Patterns of Global Terrorism 2003* (Washington, D.C.: State Department, 2004).

66. The government's figures aim at linking the increase in the foreign population to the increase in crime in the 1990s, though statistical analyses demonstrate that the connections are wildly misleading. Ryoko Yamamoto, "Alien Attack? The Construction of Foreign Criminality in Contemporary Japan," *Japanstudien* 16 (2004).

67. Keisatsuchō (National Police Agency), "Heisei 16–nendo ni okeru keisatsuchō no soshiki kaihen kōsō ni tsuite" [About the Conception for the NPA's Reorganization in 2004] (Tokyo: NPA, 2004).

68. "Ishihara tōchiji 'mayowazu utte! Ore ga sekikin o toru'" [Governor Ishihara: "Don't Wait, Just Shoot! I'll Take Responsibility"], *Shūkan Posuto*, April 16, 2004, 28–32.

69. Sassa Atsuyuki, "Chian o keishi shitekita tsuke wo ima harawasareteiru" [We Are Now Paying the Price for Having Neglected Public Order], *Chūō Kōron* 119, no. 2 (February 2004): 86–91, at 89.

70. Kokusai soshiki hanzai nado, kokusai tero taisaku suishin honbu (Task Force for Promoting Measures Against International Terrorism, International Organized Crime, and Others), "Tero no mizen bōshi ni kan suru kōdō keikaku" (Action Plan for the Prevention of Terrorism"), December 12, 2004. Available on the website of the Prime Minister's Office, http://www.kantei.go.jp/jp/singi/sosikihanzai/kettei/041210kettei.pdf. Accessed July 28, 2005.

71. See, e.g., Debito Arudou, "Here Comes The Fear," *Japan Times*, May 24, 2005. Available online at http://www.japantimes.co.jp/cgi-bin/getarticle.pl5?nn20050608a5 .htm. Accessed July 28, 2005.

72. "IC 'Gaijin' Card Shares Personal Info," *Japan Times*, June 8, 2005. Available online at http://www.japantimes.co.jp/cgi-bin/getarticle.pl5?nn20050608a5.htm. Accessed July 28, 2005.

73. "Nihon no tero taisaku, kyūsoku ni kokusai suijun e" (Rapidly Bringing Japan's Counterterrorism Measures to International Standards), *Yomiuri Shimbun*, July 19, 2005. Available online at http://www.yomiuri.co.jp/politics/news/20050718it14.htm. Accessed July 28, 2005.

74. "Iraku shien bunmin shūtai de," *Asahi Shimbun*, April 18, 2004.

75. Nao Shimoyachi, "SDF vs. NGO: An Iraqi Tale of Cost-Effectiveness," *Japan Times*, May 16, 2004.

76. Although he does not use the term "idiots," one of the most visible "Channel 2" contributors uses the discussions in the chat room to argue that the "leftist" (*sayoku*) media badly misunderstood popular sentiment against the hostages. See Nakamiya Takashi, "Dokuzen to gizen de yoron o misurōdo suru TV hōdō no gaidoku" [The Virus: Hypocritical and Self-Righteous Misreadings of Public Opinion on TV News], *Seiron* (June 2004): 74–82, especially 76–77.

77. In Japanese, Fukuda had said, "Nani ga aru ka wakaranai. Hōjin ga iraku ni hairanai yō ni yōsei shitekita." Reported in the *Mainichi Shimbun*, "Iraku nihonjin sōsoku: Fukuda kanbō chōkan kishi kaiken shōhō" [Kidnapping of Japanese in Iraq: Full Report of Chief Cabinet Secretary Fukuda's Press Conference], April 9, 2004. Available online at http://www.mainichi-sn.co.jp/seiji/feature/news/20040409k0000m010120000c.html. Accessed May 22, 2004.

78. The full text of the note was translated into Japanese and printed in the major

newspapers. "Isuramu senchi gundan no kaihō shōmyōbun," *Mainichi Shimbun,* April 11, 2004. Online at http://www.mainichi-msn.co.jp/kokusai/mideast/hitojichi/news/20040411k0000e030041000c.html. Accessed May 22, 2004. There are still several unanswered questions about the note's authenticity.

79. The most heated revelations came in the April 22 issue of *Shūkan Shinchō* (released on April 15), which sold out on many Tokyo newsstands within hours of publication. See "'Hitojichi hōdō' ni kakusareta 'hontō no hanashi'" [The 'Real Story' behind the 'Hostage News'], *Shūkan Shinchō* (April 22, 2004), 30–40. In Hokkaidō, where Imai's and Takato's families lived, the magazine ultimately removed some of the more damaging claims from its advertisements on subways in a belated effort to protect them from harassment.

80. Onishi, "For Japanese Hostages, Release Only Adds to Stress," 1.

81. Tachibana Takashi, "Koizumi Iraku hahei 'kurutta shinario'" [An "Insane Scenario" for Koizumi's Troop Dispatch to Iraq], *Gendai* (June 2004): 28–41. Tachibana is sometimes described as a Japanese counterpart of Bob Woodward; his work on the Lockheed scandal helped to expose the corruption that ultimately knocked former prime minister Tanaka Kakuei out of power.

82. Significantly, the deterioration of the security situation in Iraq had clearly shaken the noted hawk's faith in the occupation. Although he openly mentions the otherwise verboten subject that SDF soldiers might be killed and rejects it as a reason for withdrawing the troops, he argues that the government needs to consider whether civil war or the like would be reason to withdraw. See "6.30 Shuken ijō de semareru jieitai Iraku haken no 'fumi e'" [The 'Litmus Test' for the SDF Iraq Dispatch as the June 30 Sovereignty Deadline Looms], *Chūō Kōron* (June 2004): 72–79.

83. Aonuma Yōichirō, "Iraku no chūshin de ai o sakebu hitotachi" [The People Who Shriek about Love and Iraq], *Bungei Shunju* (June 2004): 148–157, at 154.

84. Okamoto Kōichi, "NGO seizensetsu no otoshiana" [The Pitfalls of NGOs' Views of Essential Human Goodness], *Chūō Kōron* (June 2004): 64–67.

85. See the interview with Imai in *Shūkan Gendai,* May 22, 2004.

7. Local Scapegoats and Other Unintended Consequences

1. Carol Gluck, *Japan's Modern Myths: Ideology in the Late Meiji Period* (Princeton: Princeton University Press, 1985), 132–33.

2. For a complete overview, see the *Yomiuri Shimbun,* "Kempō kaisei 2004–nen shian" [2004 Tentative Plan for Constitutional Revision], May 3, 2004. Online at http://www.yomiuri.co.jp/teigen/2004kenpo/main.htm. Accessed May 29, 2004.

3. Mos Def (Dante Smith), "Fear Not of Man," from *Black on Both Sides* (Los Angeles: Rawkus, 1999).

4. From "Why (What's Goin' On)," by Trotter, Thompson, Hubbard, Gray, Douglas, Bey, and Williams, on the Roots, *The Tipping Point* (Geffen, 2004).

5. Richard J. Samuels, *Machiavelli's Children: Leaders and Their Legacies in Italy and Japan* (Ithaca: Cornell University Press, 2003), 7–8.

6. Peter A. Hall and Rosemary C. R. Taylor, "Political Science and the Three New Institutionalisms," *Political Studies* 44, no. 4 (December 1996): 936–57, at 938.

7. Fawaz A. Gerges discusses these issues in "Islam and Muslims in the Mind of America: Influences on the Making of U.S. Policy," *Journal of Palestine Studies* 26, no. 2 (Winter 1997): 68–80.

8. Named for Sunshine City, the shopping complex built on the site of demolished Sugamo Prison, which housed political prisoners during the war and war criminals afterward.

women (*continued*)
79; subservience of, 202n35; welfare
for pregnant women, 56; and white
slavery trade, 86; women's groups, 64,
65
Women's Christian Temperance Union
(WCTU), 91, 208n46
Woolsey, R. James, 121, 129
World Congress against Commercial Sexual Exploitation of Children, 88, 111

yakuza (organized crime groups), 65, 77,
120

Yasukuni Shrine, 43–44, 168
Yomiuri Shimbun, 73, 135, 160–62, 168,
173, 183–84
Yoshimi Shun'ya, 39, 41
young people: cults preying on, 40, 59,
121; and economic issues, 33–34;
recklessness of, 3; and responsible
adults vs. youths, 38–41; and self-
responsibility, 176–77; and sense of
crisis, 24, 46; sexuality of teenagers, 5,
93–94; as threat, 41, 50, 59, 60, 183.
See also juvenile delinquency; schoolgirls